'This book is breath-taking in its scope, perceptioı most urgent and readable.'

Professor Michael Traynor,
in Context: Policy, Politics, Profession

'Dalal gives us a devastatingly forensic critique of the weaknesses of CBT and the supposed "science" that backs it up, and of the ruthless professional politics that have led its proponents to win the battle for the nation's souls. His term "cognitivist delusion" says it all. But in addition, as with his previous books, he lays bare the deeper intellectual and cultural histories that have conspiratorially allowed the "mental health professions" to short-change citizens in the service of materialist capitalism and a society dominated by elites.'

Professor Andrew Samuels, Department Of Psychosocial
And Psychoanalytic Studies, University Of Essex

'CBT is often presented as an alternative to psychiatric drugs for depression and other mental disorders. But in this erudite, thoughtful investigation of the "CBT Tsunami," Farhad Dalal details how it is built upon the same flawed foundation that gave us "safe and effective antidepressants": neoliberalism, the American Psychiatric Association's Diagnostic and Statistical Manual, and bad science. A refreshing, and much needed, critique.'

Robert Whittaker, Author of Mad In America

'This book is an analysis of the triumph of CBT as a method of "treating" "depression" but its argument also offers an urgent critique of the dysfunctions of our hyper-rational culture. By splitting nature from humankind, and then splitting emotion and ethics from reason in the latter, Dalal notes we have ended up with a perversion of Enlightenment values where the only things that count are the things that can be counted.'

Paul Hoggett, Emeritus Professor of Social Policy and
Chair of the Climate Psychology Alliance

'We live in alienating world where malignant individualism and rapacious neoliberal capitalism are destroying the belongingness and social cohesion that give our lives meaning, as well as degrading the planet we live on. In the therapy professions, these forces are thwarting relational ways of working, and replacing them with government-run machinery to provide industrialised therapy. This book is what we have all been waiting for: a robust, detailed and psychologically sophisticated critique of the frightening place where modern managerialism, regulation, compliance and performativity have taken us. It provides evidence that our narrow view of "evidence-based practice" is not enough.'

Rex Haigh Consultant Psychiatrist in Medical Psychotherapy,
Berkshire Healthcare NHS Foundation Trust

'This is an absolute masterpiece and should be read by anyone interested in anything to do with mental health or psychotherapy or economics or neoliberalism. Farhad has a wonderfully clear, engaging, intellectually rigorous, at times witty, style; but with a great talent for making complex phenomena easy to understand.'

Sami Timimi, Director of Medical Education Lincolnshire Partnership Foundation NHS Trust

'This book could be the Apricity that is needed in these times: in a scholarly way it honours value-based ideas, and names those ideas that have been hijacked and corrupted. Watch out! It takes no hostages and introduces no heroes; it is a great read for those of us who appreciate challenging, perspicacious and compassionate analyses.'

Professor Margie Callanan Programme Director of Clinical Psychology Doctorate, Salomons Centre for Applied Psychology

'Dalal's book provides a vital contribution to our understanding of the politics and ethics of contemporary mental health treatment, and of the managerial and reductive pursuit of happiness which is a symptom of our times.'

David Ferraro, President of the Lacan Circle of Melbourne & blogger Archives of a Divided Subject

'Under the sway of neoliberalism, the "happiness industry" is in full flow and cognitive behaviour therapy is the technology of treatment for those who fall by the wayside. In this combative and passionate book, Farhad Dalal draws on his expertise in psychotherapy and critical thinking to reveal the corruptions of argument and evidence on which the dominance of CBT is based. The book is a much-needed and timely reminder of the dangers inhabiting simplistic responses to complex social and personal conditions.'

Prof. Stephen Frosh Professor of Psychosocial Studies, Birbeck, University of London.

'With devastating irony and a poetic turn of phrase, this tightly argued yet wide ranging essay about politicised behaviourism in psychotherapy today is both highly instructive and entirely persuasive. . . . Farhad Dalal redeems the possibilities of Group Analysis from the corrosions and dilutions of neo-liberal economists and administrators. It is good to have him on our side!'

Earl Hopper, Ph.D., Mem.Inst.GA, CGP, DFAGPA. Psychoanalyst, group analyst and organisational consultant in private practice in London

'Dalal lays bare a "tragedy-in-progress" which will concern anyone for whom mental health or the direction of travel of twenty-first century healthcare is important.'

Dr. Douglas Board; Coach and Organizational Consultant; MaslowsAttic

'This is one hell of a book! Brilliantly written.

In his closely and passionately argued book, *The Cognitive Behavioural Tsunami*, Farhad Dalal issues a complex and thought-provoking challenge to the claims of Cognitive Behavioural Therapies as the pinnacle of effective psychotherapy. Implicit in his critique are such fundamental questions as: Do we have the right to suffer? Is human suffering a medical problem? Does personal happiness equate with mental health? Can one's capacity to suffer reflect mental health rather than mental illness? What does it mean to "treat" suffering?

Dalal argues against the over valuing of hyper-rationality that has come to pervade models of contemporary psychotherapy. He outlines the corruption of science in the service of politics and profit. Though written primarily within the perspective of mental health services delivery in the United Kingdom, Dalal's book mirrors the same economic and political forces seen in the United States in a once deeply personal field of human encounter, now increasingly defined, manualized, and controlled by government and market forces, insurance companies, and the pharmaceutical industry.

This book raises fundamental questions of the ethics and human essence of our psychotherapeutic endeavours that speak urgently to the future of psychotherapy.'

William F. Cornell, Author of Somatic Experience
in Psychoanalysis and Psychotherapy

'An important book for those worried about the clinical value of CBT. Dalal presents a rich and fundamental critique of CBT as well as the systems that support it. Dalal is an independent thinker who courageously challenges the DSM and the power politics of psycho-therapy.'

Dr. Robi Friedman, Past President of the International
Group Analytic Society

'Farhad Dalal's passionate and informative analysis of the questionable foundations of CBT, and of the professional and political contexts in which it has risen, is presented with his characteristic engaging directness. You do not have to agree with everything he says to be convinced of the importance of his powerfully-stated message: that the CBT behemoth, loaded high with good intentions and false hopes, should be halted.'

Barry Richards Professor of Political Psychology
Bournemouth University, UK

'Another brilliant book from Farhad Dalal! This time his target – well deserving the sue of heavy weaponry — is Cognitive Behavioural Therapy, together with the idiocies of the Diagnostic Statistical Manual. Dalal demonstrates that they are symptoms of a much more general affliction of modern society: "hyper-rationality" and the corruption of science.'

Stephen Mennell, University College Dublin

'Farhad Dalal employs critical analysis with surgical precision to debunk the mythology surrounding and supporting the science of CBT.

The book will confront, inspire, provoke and enlighten any reader with an interest in how CBT has morphed from a treatment dealing with the fear of flying and spider phobia into a powerful political-scientific movement, which claims to cure almost all "mental disorders" on an industrial scale.'

Professor Stig Johannessen, Faculty of Health Sciences,
Oslo Metropolitan University, Norway

'Farhad Dalal's book looks behind CBT's moral and rationalistic justification for its dominance in the field of psychotherapy. Dalal succeeds in illuminating the dark politics that drive this process, exposing their self-serving actions for what they are. This eloquent and fascinating book exposes the reader to the cost we are paying for this therapeutic approach: the reduction and diminishment of the human subject and the silencing of other therapeutic alternatives.'

Dr. Avi Berman, Tel Aviv University

CBT: The Cognitive Behavioural Tsunami

Is CBT all it claims to be? *CBT: The Cognitive Behavioural Tsunami: Managerialism, Politics, and the Corruptions of Science* provides a powerful critique of CBT's understanding of human suffering, as well as the apparent scientific basis underlying it. The book argues that CBT psychology has fetishized measurement to such a degree that it has come to believe that only the countable counts. It suggests that the so-called science of CBT is not just 'bad science' but 'corrupt science'.

The rise of CBT has been fostered by neoliberalism and the phenomenon of New Public Management. The book not only critiques the science, psychology and philosophy of CBT, but also challenges the managerialist mentality and its hyper-rational understanding of 'efficiency', both of which are commonplace in organizational life today. The book suggests that these are perverse forms of thought, which have been institutionalised by NICE and IAPT and used by them to generate narratives of CBT's prowess. It claims that CBT is an exercise in symptom reduction which vastly exaggerates the degree to which symptoms are reduced, the durability of the improvement, as well as the numbers of people it helps.

Arguing that CBT is neither the cure nor the scientific treatment it claims to be, the book also serves as a broader cultural critique of the times we live in; a critique which draws on philosophy and politics, on economics and psychology, on sociology and history, and ultimately, on the idea of science itself. It will be of immense interest to psychotherapists, policymakers and those concerned about the excesses of managerialism.

Farhad Dalal has been in independent practice as a group analyst and psychotherapist for over thirty years. He also works with organizations. His previous books have questioned received wisdom in a range of territories including psychotherapy (*Taking the Group Seriously*), racism (*Race, Colour and the Processes of Racialization*) and equal opportunities (*Thought Paralysis – The Virtues of Discrimination*).

CBT: The Cognitive Behavioural Tsunami

Managerialism, Politics and the Corruptions of Science

Farhad Dalal

Routledge
Taylor & Francis Group

LONDON AND NEW YORK

First published 2018
by Routledge
2 Park Square, Milton Park, Abingdon, Oxon OX14 4RN

and by Routledge
711 Third Avenue, New York, NY 10017

Routledge is an imprint of the Taylor & Francis Group, an informa business

© 2019 Farhad Dalal

British Library Cataloguing-in-Publication Data
A catalogue record for this book is available from the British Library

Library of Congress Cataloging-in-Publication Data
Names: Dalal, Farhad, author.
Title: CBT : the cognitive behavioural tsunami : managerialism, politics, and the corruptions of science / Farhad Dalal.
Description: Abingdon, Oxon; New York, NY : Routledge, 2018. | Includes bibliographical references.
Identifiers: LCCN 2018013721 (print) | LCCN 2018016067 (ebook) | ISBN 9780429457814 (E-book) | ISBN 9781138313064 (hardback) | ISBN 9781782206644 (pbk.) | ISBN 9780429457814 (ebk)
Subjects: | MESH: Cognitive Therapy
Classification: LCC RC489.C63 (ebook) | LCC RC489.C63 (print) | NLM WM 425.5.C6 | DDC 616.89/1425–dc23
LC record available at https://lccn.loc.gov/2018013721

ISBN: 978-1-138-31306-4 (hbk)
ISBN: 978-1-78220-664-4 (pbk)
ISBN: 978-0-429-45781-4 (ebk)

Typeset in Times
by Apex CoVantage, LLC

MIX
Paper from
responsible sources
FSC™ C013985

Printed in the United Kingdom
by Henry Ling Limited

Contents

Chapter I

Introduction
Hyper-rationality

Cognitive Behavioural Therapy (CBT) has come to dominate the field of psychological therapy, particularly within the NHS in the UK, but also in other sorts of institutions such as prisons and schools. This state of affairs is reproduced in many other countries across the world. If you go to your GP because of feeling depressed for some reason, in your ten-minute consultation your GP is almost certain to offer you anti-depressants or/and the 'one-size-fits-all' manualized treatment called CBT. The 'treatment' will try to teach you to replace your 'negative' thoughts with 'positive' ones. Your CBT therapist will have little interest in *why* you are depressed (perhaps you have been bereaved) because they think depression to be an illness, rather than a reasonable response to a devastating life event. According to the latest edition of the psychiatric bible, the *Diagnostic and Statistical Manual V* (DSM V, 2013), if you are still grieving *a whole two* weeks after your bereavement, it is because you are suffering from a mental disorder, because you should have come to terms with your loss by then.

How on earth did we get here? How is it that so many of the great and the good, researchers, regulatory authorities as well as hard-nosed economists and commissioners all come not only to think that there is nothing odd about this way of thinking about human suffering, but also that it is a sensible, scientific way of thinking?

In part, this has come about because in more recent times in *some* quarters of the academy, the notion of scientific knowledge itself has become progressively corrupted and degraded by the self-serving manoeuvres of a number of interest groups. This is somewhat ironic, because the function of the scientific attitude when it first emerged during the Enlightenment was precisely to expose the self-serving rationalizations of the then ruling elites to be fantastical fictions, not facts.

Once upon a time in the west . . .

Once upon a time in medieval England, anyone caught simply *reading* the Bible in the English language, would be in deep trouble, branded a heretic and quite likely burnt at the stake. The official Bible – the Vulgate – was in Latin. The Church said that to render the Word of God from 'high' sonorous Latin into the low commoner's tongue – English – was heresy as it would defile it. In this way the priest rationalized and protected his privileged position as gate-keeper between God and mammon. The Bible's impenetrability for the masses served the interests of both princes and priests, who used self-serving Biblical readings not only to claim that they were chosen by God to do his work, but also to give divine sanction to their political intrigues. Pope Urban II used biblical imagery to launch the first of the Crusades by conflating the Saracen with Satan, and in the same breath declared a *fatwah* on Jews everywhere. In June 1643, the Puritan English parliament actually passed a law – *The Covenant to be Taken by the Whole Kingdom* – which was supposed to be a Covenant with God. This celestial legal contract was an agreement between the English parliament and the Almighty, in which the Almighty agreed that the English would do God's work on earth (expanding His Kingdom), and He in turn would look after them. It was also agreed that God would replace Jews with the (Protestant, Puritan) English as his Chosen People.[1]

Having sole access to the word of God, the utterances of priests and princes had absolute authority. To question the proclamations of Kings was treason, to question the Church was heresy. Either was a sure way to book a place in the medieval torture chamber.

Then, in the late Middle Ages this despotic world order began to be challenged right across the land that would come to be known as Europe. Perhaps surprisingly, it was philosophy that was in the vanguard of this revolution. Philosophers like Locke, Hume, Descartes and Kant were amongst the first to challenge this tyranny. The radical revolution that they triggered transformed the world; it came to be called the Enlightenment because it brought the Light of Reason into the darkness of superstition. Kant cried out to humanity at large: *Sapere Aude!* Dare to think for yourself! (literally, 'Dare to know'). Intrinsic to the Enlightenment were the ideas of equality and freedom – the freedom to question, the freedom to think. And think humanity did. Rational thought became the organizing principle of society at large. Science itself grew out of this movement, bringing us unimaginable benefits in all kinds of arenas from technology to agriculture to leisure to medicine.

Physics envy: only the countable counts

But then, things began to change. Entranced by the predictive powers, advances and insights of the natural sciences, all kinds of disciplines and social practices began to suffer from a kind of 'physics envy'. And so, they began to try to emulate the empirical methods of natural scientists in order to garner for themselves the prestige of being a 'science'.

Today, it is hard to move without falling over all manner of things that claim to be scientific and evidence-based: evidence-based policy, evidence-based probiotics, evidence-based decision making, evidence-based fitness, evidence-based software engineering, evidence-based teaching, evidence-based investing, and of course, evidence-based psychological treatment.

However, the version of evidence that has come to prevail has meant that the virtues of the rationality of the Enlightenment have become perverted and distorted into a kind of hyper-rationality. Whereas Enlightenment rationality valued the freedom to think and question all things and anything, hyper-rationality uses a distorted and corrupt version of science to close down thinking. Rule-following comes to triumph over questioning and thinking. Where Enlightenment rationality brought freedom and light, hyper-rationality brings authoritarianism and darkness.

The virtues of rationality itself cannot be overstated. It has brought untold benefits to our lives and our ways of life. But the extreme versions of rationality, hyper-rationality, are corrosive to these very ways of life. As William Barrett put it, 'the untrammelled use later thinkers made of human reason [i.e. hyper-rationality], applying it like an acid solvent to all things human or divine' (Barrett, 1990, p. 26).

Hyper-rationality is the use of a reductive version of rationality in contexts that are not suited to it. Hyper-rationality insists that only evidence-based claims are valid. This sounds fine until we discover that hyper-rationality insists that this evidence be only of the arithmetic kind, because numbers and measurements are objective and real. If something can't be counted, if it can't be measured, *then it does not exist; it is not real.* This belief then allows all kinds of bizarre things to take place.

The Neem tree

For example, for over 2,000 years, components of the Neem tree have been used by farmers in India as pesticide. In 1992 an American agricultural company called 'Grace' patented a version of the pesticide. Having patented it, they claimed to be the legal owners of all such uses of the Neem tree. If any Indian farmer then used the Neem tree as a pesticide on his plot of land, then he was breaking the law and would be sued by Grace. Understandably, the farmers were outraged and took to the streets in protest. But protest counted for nothing, because in patent law, a challenge to the novelty claim of the patent could only be allowed if it could be demonstrated that the prior knowledge had previously appeared *in a printed publication*, preferably in a 'scientific' journal, at some time before the application for the patent. In other words, the legal system required *documentation*, something tangible as 'proof'. Patents are supposed to be granted when they meet the legal criteria of 'novelty, non-obviousness and utility'. In this case, the patent claim was neither novel nor non-obvious, and its utility was already well known. But this being folk knowledge, there was no evidence of the approved kind in print. Because of this, the courts declared that there was *no evidence*. The observable visible reality, the actual use of the Neem tree by farmers for millennia, was declared anecdotal and dismissed as unscientific.

In this hyper-rationalist world, it is the presence or absence of documentation that is the ultimate arbiter of truth and reality.

Encouraged by the findings of the courts, three years later two Indian researchers, Sumin K. Das and Hari Har P. Cohly at the University of Mississippi Medical Center, jumped on the same bandwagon. In 1995 they patented 'the use of turmeric in wound healing'. Being Indian, they of course, knew that Indian families had used turmeric paste for millennia to help speed up the healing of cuts, bruises and wounds. Their use of the patent law was entirely exploitative, cynical and self-serving. Astonishingly, their patent also granted them the *exclusive right* to sell and distribute turmeric. In one fell swoop, not only had they commandeered the uses of turmeric, but also all commercial activities around it. They were going to become very rich indeed.

Eventually, after years of legal battle, both patents were revoked. In the Neem tree case, the patent was revoked after a manager of an Indian agricultural company was able to demonstrate that he had been producing oil from the tree for the same use as the patent, but prior to the patent. And in the turmeric case, written evidence for its prior use was produced from ancient Ayurvedic texts from 500 BC. However, there remain a large number of patents in place on other uses of the Neem tree as well as turmeric. This kind of bio-piracy is only able to take place because the procedures and protocols of patent law are hyper-rationalist.

The point to be underlined is this: that *the idea of evidence itself is up for grabs*. What counts as legitimate evidence (real, objective data), is determined by the ruling definition of evidence. This ruling definition also has the effect of *ruling out* other kinds of evidence, even though it is also objective and there for all to see. This is the kind of hyper-rationalist reality that we find ourselves beleaguered by, in which so-called evidence or lack of, is being used to mystify and deny the existence of self-evident realities.

As things stand today, *in order for something to count, it has to be countable*. But further, and more worryingly, in some contexts the number itself becomes more real than the thing it is apparently representing, so much so that in some instances the numbers *become* the reality.

Rationality, Truth and Madness

The activity of science is supposed to be the production of objective knowledge by rational means. The 'means' themselves are a mix of observation (empirical evidence) and logical argument. CBT claims to produce scientific knowledge in this way, and on this basis assert that its claims are rational, objective and value free. In short – that they speak the truth.

Because the claims of CBT are rational, then any that question them are bound to be irrational. Why else would they deny the objective reality staring them in the face? They must be mad, or at the very least misguided. Even more, the notion of truth evokes its opposite – the lie. What this means is that anyone that questions the truth of the CBT thesis must not only be somewhat mad, in some way they must also be bad. It is in this sort of way that the evidence-based therapies buttress themselves and dismiss those that question them as deluded anti-science Luddites.

However, the arguments of this book are that the claims of CBT are not rational but hyper-rational, and that its observations as well as its logical arguments, fall far short of the standards required by good science.

Neoliberalist efficiencies

Hyper-rationality has infiltrated all levels and arenas of social life. It is the basis not only of much of what passes for psychological science, but is also the basis of neoliberalism and the ethos of New Public Management. These three territories powerfully come together, to interlock, bolster and sustain each other, to create a peculiar world view that is promoted as both normal and sensible, despite its peculiarity.

This book is primarily about the first element of the unholy trinity, about the 'science' of psychology, and more specifically about the psychology of Cognitive Behavioural Therapy. But in order to better understand how CBT has come to prosper, the book will also consider the other two components of the trinity: managerialism and neoliberalism as it was in their interests that CBT should flourish. In return, CBT supplied them with hyper-rationalist legitimations for their endeavours. In this way the argument of the book also functions as a broader cultural critique of the times we live in.

A key doctrine of hyper-rationality is a distorted and amoral take on 'efficiency'. We can see it in play in the workings of neoliberalism. To begin with, neoliberalism uses a shallow and instrumentalist definition of efficiency having to do with profit and money, to rationalize and legitimate deregulation. It follows this up by calling on efficiency again to legitimate the austerity measures that are deemed to be necessary to repair the damage done by the deregulation in the first place. The actual implementation of austerity itself is devolved to managerialist bureaucrats who do the dirty work of decimating our public services and institutions. But the dirty work of making 'cuts' and causing harm is made to look sanitary and rational by alluding to 'cuts' as 'savings' – and camouflaging it to make it look as if it is all taking place in the service of increased efficiency. These cuts then result in human distress, distress which is framed as a mental disorder. By this means managerialism and neoliberalism sanitize their activities and then, in a gesture of good will, offer CBT treatments for the unfortunates who are deemed mentally ill. It is in the name of efficiency that bureaucracies fund CBT over and above the other forms of therapy, on the basis of the claim that CBT's efficacy has been scientifically demonstrated; it also just happens to be the case that CBT treatments are inexpensive and relatively quick to implement (that is, they are 'efficient'). In sum, CBT is a managerialist creation, not the scientific one that it claims to be.

Command and control

The watchword of hyper-rationality is 'command and control'; its expectation is that we should be able to control everything: not only the world, not only the functioning of organizations, but also our very beings. This ethos is shared by both managerialists as well as cognitivists. Richard Layard, the godfather of CBT in Britain, informs us that 'Human beings have largely *conquered* nature, but they have still to *conquer* themselves' (Layard, 2005, p. 9). If we can't control something, then this is because we have yet to figure how it works. 'The inner life . . . determine[s] how we react to life . . . So how can we gain control over our inner life?' (Layard, 2005, p. 184).

Once we have learnt how to take control of our inner life, then we ought to be able to make it do what we want it to do. In this way, its command and control ethos claims to be able to conquer inner psychological life itself. As we will come to see, it is believed that you should be able to *choose* and determine what you feel and think. If you feel depressed say, then it is because you have not yet understood how to take control of your inner life. This is where CBT will come to the rescue: it will explain to you how your inner life works; it will then train you in techniques to control its workings. If, after all this, you still cannot control your inner life despite having understood the mechanism, then either this is of your choosing, or it is because you are still in the grip of your mental illness. In which case you will be the beneficiary of an additional diagnosis granted by the researchers: 'CBT resistant' (for example, Otto and Wisniewski, 2012).

Hyper-rationality is infused by two other doctrines that go along with that of 'efficiency', these being atomization and decontextualization. We will come to see how these doctrines start to play out in the course of this book.

The rhetoric of the proponents of CBT would have us believe that the reason that it has come to dominate the psychological field, is simply because it is the best in the field, the most efficient player. But as we will come to see, CBT has succeeded not because it is the best player in the game, but because (along with its allies) it has adapted the rules of the game to favour its own method. In other words, CBT's success is a political victory masquerading as a scientific one.

The virtues of CBT (and their corruption)

CBT is not entirely without virtue, and in a sense the problem is not with CBT itself, but the hype that surrounds it and the use it is put to further specific ideological, professional and political agendas. In its original avatar, the scope of CBT was limited. Its technology was developed to help people recover from phobias, such as fear of flying, obsessive behaviours, and so forth. In this it succeeds very well, and in these areas it is very often the 'treatment of choice'. Problems became apparent when CBT's ambitions expanded to colonize *all* forms of psychological suffering. As we will come to see in the next chapters, in this task CBT was aided and abetted by the merchants of happiness who appropriated CBT for their own ends.

This resulted in the production of a powerful polarization – at one pole happiness and health, at the other, mental illness and mental disorder. The dichotomy is so powerful that it makes it seem that the only available territory resides at one or other of the poles, leaving no place to stand anywhere between mental illness and mental health. This either/or dichotomization has come about in the following way.

It is true that some people inhabit alternative realities filled with terrifying para-noid delusions and the like, and as such they could be said to be 'mentally ill'. However, there is no 'opposite' to this, in the sense that there is no such thing as a state of 'mental health'. What there is, is ordinary human suffering, which we all suffer from, and which we more or less find ways to manage to live with, for better or worse. Modern CBT has colonized not only this territory, the territory of ordinary suffering by medicalizing it, it has also commandeered the territory of the genuinely mentally ill (schizophrenia, psychosis, and so on); it has lumped all this together and dumped it at the pole called mental illness. It is by this means that we find ourselves caught in the dichotomy: either you are happy and 'have' mental health, or you are not happy and therefore you 'have' a mental disorder.

In this way, CBT has joined forces with the pharmaceutical industry and psy-chiatry in their project of medicalizing ordinary human suffering, and then selling (patented) treatments for that suffering.

The structure of the book

The situation we find ourselves in is the seemingly unquestionable ruling status of CBT in the field of therapy. The work of this book is to question it. To this end, the 'unpacking' takes place in a number of different ways and directions. The deconstruction will call on philosophy and politics, on economics and psychol-ogy, on sociology and history, and ultimately, on the idea of science itself.

The official CBT narrative is an unproblematic linear one that is premised on two axiomatic beliefs. The first is the uncritical acceptance of the existence of the 'mental disorders' found in the DSM as 'facts'. The second is the belief that positivist, empirical scientific research methods are an appropriate way of searching for potential treatments and then testing their capacity to curing these self-same 'mental disorders'. On this basis, treatments for mental disorders are tested under controlled conditions by scientists. This produces scientific evi-dence regarding whether or not the treatment actually works (the evidence base). If this evidence is thought to be convincing by the National Institute for Clinical and Health Care Excellence (NICE), then it will authorize the use of a manual-ized version of the researched treatment. The treatment is manualized in order that it replicates the successes of treatment that was researched. Once a treatment is validated in this way, the job of delivering it to those troubled with a mental illness, is passed onto the statutory agency Increasing Access to Psychological Therapies (IAPT). IAPT also produces empirical evidence about its function-ing and delivery of the treatment. It produces prodigious amounts of data that appears to demonstrate that the providers are delivering outcomes at the level that the research says should be the case. This data is further scrutinized by gov-ernment bodies for example, the National Audit Office (NAO). Annual reports emerging from the NAO, IAPT and NICE all seem to confirm that all is well and as it should be in the world of CBT. The whole endeavour is evidence-based, from the bottom to the top. And the evidence repeatedly shows that everything is copacetic in the CBT world. These are simply the facts.

But linearities should always be treated with caution. They tend to be created by imposing a particular ideological reading of events to make them seem rational, inevitable and therefore incontrovertible. Ideological readings edit out the twists and turns, as well as the complexities, contradictions and power struggles, to make it appear that they were never there in the first place. The fact is, CBT's narrative about itself is a political narrative that masquerades as a scientific one.

For these sorts of reasons, the book will not begin where the official narrative might suggest: with CBT treatment and research, as this would collude with the value-free decontextualized account that CBT gives of itself. We cannot fully get to understand how the cognitive behavioural tsunami came to be, without examining the 'climate conditions' that made the tsunami a possibility in the first place. We need to get to know something about the prevailing winds and currents, and the consequences of their interactions with the subterranean shifts taking place in the tectonic plates of science, politics, economics and ultimately, psychology; all of which had to come together to make the tsunami possible. This over-stretched metaphor is a way of saying that much of this book is about the conditions and contexts that came together to produce the cognitive behavioural tsunami.

Having said that, there is the danger that the account given here will simply replace the official linear narrative with another linear narrative. The structure of the book, consisting as it does of five parts, is an attempt to guard against this. Each of the parts is embedded in a mix of particular discourses and disciplines, producing narratives that throw different kinds of light on the tsunami. But the parts do not neatly dovetail – further, each of the parts necessarily parses over the same sort of territory. This has necessitated in some repetition, in order that each of the parts has some semblance of coherence.

In **Part I: The Tsunami**, chapters 2 and 3 are an account of how the cognitivist tsunami began and how and why Layard's Utilitarian Happiness agenda came to power that tsunami. In the UK, the Cognitive Behavioural Tsunami was inaugurated in 2005 with the publication of Richard Layard's bestseller *Happiness*. A year later this was followed up by *The Depression Report: A New Deal for Anxiety and Depression Disorders* authored by Richard Layard, David Clark and other luminaries. A decade later Layard and Clark celebrated the success of CBT in their book *Thrive: How Better Mental Health Care Transforms Lives and Saves Money*.

Chapter 2, 'The Tsunami Begins', takes a close look at the substance of the Depression Report as well as the politics around it, as it was this Report that convinced the Labour Government of the day to fund CBT to the tune of hundreds of millions of pounds. Never before had any kind of psychology been supported and promoted by the State in this kind of way and to this extraordinary degree. It was the economic argument that contained in that report that won the day.

Chapter 3, 'The Merchants of Happiness', unpacks Richard Layard's book *Happiness* which was first published in 2005. Although it is well over ten years old, it remains seminal and highly influential. CBT texts that have followed have not added much to the original thesis. The reason then, for looking deeply into this book rather than other more recent texts, is because not only did *Happiness* kick off the tsunami, it is still a fair encapsulation of the CBT landscape and remains very influential to this day. The chapter will describe the kind of Utilitarian philosophy that Layard advocates, the ways that this is used to conceptualize life's problems, and the (cognitivist) solutions that follow from it.

CBT likes to present itself as unique and distinct from every other form of psychotherapy; as though it had sprung fully formed from the mind of Aaron Beck. But in fact, all the techniques of which CBT has claimed ownership are found in other models of psychotherapy. How was it then that CBT was able to construct its identity in this way? This is the question addressed by **Part II: Politics of Identity Formation**. Chapter 4, 'Master Myths and Identity Formation', introduces some of the ideas of the sociologist Norbert Elias, which are then drawn on in the following chapter, 'The "Psy" Wars'. Chapter 5 is a social history and overview of the power struggles within the 'Psy' professions in the US and UK. It details the politicized machinations between psychiatry, psychoanalysis, behaviourism, cognitivism and clinical psychology over the last 80 or so years. The weapon of choice in these battles was positivism, which they each wielded with increasing fervour, one against the other, in their efforts to prove themselves to the scientific fraternity. It was in this way that the positivist vision was fostered, which in turn facilitated the burgeoning of CBT.

Part III: Cognitivism, turns its attention to the genesis of the cognitivist conception of the human condition that has come to preside in CBT. This conception started out in the discipline that came to be known as economics. The first theories of psychology were created during the Enlightenment by philosophers who were only latterly called economists, and at the same time philosophers we would now call psychologists were writing treatises on economics. This is the territory traced by Chapter 6 – Homo Economicus. In this chapter we encounter Utilitarian economics and also Milton Friedman's neoliberalist economics, both of which continue to dominate and organize all aspects of the world we live in, including the provision of psychological treatments. But the role of economics is not limited to the part it played a few centuries ago in the genesis of cognitivism. The Friedmanesque turn that economic theory took into neoliberalism in the latter half of the twentieth century, came to play a key role in the rising fortunes of CBT. To understand how this played out requires us to engage with New Public Management or Managerialism.

Chapter 7 is a critical account of the ways in which Managerialism uses the rationalist cognitivist ideations developed in economics and CBT to inflict psychological mayhem and destruction not only on the 'workforce' but also the 'customer'. Managerialism furthers the neoliberal agenda by representing the casualties it creates as not casualties at all, but as unfortunates suffering from a 'mental illness'. It then makes the (kind) offer of treating these illnesses with CBT and the new scientific technologies of Happiness and Resilience.

Parts IV and V endeavour to get to the heart of the matter.

Part IV: Dispensing CBT, comprises three chapters. Chapter 8, 'NICE: naughty, but not nice', focuses on the body that has the task of examining evidence-based scientific claims for treatments. Based on this evidence it makes recommendations for treatments of choice – this mainly features CBT. We will find managerialism writ large in the political machinations taking place within NICE as well as IAPT. Chapter 9 is a description of CBT treatment itself. When stripped of jargon, CBT treatment amounts to little more than the injunction: think differently, feel different. Chapter 10 uncovers the hyper-rationalist managerialist practices being deployed within IAPT. These practices not only end up short-changing patients by significantly diluting the intensity and duration of treatments that they are entitled to, they also put practitioners under unbearable amounts of stress. But the art of managerialism is one of making it appear that none of these things are happening and that the institution is meeting all its goals and targets.

Part V: CBT Research focuses in on the research itself – the head of the beast as it were. Ben Goldacre's notion of 'Bad Science' is insufficient for the situation we find ourselves in because bad science can be the result of ineptitude and incompetence. The more accurate term for the prevailing situation is 'Corrupt Science'; this being when bad science is deliberately and wilfully promulgated as 'good'. This is the kind of science that prevails in the CBT landscape; it is both corrupt and deceitful. But one cannot fully understand the extent and depth of the corruptions without contrasting it with good science, which is the subject of chapter 11. Chapter 12, 'The Corruptions of Science' is then better able to delineate some of the chicanery used to bewilder us into thinking that Bad Science is Good Science.

Finally, Chapter 13 introduces 'third wave' CBT and looks at two interlinked studies which found Mindfulness Based Cognitive Therapy (MBCT) to be efficacious in the prevention of Depression. The fact that the second study replicated the results of the first was greeted with much excitement and was convincing enough for NIICE to approve its use as a preventative measure in certain circumstances. MBCT has gone through all the scientific requirements; it sits on the list of IAPT approved therapies and is considered to be a great CBT success story. This chapter looks closely into these studies and finds the situation to be otherwise. It is these findings that give the final chapter its title: 'Statistical Spin; Linguistic Obfuscation'.[2]

Note

1 Chosen then, but alas, no longer. Ronald Reagan (and more recently, Donald Trump) declared that the celestial baton had moved to the USA. 'Can we doubt that only a Divine Providence placed this land, this island of freedom, here as a refuge for all . . . who yearn to breathe freely? . . . God Bless America'. R. Reagan, 17 July 1980, Address Accepting the Presidential Nomination at the Republican National Convention in Detroit, http://www.presidency.ucsb.edu/ws/?pid=25970.

2 A version of chapter 13 was previously published in *The Journal of Psychological Therapies in Primary Care* 2015, 4, pp 1–25, 'Statistical Spin: Linguistic Obfuscation—The Art of Overselling the CBT Evidence Base'.

Part I

The tsunami

Chapter 2

The tsunami begins . . .

Reverse engineering: hugs, tails and unhappy dogs

On arriving at a conference on 'Happiness', we were greeted by a number of smiling people, each carrying a placard announcing, 'Get Free Hugs Here!'. Curiously, not many of the delegates took up the free offer. Over two days we were repeatedly told that there was now a *Science* of Happiness which had not only discovered what made people happy, it could also teach unhappy persons the skills which would make them happy. What's not to like about a science that advocates that one's happiness is at least, if not more, important than money? The scientific 'discovery' behind the offer of a free hug was the fact that happy people tend to have more physical contact than unhappy ones. Sure, I wanted to be happier, but for some reason I was not drawn to the idea of hugging and being hugged by a random stranger.

The so-called 'scientists of happiness' have forgotten the first lesson of empirical science: that correlation is not necessarily causation. For example, we observe a dog wagging its tail. We notice that only happy dogs wag their tails. We notice that unhappy dogs do not wag their tails. We deduce from this, that if unhappy dogs wagged their tails, they would become happy. We develop a treatment protocol which teaches unhappy dogs to learn to wag their tails. If they learn how to wag their tails, and then *choose* to wag their tails, then they will become happy. Q.E.D.

The offer of free hugs is born out of exactly this kind of error. CBT techniques assume that it is possible to use this kind of reverse engineering to change feeling states. Happy dogs wag tails; therefore tail wagging should generate happiness. Happy people tend to have more physical contact; therefore increased physical contact will generate a feeling of happiness. Of course, all this is based on the premise that it is possible to *reengineer* human behaviour in this mechanistic way in the first place.

But a hug is no abstraction. I do not feel better for hugging anonymous strangers; that would be a form of prostitution. On the other hand, I do feel happier and better when I hug and am hugged by those who are meaningful to my emotional life. Moreover, and most importantly, the impulse to hug is an *expression* of tender feelings for the other, and not an instrument to increase *my feelings of wellbeing*.

This is our first glimpse into the mechanistic mind-set that is CBT. Actions are stripped out of their contexts, contexts which make actions meaningful. Stripped of meaning, actions become empty instrumentalized techniques, so-called 'skills'. Is hugging a skill? When a hug is reduced to technique to *make myself* feel happier, then the role of other person is rendered functional rather than meaningful: they are simply an object to be used in the service of adjusting my emotional state.

The father of this new Science of Happiness and Positive Psychology was Martin Seligman, one-time president of the powerful American Psychological Association. He used his time in the presidential office to place positive psychology at the centre of the Association's concerns.

However, the first claim to fame of this advocate of happiness was the infliction of unhappiness in the name of science. Seligman started his career in psychology by torturing dogs to the point of what he called 'learnt helplessness' (Seligman, 1972). He did this by giving them electric shocks at random through the floor so that they were unable to escape the shocks by jumping away. This was done repeatedly until the dogs resigned all hope and lay down on the floor even whilst being shocked, simply whining. His great finding was this: that when these dogs were put in new situations where there was the possibility of escaping from the shocks, they did not try to do so. They had truly given up. The dogs were now deemed to have *learnt* helplessness. Seligman supposed that there was a corollary between learnt helplessness and depression. He thought that depression was a form of learnt helplessness due to having lived through previous experiences of helplessness. Depression was now being defined as being stuck in a state of *imagined* helplessness despite a change of circumstances. *Depression then becomes construed of as the opposite of happiness.*

The Happiness ethos has proliferated into all kinds of territories and to an extraordinarily degree. It has found favour not only with those involved in the 'health' industry, but also governments and HR departments within organizations globally. Journalists, universities, GPs and politicians all refer to it and its sister discipline – Cognitive Behavioural Therapy (CBT) – as established scientific fact.

The unlikely figure behind this seismic cultural shift that made the psychological wellbeing of citizens politically respectable was not a psychologist, but an economist called Richard Layard.

A chance meeting . . .

Layard was born in 1934 into the privileged classes. Despite being educated at Eton and then Cambridge, his sympathies lay with the disenfranchised; his values were those of the Labour Party. He played an influential role in the expansion of university education in the 1960s. At the London School of Economics, he specialized in unemployment and inequality.

Richard Layard was a Utilitarian and of the view that it was in the nation's economic interests to support and promote the psychological wellbeing of their citizens. He was casting about for how to go about doing this. Then one evening in 2003 at a tea party for the great and the good at the British Academy, Layard bumped into David Clark a leading figure within the world of CBT. It was this chance meeting that would light the fuse that was to trigger the CBT tsunami.

Very quickly they discovered that their interests dovetailed. They realized that by working together they could further each of their interests, Layard's agenda for happiness and Clark's desire to advance the fortunes of CBT. An opportunity arose almost immediately after this meeting in 2004 when the Government's regulatory body, The National Institute for Health and Care Excellence (NICE) gave CBT its seal of approval, recommending it as the best of all psychological treatments for anxiety and depression.

Layard and Clark used this moment to produce a short but powerful manifesto, 'The Depression Report: A New Deal for Anxiety and Depression Disorders' (2006), calling for a change in the Government's priorities regarding its citizens' wellbeing.

Layard, as a part of Labour Party aristocracy, had direct access to Cabinet Ministers and the Prime Ministers at that time, initially Tony Blair, and then his successor, Gordon Brown. The manifesto itself was published under the auspices of the Mental Health Policy Group at the Centre for Economic Performance (of which Layard was the Director) at the prestigious London School of Economics. This combined with the list of nine authors, all high-status establishment figures, not only gave the *Depression Report* immediate prestige and credibility, it also allowed it to make its way onto the agenda of the Cabinet.

The Depression Report: A New Deal for Anxiety and Depression Disorders

The argument of the Report and its recommendations, written in clear, concise and compelling language, was convincing enough for the hard-nosed and hard-pressed Exchequer to release hundreds of millions of pounds. It is worth going through the report slowly otherwise we will be swept up by its powerful rhetoric, as was the government of the day.

At its most condensed, the Report claims that *CBT is the royal road to happiness*. The slightly less condensed version of the report is this: It begins with the assertion that the natural state of persons *should* be that of happiness. This is 'mental health', a corollary of physical health. Someone in a state of mental health will be in a positive state of mind most of the time quite naturally, without efforts. If someone is not able to do this, if they are not-happy, then this is because they are suffering from a '*mental illness*'. The treatment for this illness is CBT.

The point bears repeating: unhappiness is a symptom of a mental disease called depression or anxiety or something else. Treat the illness, disperse the symptom, and you will once again be happy. This is how human suffering has become medicalized. The Report begins by describing the scale of the *problem*.

> depression and chronic anxiety are the biggest causes of misery in Britain today . . . [and that] *one in six of us would be diagnosed as having depression or chronic anxiety disorder,* which means that one family in three is affected.
>
> (Bell et al., 2006, p. 1; emphasis in original)

The *solution* put forward in the report is a trumpet call for the 'new' '*evidence-based psychological therapies that can lift at least a half of those affected out of their depression or their chronic fear*' (Bell et al., 2006, p. 1; emphasis in original). They go onto say that:

> These new therapies are not endless nor backward looking treatments [for which read psychoanalysis]. They are short, forward-looking treatments that enable people to challenge their negative thinking and build on the positive side of their personalities and situations. The most developed of these therapies is cognitive behaviour therapy (CBT).
>
> (Bell et al., 2006, p. 1)

There is unfortunately a problem with this solution, which is that

> we do not have enough therapists. In most areas waiting lists for therapy are over nine months, or there is no waiting list at all because there are no therapists . . . The result is tragic . . . at least half of them could be cured at a cost of no more than £750.
>
> (Bell et al., 2006, p. 1)

The solution to *that* problem, says the Report, is that the government should invest in training '10,000 new therapists within the next seven years. *Some 5,000 of these should be 'clinical psychologists'* (Bell et al., 2006, p. 10; emphasis in original).

The 'business case' for pursuing this course appears to be a no brainer:

> someone on Incapacity Benefit costs us £750 a month in extra benefits and lost taxes. If the person works just a month more as a result of the treatment, the treatment pays for itself . . . we . . . have a solution that can improve the lives of millions of families, *and cost the taxpayer nothing.*
>
> (Bell et al., 2006, p. 1; italics added)

> *the total loss of output due to depression and chronic anxiety is some £12 billion a year . . . Of this the cost to the taxpayer is some £7 billion . . .*

These billions of pounds lost through inactivity are a huge cost when compared with the £0.6 billion a year which a proper therapy service would cost.

(Bell et al., 2006, p. 5; emphasis original)

Who would not invest 60p in order to earn £7.00? That's a dizzy 1166 per cent return – a stockbroker's dream. It is perhaps not surprising that the government of the day should have taken the 'findings' of the Report seriously, as it was backed by nine 'experts' – prestigious scientists and influential members of the establishment. The government took the Report at face value, believed it and proceeded with its advice. The advice being that not only could the government increase the wellbeing of the inhabitants of the nation, but also in pursuing this good deed, the economic benefits were such that *it would end up with more money in the bank than it started out with.* So it came to pass that the UK government went ahead and poured millions upon millions into this venture, training the requisite number of CBT therapists and rolling out the therapies through the institution called IAPT – Increasing Access to Psychological Therapies. A key reason as to why the Report was so readily embraced, had to do with the fact that the ground had already been well prepared a year earlier, with the publication of the economist Richard Layard's hugely popular book: *Happiness: Lessons from a New Science.* It is with this work that the Cognitive Behavioural Tsunami really began. Although the book is now over ten years old, CBT texts that have followed it merely reproduce the same thesis. Further, the book and its author continue to have enormous influence on politicians and the public generally. For these sorts of reasons, it is well worth looking more deeply into it.

Chapter 3

The merchants of happiness

Fin de siècle 2000 – a Baron rewarded

With the coming of the new millennium, the Labour Party rewarded Richard Layard with a life peerage. Henceforth, titled as Baron Layard of Highgate, he had a right to sit in the House of Lords until his dying day. Layard was being rewarded for the contributions he had made to developing policies for Tony Blair's vision of New Labour with its affection for neoliberalism. In particular the Peerage was recognition for the policy on unemployment that Layard had developed and which the Labour Party had enthusiastically embraced: 'The New Deal'. The intention of this government policy was to reduce unemployment by providing the unemployed with training which would reacclimatize them to the idea of work and the workplace. For Layard, the New Deal was the fruition of his lifelong academic interest in the subject of unemployment.

Labour's New Deal resembled Roosevelt's New Deal only in name, not in spirit. Whereas Roosevelt's New Deal (1933–1945), countered the Great Depression by putting financial resources into programmes that actually helped the desperate unemployed, Labour's New Deal became a coercive instrument that was used to bully, intimidate and harass the unemployed. It was able to do this in part by mobilizing notions of mental disorder, depression and happiness, which underpinned by a hyper-rationality, was used to construct a very particular and pernicious narrative about the psychology of the unemployed and the causes of unemployment.

On first reading Layard himself comes across as a decent enough man who thinks that 'costs and benefits should be measured in terms of happiness not money' (Layard, 2005, p. 126) and that 'happiness should become the goal of [social] policy' (Layard, 2005, p. 147). He is against poverty and 'rampant individualism'; he is for the redistribution of wealth; he is against the rat race and the stresses it generates. Although these sentiments are aligned with those of the Labour Party, as we will come to see, at bottom he holds deeply conservative values.

But whether he be conservative or progressive, he set off a pernicious chain of events that have been calamitous for our society. The causes of that calamity are not the sentiments of goodwill in themselves; rather they have to do with the way that problem is initially conceptualized: mental illness; the solution advocated: CBT; and finally, with the way that the solutions are implemented: New Public Management. Implicated in all of these we will find our new friend, hyper-rationality.

Although Layard is an economist, his primary agenda is a *moral* agenda: the enhancement of the happiness of the nation. His secondary agenda is a *psychological* agenda: CBT is the psychological *means* of achieving the moral *end* of happiness. Being neither philosopher nor psychologist, his understanding of both is not only simplistic, it is also deeply flawed. Even a cursory reading of *Happiness* reveals any number of contradictions and confusions, with everyday homilies passed off as scientific discoveries.

I begin with the moral philosophy called Utilitarianism, as that is the foundation for Layard's happiness agenda.

Utilitarianism: the arithmetic of happiness

Although many a philosopher might think otherwise, Layard blithely declares that

'[Jeremy] Bentham was one of the greatest thinkers of the Enlightenment. The best society, he said, is one where the citizens are happiest. So the best public policy is that which produces the greatest happiness . . . This is the Greatest Happiness principle'.

(Layard, 2005, p. 5)

In a nutshell, Utilitarianism is the principle of 'the greatest good for the greatest number'. Here we have it: number. The introduction of numbers means that ethical predicaments can now be reduced to, and solved by arithmetic calculation. We can see why this sort of philosophy might be appealing to positivists everywhere, not only economists, but also cognitivists. It goes without saying that anything with numbers will be especially appealing to the hyper-rationalists.

Layard reproduces and fosters the one-dimensional view of humanity that is found in economic theory (see chapter 6), this being that human beings are primarily autonomous, *rational* agents capable of rationally determining their destinies. 'We are active agents who both shape our situation and *control our response to that situation*' (Layard, 2005, p. 73; italics added). If you are one of the unfortunates who find this difficult to do, then it is likely that you are suffering from a mental disorder. But I am getting ahead of myself.

As rational beings, Layard thinks that people make ethical decisions on the basis of a '*rational calculus*' which is a simplified version of Jeremy Bentham's *felicific calculus*. But how should we *calculate* what we ought to do next? Calculus is a big word evoking a picture of fearfully complex mathematical calculations.

While Bentham's calculation took account of a mix of elements such as the duration and the economics of intensity of emotion, Layard's calculations on how to decide between ethical alternatives is very simple; they 'simply' consist of addition and subtraction: 'We . . . simply add up the happiness of all concerned' (Layard, 2005, p. 121). He helps us out with an example:

> I . . . promised to attend my daughter's play, but my mother is taken to hospital. How should I use my time? . . . Obviously I should figure out whose feelings would be most hurt if I did not come. That is the Benthamite solution'.
>
> (Layard, 2005, p. 116)

Phew. That was easy.

But wait. *Should* ethical decisions be based now on whose feelings would be most hurt? Is it not possible that the right ethical decision might be the more hurtful one? And how will I set about calculating 'whose feelings would be *most* hurt'?

There is neither psychological depth nor any moral complexity in the Layardian universe; there are no such things as ambivalence or moral dilemmas because they are easily resolved by the arithmetic of happiness. For example, 'Oppression is one of the most potent sources of misery. Consequently, the Greatest Happiness principle would strongly condemn the oppression of *any* group or individual' (Layard, 2005, p. 122).

Test out this platitude in relation to the powerful short story penned many years ago (1973) by the great science fiction writer Ursula K. Le Guin: 'The Ones Who Walk Away from Omelas'. The citizens of a city called Omelas are happy and cultured; everything about the city and its inhabitants is delightful. However, we soon discover that this edifice of light and delight requires that a child be perpetually tormented in filth and misery in a dark underground cave below the city. Without the suffering child, the glory of the Omelas would collapse. In order to continue living in Omelas, each citizen is taken to the dungeon and shown this child. On seeing the child, some decide to walk away.

How would Layard 'add up' the happiness of an entire city (millions of people) and weigh it up next to the misery of a single person? If we were to find for the suffering child (as well we might), then in no way could we have said to have '*simply* added up the happiness of all concerned'. This kind of situation is the Achilles heel of Utilitarianism. Layard tries to get around this by allocating a 'weight' to the happiness of an individual depending on how wealthy they are: 'an extra dollar gives more happiness to the poor than the rich' (Layard, 2005, p. 136). The dollar 'weighs' more for the poor person because it means more to them.

But what will the *scientific* process of adjusting the 'weight' look like? Layard tells us that the 'weight' one allocates to a person's issues will depend on how much one *cares* about them: 'The impartial spectator would *surely care* more about what happened to the miserable person than to the person who was already happy. He would therefore give a different "weight" [to each]' (Layard, 2005, p. 122; italics added).

The more you care about something, the more weighty it is. I well understand what is meant by this as a metaphorical way of speaking; he claims however, that he is not speaking metaphorically, but objectively. By the device of using the term 'surely' he bypasses the question of the basis on which one cares more in one circumstance over another. 'Surely' he is beholden to describe the *'Science of Care'*?

In putting all his ethical eggs in a rationalist basket, Layard is following in the footsteps of Immanuel Kant, even though he makes no mention of him. However, Layard is 'Kantian-Lite', giving no indication that he is deeply at odds with another 'one of the greatest thinkers of the Enlightenment' (and to many, a much greater thinker than Bentham). For example, here: 'There may be a conflict between the rules. If a Nazi stormtrooper asks us where we think a Jew is hiding, we should *surely* invent a plausible lie' (Layard, 2005, p. 124; italics added).

That word 'surely' again. If I decided not to lie, then 'surely' I would be being unethical; or would I? Kant would not only fundamentally disagree with Layard's strategy, he would condemn Layard's stance as utterly immoral. Kant insists that we should never ever lie in such a circumstance, in part because we do not know how things will turn out. While I do not agree with Kant on this matter, nor do I think the answer to be the simplistic one advocated by Layard.

There is a deep point to be made here, which has to do with the reason for Layard's smug self-assured tone when he claims that all sensible people would *surely* invent a plausible lie. He is only able to be so confident in his assertion because he is positioning himself outside the scenario, as the afore mentioned 'impartial spectator'. There can be no repercussions for a detached, impartial spectator for the lie because they are outside and above 'the system' and untouched by consequences. But in reality, we are always embedded and implicated actors. In our day to day lives we do not have the luxury of being removed from these kinds of moral dilemmas. Who is the stormtrooper asking, and where are they standing? Presumably the stormtrooper is asking this of a German citizen during the Nazi era (or someone in one of the occupied territories) in the 1930s or 1940s. Let us assume that this German citizen did not have Nazi sympathies. If he or she had dared to protect the Jew by lying to the stormtrooper, and if the lie was found out, then the citizen as well as their entire family would very likely find themselves consigned to one of the death camps. To lie in this circumstance is to take a huge risk, as many a German did and paid the ultimate price; there were many such German citizens. I am not convinced that I would have had the courage to do the same in that kind of situation – there is no 'surely' here for me. Nor do I think that Layard knows what he would actually do in that kind of circumstance: if by lying, he was not just protecting the Jew from the safety of detached impartiality, but he was also putting his own life as well as the lives of his loved ones at real risk. What would his impartial rational calculus have him do then?

So much for moral philosophy. Let us turn next to science and psychology.

The science of happiness

Layard boldly asserts 'what matters ultimately is what people *feel*' (Layard, 2005, p. 6).

If so, then feelings are a serious problem for a science that will only take account of the measurable and countable. How do you measure an intangible subjective feeling? Until recently there was no way to measure feelings, particularly happiness. And so *feelings* of happiness were of no account to Science, until . . .

> Scientific breakthroughs . . . transformed the way we think about happiness. Until recently, if people said they were happy, sceptics would hold that this was just a subjective statement. There was no good way to show that it had any objective content at all. But now we know that what people say about how they feel corresponds closely to the actual levels of activity in different parts of the brain, which can be measured in standard scientific ways.
>
> (Layard, 2005, p. 12)

This is the exciting news – a particular part of your brain lights up when you are feeling happy. You will be much relieved to know that it is now official: The *feeling* of Happiness has now been proved to exist! 'Happiness is an objective dimension of all our experience' (Layard, 2005, p. 224). Not only does happiness exist, but 'psychology and brain science are beginning to give us the tools to arrive at *precise answers*' (Layard, 2005, p. 13).

The reason that Layard is so excited is a hyper-rationalist one. The highly influential Viennese circle of Logical Positivism had decreed that only the tangible and measurable could count as science. Layard is excited because now there is a visible 'objective' trace of emotionality. Therefore, the emotional life is demonstrated to be 'real', and now it can be studied by Science. In the hyper-rationalist account, prior to this, the emotions simply did not exist; as in the story of the Neem tree (see chapter 1), the lived experience of an emotional life counted for nothing. These points and issues will be developed further as we go along.

In case you were wondering quite what happiness *is*, he tells us: 'Happiness is feeling good, and misery is feeling bad . . . that feeling can now be measured by asking people or by monitoring their brains' (Layard, 2005, p. 6). These oversimplifications contain not only half-truths but also outright falsehoods. It is in this way that CBT manufactures and sustains its mythology. For one thing, it is quite untrue to say that the levels of activity in the brain 'can be *measured* in standard scientific ways' which give us 'precise answers'. All we can do is to notice a *correlation* between an experience and electrical activity in a particular part of the brain. Correlation is not measurement. Nor is it particularly surprising to discover that there are neurological and physiological correlates to one's emotional and mental life. Humans are bodies after all, and brains are a part of the body. What would be mysterious is if no cerebral activity were visible in tandem with lived experience.

Strangely, I often feel convinced by an experience of happiness, be it in another person or as a feeling within myself. I seem to require no further so-called objective evidence to substantiate its reality. I seem to be able to recognize the experience without the aid of brain scans or questionnaires. Am I deluded?

According to Layard the problem that humanity is blighted with is this: 'for some people it seems impossible *to be positive* without some physical help. Until fifty years ago there was no effective treatment for *mental illness*' (Layard, 2005, p. 9). Almost all the difficulties with the Happiness/CBT theses are encapsulated in the linkage between these two sentences. The subject of the first sentence is 'positivity', and that of the second sentence 'mental illness'. The two are conflated to produce the cognitivist belief that you should primarily be in a positive state of mind, and if not, then there is something wrong with you: you are suffering from *a mental illness*.

There is no place for ambiguity and ambivalence in CBT psychology; it is linear and one dimensional; it has no patience with complexity. 'Happiness is a single dimension of experience . . . *it is not possible to be happy and unhappy at the same time*' (Layard, 2005, p. 21; italics added). The treatment draws on the command and control ethos of hyper-rationality, so that the treatment is also devoid of complexity. 'Human beings have largely *conquered* nature, but they have still to *conquer* themselves' (Layard, 2005, p. 9). Layard continues 'The inner life . . . determine[s] how we react to life . . . So how can we gain control over our inner life?' (Layard, 2005, p. 184). The answer is CBT which we can use to 'train ourselves in the skills of being happy' (Layard, 2005, p. 189). These skills consist of techniques which train us to 'directly address our bad feelings and *replace* them by positive feelings, building on the *positive force* that is in each of us, our better self' (Layard, 2005, p. 188).

Operationalism: the Borrowers (borrowing from physics – again)

There is another point here which is easy enough to miss when Layard says 'feeling can be measured by asking people'. No doubt you have been doing this your whole lives; asking people: 'How are you?'. But Layard's kind of asking is scientific – unlike yours. But if you were to ask, 'how depressed are you on a scale of one to five', then that is scientific, *because the answer is a number*. By this subterfuge a subjective experience is given the gloss of objectivity.

This kind of 'measurement' practice in psychology and the social sciences generally, has its antecedents in physics, from which it has been borrowed. But that which has been borrowed – the principle of *operationalism* – has become distorted. The notion of operationalism in physics came about in the following way. Entities like the atom or electron are too small to study directly. So what physicists do is measure the *tangible effects* of interactions taking place in inaccessible realms, say by measuring how hot the atmosphere has become after some atomic reaction. So in its first incarnation, operationalism is a means by which we make inferences about something that is not directly accessible through tangible effects which are accessible.

It is quite reasonable to say that if we cannot *see* or *experience* something, then we have no way of knowing whether or not it exists. Claims that the world is populated by fairies fall into this category. We cannot assert that fairies exist, but nor can we say with full certainty that they do not. The position we are left in is agnostic – not knowing this way or that.

But when the positivists within psychology and the social sciences generally got hold of operationalism, they amputated one half of it and turned it into something else altogether. In this second incarnation, operationalism becomes rigid and puritan. In this incarnation it is not just declaring that things have to be shown to be tangible before we need take account of them, but that they have to be shown to be measurable in ways that accord with certain protocols. If it cannot be measured in these ways, then it is discounted. In this way operationalism has been co-opted by the positivists in the service of the belief that *only the quantifiable may count as science*.

The wisdom of this stance seems reasonable enough in the fields of physics, engineering, technology and chemistry. However, even in these fields there are ongoing arguments about the usefulness of the principles of operationalism and its limits.

Psychology however, is untroubled by these complexities, as it takes up a simplistic version of operationalism in order to make itself seem more scientific. Intangibles of the inner life (emotions, aspirations, satisfaction, etc.) are *operationalized*, that is 'measured' by the tangible. Mostly what these measurements consist of are questionnaires consisting of questions requiring a numerical answer. These numbers get added up to give a 'score', which counts as measurement. The questionnaires themselves are referred to as 'instruments', by which device they are given the semblance of scientific sounding credibility. This kind of practice is become so integral to the study of academic psychology today, that it is almost impossible to question its validity.

Green, a critic of operationalism in psychology, points out that one of the initial intentions of operationalism was *to do away with subjectivity* by only attending to the objective measurable. But what psychology has done has been to turn operationalism on its head and 'Instead of replacing "metaphysical" terms such as "desire" and "purpose" [they] used it to legitimize them by giving them operational definitions' (Green 2001, p. 49).

Mind that (dammed) gap

Ironically for a discipline that prides itself on being an empirical evidence-based science, CBT seems determined not to have anything to do with the material world. Proponents of CBT continually tell us that the problem is not out there; it has little to do with life circumstances. The problem is within: it either has to do with the faulty way you think about things, or with your faulty genes. I begin with the first of these.

CBT is confused as to whether unhappiness is in itself an illness, or whether it is a symptom of an illness. Sometimes it is one, sometimes it is the other, and sometimes it seems that people are unhappy for an entirely different reason: our 'habit' of comparing ourselves with others – social comparison.

There have been numerous epidemiological studies, one of the more recent being *The Spirit Level* (Pickett and Wilkinson, 2010), which show that the more unequal a society is, the more unhappy it is in the sense that it is prone to a whole range of social ills, from teenage pregnancies, psychological and physical health problems, increase in prison populations, street violence, and so forth. One would think that the obvious solution would be to reduce the social and economic disparities between the rich and poor. Layard and Clark's 'solution' avoids troubling itself with inequality or redistribution. Instead of addressing the causes of inequality, their solution is to change the thoughts of individuals, so that they are no longer troubled by the conditions they live in. We can see why their thesis is so appealing to the neoliberal elite. 'If happiness depends on the *gap* between your *perceived* reality and your prior aspiration, cognitive therapy deals mainly with the perception of reality' (Layard, 2005, p. 197; italics added).

Because the problem lies in our tendency to compare ourselves with others, we can solve the problem quite simply, by doing away with the 'gap'. The problem is not reality *per se*, but your *perception* of reality. Layard continues 'We constantly distort our perception of reality by unhelpful comparisons. So, one 'secret of happiness' is to enjoy things as they are without comparing them with anything better' (Layard, 2005, p. 49). There are many such secrets soon to be revealed.

Layard then muses upon why it is that women are still complaining about their lot even though their *absolute* situation has improved considerably over the last decades:

Women, whose pay and opportunities have improved considerably relative to men, but whose level of happiness has not . . . perhaps women now compare themselves more directly with the men than they used to and therefore focus more than before on the gaps that still exist.

(Layard, 2005, p. 45)

The problem is that dammed 'gap' again. If only women would learn to stop looking at the gap, they would enjoy the privileges that they have accrued and then, surely, they would be happy.

The trouble, is that 'People compare themselves . . . with people close to themselves . . . [their] "reference group"' (Layard, 2005, pp. 44–5). Layard uses this to explain why the rich tend to be happier than the poor. And it is not because as you might have foolishly supposed: that the rich are less troubled with life's hardships because they are more able to indulge their desires. Layard reasons otherwise:

The rich are so near the top that their reference group is likely to include people who are poorer than they are, while the poor are so near the bottom

that their reference group is likely to include people who are richer than they are. This helps to explain why the rich are on average happier than the poor.
(Layard, 2005, p. 45).

It's that dammed 'gap' yet again. It seems that we cannot *not* compare. The answer to this existential predicament is only now revealed by Layard: Stop comparing! 'So one "secret of happiness" is to enjoy things are they are *without comparing* them with anything better. Another is to find out which things really make us happy' (Layard, 2005, p. 53). Two secrets for the price of one. And if you can't hold back from comparing, then you can fall back on the third and most important of the secrets: *only compare downwards*. 'one secret of happiness is to ignore the comparisons with people who are more successful that you are; *always compare downward, not upwards*' (Layard, 2005, p. 47; italics added).

Unless of course you were unfortunate enough to be truly at the bottom of the pile, in which case it would be best if you could revert to the earlier secret: refrain from comparing altogether. In effect Layard is saying, be content with your lot. And if you are not, CBT will help you learn to be content. Because apparently 'There is as yet *no clear evidence* to show that inequality as such affects the happiness of individuals in a community' (Layard, 2005, p. 52; italics added).

Happiness is but a state of mind; a mood. So simple. So many secrets – secret no longer.

***

There is a further psycho-social predicament that humans suffer from which adds to their unhappiness – adaptation. Our happiness and pleasure in new goods – say a new car or computer – quickly palls and apparently, we revert back to our natural (measurable of course), set point of happiness. However, 'Other experiences do not pale in the same way – the time we spend with our family and friends, and the quality and security of our job' (Layard, 2005, p. 49). He does not trouble us with reasons as to why he thinks friends and family do not pall. Instead he reveals to us yet another secret: 'the secret of happiness is to seek out those good things that you can never fully adapt to . . . sex, friends and *even to some extent* marriage' (Layard, 2005, p. 49). But alas, relationships with children are a different matter altogether. Because apparently, unlike sex and friends, they pall on us in the same way as do cars and gadgets. He says: 'There is indeed great rejoicing when children are born. Yet within two years parents revert on average to their original level of happiness' (Layard, 2005, p. 66).

What could the moral of these cautionary tales be? Have sex with your friends but don't bother procreating?

Genetic determinism: blue genes

The other reason proposed for unhappiness is biology: the reason you are unhappy is because of your genetic makeup. Here too material social conditions are kept well out of the picture. In brief: It's your genes that give you the blues.

CBT goes out of its way to say over and over again that life experience has little to do with human suffering. 'Under the influence of Sigmund Freud, many people used to think that the first six years of life were critical for our happiness in life, and that little else mattered . . . [it turns out that] Upbringing still matters, though less than was once thought' (Layard, 2005, p. 59). And apparently 'As adoptees progress through life, the effect of their adoptive parents fades and the effect of their genes increases' (Layard, 2005, p. 59).

Layard cites studies that claim to show that one's capacity for happiness is pegged at a certain level by nature – that is, one's genes – and that level remains broadly stable despite the ups and downs of life, income and health. 'Since the 1960s it has become increasingly clear that genes play a significant role in all mental illnesses (Layard and Clark, 2014, p. 92). Hand over fist, mistruth follows exaggeration. 'We are now at a stage where individual genes have been identified which can predispose to depression or bad behaviour' (Layard and Clark, 2014, p. 97).

If bad genes cause bad behaviour, then good genes will give you good experiences. 'People with good genes also tend to get good experiences. Their parents are good at parenting. Their own niceness elicits good treatment from other people' (Layard, 2005, p. 58). Presumably the parents of children who have good genes are good at parenting because they have the good genes that they have passed onto their offspring.

Many are likely to balk at the kind of genetic determinism that is being promulgated by Layard, Clark and others. In part because of its sorry history and the insidious uses genetics has been put to over recent centuries to legitimate racism, sexism, anti-Semitism and the criminalization of the poor and dispossessed. Anticipating this, Layard lays claim to the moral high ground. 'Why talk about genes at all? *Because we are interested in the truth*' (Layard, 2005, p. 56). Thus, by implication, those who question Layard's love affair with genes, are not particularly interested in truth, and (unlike Layard) are ideologically driven.

Despite claims to truth and to scientific rigour, pretty much each and every one of these statements on genetics is false. No single gene has ever been found for depression, schizophrenia or anxiety. CBT has replaced what it has called psychoanalysis's unsubstantiated speculations about the inner psychological world, with its own substantiated speculation about the inner biological world.

If we follow Layard to the bitter end (and it is bitter), it is hard not to come to the conservative conclusion that ultimately, breeding tells. Those who prosper and are happy do so because of their good genetic makeup. And those that don't prosper and find it difficult to achieve the goal of happiness, do so because of their bad genes.

***

It turns out that there is yet one more reason as to why people are prone to feeling anxious and depressed. This is something left over from early human history:

> It was important to be on guard when man first evolved on the African savannah. When you are in danger of being eaten by a lion, it is a good idea to be extremely cautious. Even depression may have had some function . . . [but] nowadays these mechanisms of anxiety and depression are much less essential that they were in the African savannah. By using our brains, we have largely conquered nature . . . *Much of our anxiety and depression is no longer necessary*. The great challenge now is to use our mastery over nature to master ourselves and to give ourselves more of the happiness that we all want.
>
> (Layard, 2005, p. 27 italics added)

In other words, our feelings of anxiety and depression are an unfortunate residue from our pre-history; they are unnecessary in these civilized times, they make our lives needlessly difficult – they make us ill.

Cognitivist social policy: 'blessed are the poor . . .'

Although when examined many of these claims and assertions turn out to be absurd, they nevertheless have provided the rationale for some of the social policies put forward by both the Labour as well as the Conservative parties over the last decades. The New Deal being the most prominent of them. For this reason, it is worth a brief look at some of Layard's assertions about social conditions in general.

Layard's attitude towards women and the poor are somewhat problematic. He addresses the question of whether mothers of young infants should stay at home rather than work. He says in passing, 'There should be no social pressure on parents to work, *unless they are living on benefits at other people's expense*' (Layard, 2005, p. 178). It is worth giving that sentence another parse. Only those *not* living on benefits should be free of pressure to work. But if they are not living on benefits, then they either they have money in the bank or they are being supported by someone who has money or is in employment. In other words, they have the luxury of being able to *not* work.

There is a big difference between choosing not to work and being unable to work. To be on benefits however is not a luxury whatever the tabloids might scream. Layard reveals that he thinks that those on benefits are feckless shirkers, the undeserving poor. The outcome then of his proposal, is that children born to those on benefits are said to be *undeserving* of having a mother at home during their early years. Meanwhile the children of the relatively well to do will be the beneficiaries of Layard's child rearing proposals. No wonder New Labour admired him.

Layard is nostalgic for the 'good old days' and their conservative moral certainties. For example, he bemoans 'The decline of Christianity . . . [which] has left a moral vacuum' (Layard, 2005, p. 92), and complains that,

> In recent decades it has become increasingly difficult for teachers to teach moral values as *established truths,* rather than as interesting topics for discussion. We have to pull back from this situation and teach the wisdom of the ages as well-established principles.
>
> (Layard, 2005, p. 200)

One such established truth appears to be that marriage is good for you and cohabitation is not. This is because 'People become happier as a result of marriage' (Layard, 2005, p. 65), and although 'cohabitation is becoming much more common, it has not so far proved as stable a form of relationship as marriage' (Layard, 2005, p. 66). In many places we catch a glimpse into his preoccupation about marriage and its parlous state in contemporary society. For example, 'If you feel low, there are centuries-old philosophies to help. Better to seek the beauty within than to have an affair' (Layard, 2005, p. 235). He tells us that affairs are more likely these days in part because of the contraceptive pill, the advent of which 'made extramarital affairs a lot safer' (Layard, 2005, p. 84). A contributory factor to marital breakdown is that women 'are now as educated as their husbands and have the same need to use their brains' (Layard, 2005, p. 85), from which 'new dangers to marriage arose just as women's economic opportunities made splitting up less financially devastating' (Layard, 2005, p. 74). Technology was also to blame. Labour-saving devices meant that more mothers could take jobs. However, 'many men felt that they got less attention than before from their wives . . . [resulting in] greater . . . dissatisfaction. It was also becoming easier to split up . . . [there was less] *financial pressure on the wife* to stay in an unhappy marriage, and likewise the *moral pressure on the husband* to remain' (Layard, 2005, p. 84).

Another reason for married couples staying together (according to Layard), is because children from single parent families are more prone to criminality and mental illness.

> If by sixteen you are living with only one of your biological parents, you are more likely to suffer from multiple disadvantages . . . more likely to have a criminal conviction . . . twice as likely to leave school with no diploma . . . have a child in your teens . . . [and] likely to be doing nothing at the age of twenty.
>
> (Layard, 2005, p. 61)

Leaving aside the truths of these assertions as well as the confusions between cause and correlation, the point is this: he is now talking about children being damaged by *life experiences*. The only way it is possible to square this genetic circle is by saying that it is the bad genes in the children in the first place that is the cause of them being adopted and living in single parent families.

Part II

Politics of identity formation

Chapter 4

Master-myths and identity formation

Absolute beginnings

Victors write history to give accounts in which they are the heroes of the piece. The victor's history is imposed as the real and only history, annihilating all alternative accounts of events. The ideological function of these sorts of histories is to create mythologies about the victors – that they are the good guys. This narrative works back to reinforce the very mythology that created it in the first place; it does this by making it appear that the narrative is simply an objective telling of a factual story. As Roland Barthes said: 'myth has the task of giving an historical intention a natural justification . . . and making contingency appear eternal . . . it has emptied it of history and has filled it with nature . . . *myth is depoliticized speech*' (Barthes, 1984: 142; italics added).

The victors not only have the possibility of establishing their mythology as the 'true' and only history, they also have capacity to determine where the story begins. This we are all bound to do to; to make any narrative comprehensible, we are bound to make a start somewhere. This sharp cut inserted into the infinitely long process of existence itself, is described by the sociologist Norbert Elias as an 'absolute beginning'. So when we say: 'In the Beginning' we have to keep in mind that this beginning is one of convenience and that always something has proceeded it. But Elias tells us that the choice as to where and how one creates a beginning is never innocent and merely functional. Its placing has an ideological function as well. A key function of the absolute beginning, is to expunge what has gone before as though it had never existed. In this way the beginning is made to look absolute.

The master-myth of conquerors, be they conquerors of colonies, scientific disciplines or religious movements, is that before we came there was only darkness and confusion into which we brought the light of reason. In some master-myths the hero is flawed, makes mistakes and struggles painfully towards the Holy Grail. In others, the hero is a superhero whose progress is relentless and flawless.

Thrive: The Power of Evidence-Based Psychological Therapies (Layard and Clark, 2014) published to coincide with the tenth anniversary of the CBT revolution, is a master-myth of the latter kind. It is a story of relentless progress entirely devoid of errors, wrong turns or mistaken hypotheses. Like victorious generals, Layard and Clark rehearse and reinforce the rationales first put forward in *Happiness* and The Depression Report and look back at the successes of their campaign strategy called Increasing Access to Psychological Therapies (IAPT). Reading this work, it would seem that the 'science' put forward ten years previously was utterly fool proof; no adjustment has been required. The tone of conviction and certainty with which they describe their endeavours is absolute. However, when we peek behind their absolute beginning, we will see that their version of events is not just biased, but wilfully misrepresents things to present a picture in which they and CBT are the saviours of the world. Alternative viewpoints are either not mentioned at all or dismissed in a cavalier fashion. By proceeding in this fashion, Layard and Clark are following a well-established strategy that has been tried and tested by colonialists and imperialists of old.

Terra nullius – politics

When the European adventurers stumbled across dark continents and 'new' worlds, they managed the extraordinary feat of perceiving lands full of people and ways of life as empty of both, as 'No Man's Land', as *Terra nullius*. And being empty, they claimed them as their own. They pronounced these lands to be in a state of Nature, and not just lawless but devoid of law. And so they saw it as their moral duty to bring the land and its inhabitants into the orbit of Law and Reason. The ways of the native were deemed to be primitive, irrational, uncivilized and immoral – ways to be replaced by the enlightened ways of the colonizer.

However, at the same time that the native and their ways were being discounted and denigrated, they were simultaneously being exploited for their labour and plundered of their riches – material, spiritual and intellectual. The colonizer made free not only with the flora and fauna, but also with their agricultural and other forms of knowledge accumulated over untold generations (e.g. turmeric and the Neem tree). In doing so, the colonizer did not think of themselves as plundering or stealing, rather, they conceived of themselves as engaged in the activity of science. They saw themselves as bringing order to disorder, as bringing the light of reason into the darkness of superstition. History itself was thought to begin with the colonizer stepping onto the virgin 'new' land. As far as the colonizer was concerned, there was no *his*-story and certainly no *her*-story, there is only *our*-story.

Psychologica nullius – psychological sciences

Exactly the same thing has taken place in the fields of psychology and psychotherapy. According to CBT mythology, the field of psychology before the advent of CBT was almost empty of knowledge as well as authorities, it was *Psychologica nullius*. 'Almost' because they do allow for the prior presence of behaviourists.

As with the Neem tree, all psychological knowledge that pre-existed the advent of manualized CBT which was *not in the approved form*, was readily dismissed and discounted as anecdotal. And as in the colonial situation, CBT viewed the land of psychology as virgin and empty. There was nothing of any note until recently: 'Scientific methods have only been widely applied to designing therapies for about twenty-five years' (Layard and Clark, 2014, p. 255). And it was only 'in the 1960s and 1970s [that there were] . . . major breakthroughs in psychological therapy. The most important of these was what is now called Cognitive Behavioural Therapy' (Layard and Clark, 2014, p. 7).

Because this land was empty, its resources belonged to no one; therefore, they were there for the taking. In this way all kinds of psychotherapeutic practices and techniques which have developed over the last century have been hijacked, colonized and appropriated by CBT.

For example, Layard and Clark claim 'role play' to be a technique specific to CBT. They make no mention whatsoever of any of the many other therapeutic schools (drama therapy, psychodrama, Gestalt) that have previously honed role play techniques over many a decade. By this device they commandeer 'role play' to make it both, the invention as well as the property of CBT.

Similarly, they manage to annihilate the entirety of hundreds of years of thinking about the emotional significance of early family life. In their account, the extraordinary discovery that *family life matters* happened first in 1964, when a CBT researcher 'George Brown, a British psychologist, discovered that the family environment in which a person lives has a big influence on whether they relapse in the face of stress' (Layard and Clark, 2014, p. 30).

Their rendition of the history of cognitivist psychology is one of heroic struggle against overwhelming odds and against the forces of superstition and darkness. '[CBT is a] product of a whole community of people who have been struggling to bring evidence-based psychological therapy to the millions of people who need it' (Layard and Clark, 2014, p. ix). After years of heroic struggle, CBT eventually saved the day.

They tell us that the 'facts we lay out are in many cases quite remarkable – indeed after many years in the field some of them still amaze even us' (Layard and Clark, 2014, p. 4). Many of these facts are indeed remarkable for their novelty, but not for the reasons given by Layard and Clark, rather for the perverse way that they represent reality and the way that history is rewritten. For example, they mention Pavlov approvingly saying 'the Russian physiologist Ivan Pavlov . . . showed that fears in animals could be extinguished by exposing the animal to the object of its fears in a gradual way' (Layard and Clark, 2014, p. 9). This is a somewhat peculiar depiction of Pavlov given that he is best known for using electric shocks to *produce* fears rather than for finding ways of benignly extinguishing them. Pavlov won his Nobel Prize for his work on the study of the digestive system which involved using surgical techniques to relocate the salivary glands of dogs outside their bodies, so that the saliva could be gathered and measured. He then went on to put dogs under intolerable stress by torturing them with electric shocks in order to find ways of and manipulating their responses. As already mentioned, the Happiness guru Martin Seligman followed in these self-same distasteful footsteps to also torture dogs with electricity to produce the 'condition' he called 'learned helplessness' – a finding that was put to good use by the CIA in the torture chambers of Guantanamo Bay (Ferraro, 2015).

Their master stroke however, was the appropriation and colonization of the term 'therapy' itself, swiftly followed by the colonization of the term 'talking therapy'; by this device CBT positioned itself as *the* and *the only* 'talking therapy', and the only therapy worth talking about. In previous incarnations however, cognitivist treatments were called 'training' delivered by 'instructors'. These terms – training and instructors – are much more honest because they fit with the intention of CBT treatments to train the mind to function differently. We will find this to be the case in the final chapter. The therapy 'Mindfulness Based Cognitive Therapy (MBCT)', was initially known as 'attentional control training' delivered by 'instructors' rather than therapists.

It seems to me that the reason behind the change of term from training to therapy is because therapy sounds more prestigious as it evokes connotations of cure, whilst training evokes connotations of symptom management. But as Shakespeare once almost said, 'a training by another name is still a training'.

Lumpy soup: identity formation

Master-myths are stories of identity formation: they tell us: who we are, why we are, how we came to be, and why we are rightfully here. So what makes CBT, CBT?

CBT sets itself apart from, and above other psychotherapies by manufacturing for itself a very particular identity: that of being evidence-based and differentiates itself from all the other therapies that are, allegedly, not evidence-based. But identity formation is not as straightforward as it is made out to be, as in the simple naming of things that exist as unproblematic givens 'out there' in the world; things like apples and oranges. Am I similar or different to you? Of course, I am both. I am similar on the basis of some attributes (perhaps ethnicity, perhaps religious affiliation or lack of) *and at the same time* different to you on the basis of some other attribute (perhaps gender, perhaps colour). This is to say that things are never similar *or* different. They are *always both*. And so, there is always a choice as to which similarity or difference we will emphasize and amplify. It is in this way that we generate particular versions of 'us' and 'them'. The choice as to which we amplify, is determined in part by the ends we desire, which in turn are informed by the ideologies we embody.

The National Front, UKIP and others claim that they are fighting to preserve something they call Englishness – English culture, English heritage, the English race. But as soon as we try to get a hold of English culture, it disintegrates into a number of differing, overlapping, conflictual English cultures, urban vs rural cultures; secular vs religious; Northern coal miner vs London fashionistas vs Labour Union activist vs football fans vs Oxford don vs assembly worker, and on and on.

It is also the case that very many characteristics of English culture are also shared by other cultures. Precisely because it is impossible to say what English culture *is*, the focus is shifted to what *it is not*. By this device, the notion of English culture is given the illusion of substance and coherence. Similarly, the Untouchable has a very different experience of Hindu culture from that of the Brahmin; Moslems of one kind kill those of another kind as do Christians and Communists, and on and on. There are untold formal and informal markers that are used to include and exclude good people from bad, differentiating an 'us' from a 'them'.

Hopefully, what is becoming clearer through this brief discussion, is that identity formation is primarily a process of *differentiation* rather than of coalescence. The same sorts of processes of inclusion and exclusion continually take place in all kinds of identity formation from schools of philosophy to professional designations to teenage fashions. If we look a little closer into the identity called CBT, we will see that it manufactures and sustains its identity in exactly this sort of way.

The CBT literature habitually describes its identity history as consisting of a series of waves. The first wave was behaviourism; the second wave was initiated when cognition was bolted onto behaviourism and CBT came into existence. When all the fancy language is stripped out, the ethos of the second wave is primarily that of thought control: catch your negative thoughts and replace them with positive ones. In contrast, third wave CBT treatments promote various forms of acceptance of inner turmoil. The techniques that are taught are in fact meditative strategies drawn from ancient Eastern philosophies such as Buddhism and Hinduism. This is why in the third wave we find an abundance of terms like attachment, compassion, mindfulness, and acceptance.

Given that the ethos of the second wave *sharply contradicts* that of the third wave, control and annihilation *vs.* compassionate acceptance, the first question to be asked is: what characteristics do the 'waves' share that allow them both to be called forms of CBT? It seems to me that their shared characteristics have little to do with actual content (as the values and forms of the 'waves' are so divergent), and more to do with the ways in which the 'treatment' is legitimated and promulgated. To count as CBT, the treatments have to fulfil four conditions. Whist the first three are necessary, the fourth is desirable.

The first condition is that the treatments have to be didactic and directive; they are 'trainings' in which experts train the recipients in the practice of certain mental techniques. Second, the treatments have to be 'tested' in accordance with the conventions of positivist empirical science. Third, if they are found to be efficacious, the treatments themselves should be manualized so that all practitioners closely follow in the footsteps of the study itself. And finally, it helps if the name of the treatment includes the word 'Cognitive' in some way, and so we have treatments such as 'Mindfulness Based *Cognitive* Therapy'.

In addition to Mindfulness, there are a number of other alphabetty (a term coined by the psychiatrist Rex Haigh) third wave therapies out there; CFT – Compassion Focused Therapy; DBT – Dialectical Behavioural Therapy; ACT – Acceptance and

Commitment Therapy; FAP – Functional Analytic Psychotherapy; MCT – Meta Cognitive Therapy, to name a few.

There is something more to be said about the relationship of the third wave to the Eastern philosophies that it makes use of. Recall the story of the Neem tree. CBT has stripped out and appropriated meditative practices from the philosophies and meaning worlds that have generated them and reduced them into sets of techniques and skills to be learnt. In effect, the philosophy and practice of Mindfulness has been colonized by the device of giving it the gloss of 'Science'. Knowledge and expertise no longer reside with monks and mendicants who have put in lifetimes of practice to achieve something akin to the state of Mindfulness. Now all one has to do is to take a twelve-week course to achieve the same ends.

In proceeding in this way, not only have these practices have been instrumentalized, but worse, the end to which they have been instrumentalized is a perversion of the very philosophies that generated them. In Eastern philosophies, the purpose of meditative practices is to help the meditator to work towards the state of Nirvana, which requires the dissolution of the Self. In CBT practice, Mindfulness and the like are being used in the service of reinforcing the Self. But worse is to follow. In the very same breath as mentioning the Buddha, Layard, and Clark celebrate the fact that, 'The Resilience Programme [which utilises mindfulness] is now being used for every soldier in the US Army, with the aim of reducing the incidence of post-traumatic stress disorder after traumatic experiences on the battlefield' (Layard and Clark, 2014, p. 230).

In other words, the Buddhist practice of mindfulness is being used to turn human beings into more efficient, more resilient, killing machines.

***

Today, before the regulatory authorities will even deign to entertain the possibility of validating some mode of therapy, that therapy has to demonstrate its worthiness by accruing an empirical evidence base. This is the gateway through which all hopeful psychotherapies have to pass. However, in trying to pass through this gateway, life itself gets distorted.

For example, I have decided on an experimental protocol to distinguish that which is edible from that which is not. To this end I have decided that only those substances that I am able to pick up with chopsticks will count as food. So according to this 'protocol', soup could never count as food. It matters not to me if you say that you have eaten soup and been nourished by it. *Because* your form of evidence falls outside my experimental protocol, I think it anecdotal and hearsay. Your form of verification, which is your experience (you did ingest it, you enjoyed its taste, you felt nourished, your hunger was assuaged, you did not die), none of this has any legitimacy in my protocol; this is simply anecdotal evidence; so what you say counts for nothing.

If it is just silly old me that thinks this ridiculous thing, then it is not so important for the fate of the world. But if powerful persons, disciplines, institutions and governments also come to think this and advocate for it, then this way of proceeding is become a paradigm. Paradigms powerfully lock in certain ways of thinking and practicing as legitimate, and in the same moment exclude and lock out everything else. However ridiculous the chopstick protocol, this is nevertheless exactly what has been taking place in regard to CBT and NICE. None of the alternatives are granted a voice in the overly medicalized frame of reference legitimated by NICE. More on this in chapter 8.

Within this paradigm, the form of psychotherapy that I and many others practice is soup. Because it cannot be grasped by NICE's positivist chopsticks, it simply does not exist. In order to enter the paradigm, I have to find a way to *lumpify* the soup so that it may be grasped by chopsticks. However, if I am able to do this, what is being captured *is no longer soup*. In becoming lumpified, the soup has become something else. In order for it to be made measurable in this way, it has to be distorted, so much so, that once distorted, it is no longer recognizable as itself. Today, this is what many schools of psychotherapy (including psychoanalysis) are trying to do, lumpify their practice, so that it can be picked up by NICE's positivist chopsticks and be counted as legitimate practice.

Rationality and power

We have seen why the impossibility of precisely delineating who or what 'we' *are*, necessitates a shift of attention onto what we are *not*: onto 'them'. But as we have also noted, the differentiation of an 'us' from a 'them' is a constant and necessary work. Necessary, because both, the similarities between the 'us' and 'them', as well as the differences within the 'us', continually threaten the integrity of the 'us'.

The point bears repeating: identities are not simply found, they are forged out of power struggles emanating in the interactional field. The conventional narrative of scientific 'progress' is the rationalist one: science progresses, step by step, in accordance to emerging evidence. Eventually the better idea overwhelms and replaces the weaker one. This is the case with the rhetoric emanating from CBT. It claims that it is being backed by the authorities because it has provided scientific evidence of its treatment successes – something which the other psychotherapies have singularly failed to do.

But ideas and professions are not distinct from each other. Professional bodies forge their identities in part through affiliations to specific ideas and against other ideas. The status of a professional group rises and falls with the fortunes of the ideas that they affiliate themselves with. The rationalist narrative obscures the narrative in which self-interest and power-relations permeate and influence the directions taken by the rational. But this kind of influence tends to remain unrecognized and unregistered as its features would seriously undermine the values of the rationalist ethos.

I begin by introducing perspectives put forward by the sociologist Norbert Elias as they will be invaluable in helping us understand the seemingly non-rational twists and turns of the story. Elias gives power relations a key role in the organization of society and its artefacts.

Norbert Elias and the charisma of power

Power is charismatic – power is sexy. And those that are cloaked in it somehow come to glitter; we tend to defer to them, we find ourselves admiring and emulating them; and mostly we do all of this without being aware that we are doing so, and why we are doing so.

It is embarrassing to admit, but true nonetheless, that whatever the actual attributes of the more powerful, often enough we find ourselves to a greater or lesser degree, unthinkingly emulating them, *despite our rational and ethical faculties*. But there something even more troubling here: our very rationales and ethics are in part formed and informed to some degree by the ruling ethos. It is the powerful who decree what is good and what is bad, which we somehow come to take in at a deep level; it is what we come to think, feel and believe to be the case. What I am describing here is nothing other than the workings of ideology.

Mostly, what is decreed to be 'the good' is, by definition, that which is in the interests of the more powerful; it is the rulers who decree what is good and what is outlawed. This is clearly evident when we look at ruling religious factions – be they Christian, Moslem or Buddhist. In one context to be Sunni is good, in another Sunnis are to be exterminated. In one context Protestants are devils, and in another it is the Catholics.

This same pattern can be found in politics too. The current Conservative Government in the UK drafts more and more measures that make protest and criticism of its politics illegal and punishable. In doing so it is positioning the ethical actions and protests of some of its citizens as morally wrong. To have any chance of prospering in a particular 'system', one has to demonstrate one's allegiance to, and go along with, the ruling ethos.

To repeat the point: what is being spoken of here is not fear driven compliance, a pretence that one believes X, in order to be looked on favourably by a group of Xs (although that too takes place). But the more profound situation, wherein one actual comes to believe and experience the world according to the Xs. In short, we are susceptible to being turned by the charisma of power.

The point is a deep one, and pertinent to the discussion that follows regarding Science, and its privileging of fact over value. The deep point is this: that often enough we are drawn to a course of action that gives succour to the ruling values, rather than by the 'facts', and sometimes *even despite the facts*. To put it in plainer language – nothing succeeds like success.

But in arguing against the rationalist version of things, there is a danger that I overstate my case; let me rectify that now: We humans are not entirely sheep, blindly believing and following the dictates of the more powerful. We are also thinking, Kantian beings, capable of examining, questioning and changing our conditions of existence. We are children of the Enlightenment – but not entirely, and much less so than the positivists suppose.

This then is the claim: *what we come to think of as good and pursue, is shaped as much by the vagaries of the political landscape as anything else*. All this is also true of the discourses known as Science and their legion of positivist claims such as that their decisions and directions are driven by facts and not values; that these facts are discovered by dispassionate investigators who are seekers of objective truths; that these truths are discovered and established through rigorous and repeated testing and probing; that the scientific establishment would regretfully but readily give up on any established belief (however cherished), as soon as there is any evidence that contradicts it. This is the mythology of Science. Behind the mythology lie politics, human frailty and self-interest.

Norbert Elias and *The Civilizing Process*

In his epic work *The Civilizing Process*, Elias laid bare some of the workings of power-relations through an examination of (amongst other things) the history of manners in the land that was to become known as Europe.

He showed us how identity itself was being continually forged out of the workings of power-relations. He did this by tracking the vicissitudes of the distinction between the aristocrat and the commoner – and specifically the well to do commoner, those belonging to the middle or professional classes.

The aristocrats (the more powerful), distinguished themselves from the commoners by a range of means from ideas and beliefs, to codes of everyday practice (gestures, accents, dress, etiquette). For example, that their blood was different to that of the commoner and should not be mixed with theirs through marriage – true even today. Both, the more powerful as much as the less powerful, believed that those who had power superiority had it *because they were superior beings*.

The commoner, drawn to the ways of the charismatic aristocrats, tries to emulate them in any number of ways from speech to etiquette. This results in the distinctions between the aristocratic 'us' and hoy polloi 'them' becoming blurred; consequently, the identity of the aristocrat is somewhat eroded. The aristocrats then set about bolstering their identity by re-establishing the distance between themselves and the rest. This they manage by further elaborations in their systems of etiquette and so on. In time this too comes to be incorporated by the commoner, which in turn continues to drive repeated cycles of elaboration by the aristocrats followed by its emulation by the commoner.

This movement is most clearly shown to us by Elias through the shifts in etiquette at the dinner table. In the Middle Ages people used their hands to take food from a common bowl and place it directly in their mouths. Each person dipped their bread into the common bowl repeatedly, picked out meats, put back partly chewed food, and so on. Progressively, plates were introduced, injunctions increasingly prohibited the use of the hands to eat and to serve, and instruments for eating and serving were made more complex. Eventually, further rules were prescribed on how the instruments were to be held, not 'with the whole hand, like a stick; you should always hold them with your fingers' (La Salle, 1729, cited by Elias 1994: 78).

We can see here how the aristocrat's attempts to preserve distinction were being continually eroded by the commoner's desire to emulate them, and why this escalating 'arms war' drives the requirements of etiquette of the more powerful in directions that are increasingly complex, elaborate and intricate.

What we are witnessing here is the process in which identity is being forged out of the vicissitudes of power relational struggles. *Importantly, all this is taking place with no conscious thought; there is no deliberate intention or design here.* The aristocrats are not deliberately saying: 'we will now invent a new kind of fork to eat cake with, because that will help us maintain our distinction from the commoner'.

This kind of unconscious movement towards the more powerful (and therefore more charismatic) is found everywhere in human life. For example, the directions being taken by some forms of modern music can be understood as manifestations of this kind of process. The leading lights of jazz push the boundary of what is considered to be musical by some improvisational innovation. This novel form is emulated by the 'ordinary' jazz musician because of the esteem that they hold the innovator in. This in turn provokes those at the cutting edge to further innovate to retain their position at the cutting edge. And so it has come to pass, that what is understood as musical in these territories, is a long way away from any notion of 'the tune' itself. In some settings improvisation is privileged over harmony to such a degree that it can result in a form of music, which to my untutored ear, sounds like random noise.

In art too, the movement has been away from representation (which is looked down on by many contemporary artists), and towards increasing abstraction. High street fashion too works in exactly this way. Haute couture is emulated by the high street department store, and in a moment, we find ourselves (despite ourselves) loving flared trousers and platform soles, and in another, thinking them ridiculous. The speed of change reveals just how vulnerable we are to this process – despite our rational capacities. The thing is that when we are in the grip of a particular world view (or fashion even), that particular perspective tends to seem to us to be an eminently sensible one. Our rationales for actions are often post hoc rationalizations. For example, Elias has shown that the earlier rationales regarding eating habits had less to do with hygiene and more to do with social standing. For example, 'If everyone is eating from the same dish, you should take care not to put your hand into it before those of higher rank have done so' (De Courtin, 1672, cited by Elias 1994: 75) and 'It is a far too dirty thing for a child to offer others something he has gnawed, or something he disdains to eat himself, *unless it be to his servant*' (Calviac, 1560, cited by Elias 1994: 74).

The rationale of hygiene (although true) came much later; it was in a sense an afterthought.

The function of shame

Shame plays a critical role in all of this. Its workings are seen most clearly when looking to the more banal context of codes of dress. Shame phenomena are clearly visible not only when one looks back at the conventions of Court Society, but also today in formal settings as well as the day to day vagaries of fashion. All this is particularly the case with adolescents. To wear the wrong kind of trainer can all elicit taunts and mockery from peers. These are activities of shaming. The pressure to be 'in', to be 'cool' is severe and cannot be overestimated. But shame can also arise within oneself, without being actively sham*ed* by others. Shame is the response that arises within one, when deviating from norms that one subscribes to. I need to stress that in speaking of 'subscribing', I am not referring to a conscious rational and cognitive decision; rather I am referring to deep unconscious processes that are integral to our human sensibility.

One feels ashamed when one deviates from established norms, however capricious they might be. In one moment I feel cool wearing platform shoes and flares. In the next moment they suddenly seem utterly ridiculous and are consigned to the bin.

Shame then is an aspect of the self-policing and other-policing activity that we are all unconsciously mired in. Metaphorically speaking, shame is the mechanism which entices us back towards and into ruling norms.

But it is not all plain sailing for the more powerful ruling elites. Their authority and privileges are constantly being challenged by cultural movements that explicitly challenge the ruling norms and those that embody them. Hippies, Black Power, feminism and punks come to mind. In these processes we are witnessing power-relational struggles playing themselves out. We are witnessing the means by which the marginalized gather together to challenge the hegemony of the centre. Each position is in a manner of speaking, a paradigm; each constitutes a discourse that advocates particular sets of values, beliefs and practices; and being discourses, they are self-validating. Each can be called a culture. The centre deals with them in one of two ways.

First, it mocks and demeans those who challenge its authority, portraying them as misguided and deluded, or as mad, bad and dangerous. Elias names this a 'gossip process'. Elias tells us that gossip draws on instances of the 'the best of the best' to enhance the image of the 'us', and the 'worst of the worst' to denigrate and mock the 'them'. In this way gossip is used to maintain the 'us'/'them' divide. Gossip mobilizes shame to shame those who transgress the division. On the other hand, the centre also colonizes that which challenges it, thus appropriating it. In taking ownership of it, the centre makes it seem that that has always been its rightful place.

In the story that follows, one of the things we will get a chance to see, is how gossip is employed to maintain a division between a good 'us' (CBT) vs bad 'them' (psychoanalysis). We have already witnessed the other strategy in play, colonizing techniques from the therapies it denigrates, to claim them for itself.

Science is driven (in part) by these kinds of power relational processes. *Where power lies, there we will be drawn*. Today, the conventions that have become established within the 'court societies' of Science, are intensely positivist and reductionist. In this court only the observable and measurable is granted validity by the ruling ethos, and so quantitative research methodologies become sanctified as the only road to truth. On the basis of the Eliasian argument just elaborated, we can see why all are likely to scramble to clothe themselves in the same attire as the ruling elites, to make themselves respectable and acceptable to those that rule the Scientific Courts. When ideas are supported by the respected in our scientific societies, the ideas themselves become respectable.

Eliasian gossip mills: the manufacture of opposites

One way of manufacturing an 'us' is by insinuating a rupture that makes it appear that the 'us' is distinct from 'them'. The 'them' are distanced by portraying them in a dark and peculiar light which makes them look grotesque. In contrast the 'us' are bathed in lighting that makes them look appealing. In the language of Norbert Elias, the different kinds of light are being generated by gossip mills. When the 'us' has emerged out of the 'them', it becomes particularly necessary to reinforce the distinctions between the two because of the constant danger that they will become one again. In the project of differentiating itself from psychoanalysis, CBT has generated a number of such oppositions. But as we examine them, we will see that they are less convincing than the rhetoric makes them out to be.

Gossip mills come in many forms, not just the stereotypical ones made up of busybodies conversing across garden walls. The most effective gossip mills are the ones that disguise themselves as disseminators of factual science.

Cause and maintenance

As we have previously noted, CBT texts tend to parody psychoanalysis as end-lessly and fruitlessly rummaging about in the past, looking for the root causes of difficulties. According to CBT accounts, this is *all* that psychoanalysts do, and it is *the only thing they ever do*. 'Freud's view [was] that successful treatment should focus on identifying the origins of a mental health problem' (Layard and Clark, 2014, p. 136).

CBT says that to look for causes is a waste of time. CBT treatments claim to focus almost exclusively on the question: What keeps the problem going? The *reason* why you might be depressed is of less consequence to CBT than how you *keep* yourself depressed. They call this 'maintenance': '[Research shows that the] treatments that are most effective are generally those that focus on the psychologi-cal processes that are known to maintain the condition, rather than on the original cause' (Layard and Clark, 2014, p. 176).

The focus on 'maintenance' turns depression into a technical problem rather than a moral and ethical struggle with meaning making. To this way of thinking the mental illness called depression has no more meaning than any other physical illnesses which infect innocent persons. It is not 'necessary to know what caused the cancer – you cure it by cutting it out . . . Similarly, infections are often cured with antibiotics, *without knowing their causes*' (Layard and Clark, 2014, p. 109). It really does not matter why you got depressed. What matters is to be cured of it. 'It may not be necessary to know why this person has blocked arteries – you cure the breathlessness by putting in a stent' (Layard and Clark, 2014, p. 109).

In order to maintain the dichotomy, CBT has to continually assert that practitioners of CBT *have no interest in cause*; CBT texts habitually mock those who think that there is some virtue in thinking about how the situation has arisen: 'if you want to put out a fire then you had better tackle what keeps it going – heat, fuel, oxygen etc. – rather than look for the match that started the fire' (Westbrook et al. 2008, p. 40). But now, having made this opposition between cause and maintenance, they are unable to hold to it:

> someone who was frequently criticized in front of other children by hypercritical adults may have difficulty dealing with authority figures at work. *Once this cause is established*, a simple technique might involve selectively focusing on everything about the authority figure at work that is different from the critic in one's childhood. *If this is not helpful, more detailed discussion of the early trauma may be indicated in order to reduce its emotional impact.*
>
> (Layard and Clark, 2014, p. 146; italics added)

They also allow that a 'first episode of depression is often triggered by *an adverse life event* (loss of a job, break-up of a relationship, death of a loved one) or by chronic stress (ongoing financial difficulties, bullying at work)' (Layard and Clark, 2014, p. 153; italics added). This first episode, which is where 'helplessness is learnt', is said to be the basis for all future episodes of depression. These secondary depressions have no external causes, they are just the reproduction of habituated negative thought patterns of the 'learned helplessness' kind found by Seligman. It becomes clear that when they are arguing for the irrelevance of 'cause', they mean emotional or life situational cause, in other words they are doing away with meaning. In the main CBT treatments are designed to treat those who are suffering when there is no 'adverse life event' evident. Many CBT treatment centres explicitly exclude from treatments people who are depressed for *reasons*.

Clearly then, 'cause' and 'reason' do matter to CBT; their claim that there is no need to attend to the causes of distress is plainly false. It is also mischievous gossip on their part, to assert that psychoanalysis does not attend to the present and 'maintenance'. The whole ethos of the 'transference' which is central to psychoanalytic treatment is based on the belief that problems of the past play out in the present. Say a patient comes for psychoanalytic treatment because he feels intimidated by authority figures. During treatment, the patient is likely to experience the analyst in a similar way, even though this particular analyst (let us say) is not an intimidating presence. The patient is thought to be 'transferring' an experience from another situation into the present. When this experience in the here and now is analysed, then a link is made with the fact that the patient had (say) been bullied terribly by his father when he was a child. The idea is that as this is unpacked and understood in the present, it will free the patient to experience future authority figures more realistically and so be able to respond more appropriately. *In these ways the psychoanalytic treatment can be construed of as examining and dismantling the habituated ways in which the problem is maintained.*

With this Eliasian schema in mind, let us look at how things played out between and within the 'psy' professions over the last hundred or so years in the UK and US as this will shed light on the political reasons that lie behind the advancement of CBT.

Chapter 5

The 'psy' wars

The protagonists in the story that follows are the professions of psychoanalysis, psychiatry, medicine and clinical psychology; and the story itself has to do with their struggles to gain and retain scientific respectability. The rationalist history of CBT and psychology casts itself as an objective history of science and method. In contrast, this narrative brings an Eliasian perspective to bear on the power struggles between the professions, to show how and why CBT came to profit, and how cognitivist clinical psychology came to prosper as an outcome of these struggles.

Fin de siècle psychoanalysis – 1900

The Freudian revolution flickered into life at the turn of the twentieth century, and very quickly swept across the 'Western' world. In the early part of the twentieth century, it reigned supreme as the only credible way of thinking about the human psyche. In the US, by the 1930s, the treatment of choice for almost all psychological ailments was that of psychoanalysis. The treatments were delivered in the private setting by psychoanalysts and in hospital settings by psychiatrists – psychiatrists who were almost entirely psychoanalytic in their outlook. The dominance of psychoanalysis in the clinic as well as in the culture at large was indisputable. Psychoanalysis accrued extraordinary amounts of mystique and prestige and was feted by the intelligentsia, Hollywood and the film and media industry generally. But it was a hierarchical profession in which only medical doctors were allowed to train as psychoanalysts, and then as only certain kinds of psychoanalysts. In the US the profession rigidified to become increasingly authoritarian, dogmatic and conservative in its outlook. There were of course dissenting voices from within the psychoanalytic community, but these were readily sidelined and ignored by the main stream.

Money (as ever) was key. It was expensive to train first as a medical doctor, and then as a psychoanalyst. It was no surprise then that psychoanalysts, like the rest of the medical profession, were largely, but not entirely, drawn from the privileged classes. They had the situation sown up – they were beneficiaries of the prestige accruing to psychoanalysis mixed in with the fact that the profession was a 'closed shop'. It was also the case that the analyses of patients were (and remain) extraordinarily costly – five times a week for ten and more years not being unusual. To be able to partake of psychoanalytic treatment, one had to be either very ill and institutionalised, funded by health insurance companies, or extremely wealthy.

Critical to this whole story is the turn taken by Freud early in his career from the external social world to the internal psychological world. The profession followed him into the turn where the classical form of psychoanalysis remains marooned to the present day.

In his early theorizations Freud gave actual life experiences a significant role in the creation of neurosis. For example, the idea that infants and children might be damaged when brought up by abusive parents. But then Freud changed his position and came to think that the sources of neuroses were not to be found in actual lived events, but in fantasy. Freud thought that humans were born with instincts that were in perennial conflict with each other. These instincts and their conflicts gave rise to fantasies and desires that could not be expressed in civilized society. The most famous of these is perhaps the 'Oedipus complex' wherein the child is said to desire the parent of the opposite gender. Because the very thought was taboo, the desire was repressed and made unconscious; this sort of repression is the source of neurosis.

Crucially, Freud also came to think that reports of abusive parents were born of fantasy not reality. He thought that infants and children projected their sexual and hateful instincts into their parents, who they consequently came to experience as sexual and hateful. The work of psychoanalysis was in part, to reveal the reality behind the fantasy, so that eventually the parents would come to be viewed in a more realistic light. Freud and the psychoanalysts that followed him were emphatic: the causes of the difficulties of social life will be found in the difficulties residing in the psyche. In other words, the external social world could only be understood by looking to the internal psychological world.

For these sorts of reasons, psychoanalytic treatment came to focus almost entirely on the internal world of patients, as this was where the sources of disturbances were thought to lie. Psychoanalysis made a powerful dichotomy between the internal (psychological) world and external (social, political) world, and gave precedence to the internal/psychological over the external/socio-political. The social was the effect of the psychological. Henceforth it became psychoanalytic blasphemy and treason to give any credence to the idea that actual external events played a role in the creation of psychological distress. When analysts found themselves seduced by this error, it was regarded by the profession as 'acting out'.

It was during this time, whilst the classical psychoanalytic empire was at its imperial height, that the tide began to turn against it. Even as psychoanalysis was being feted by Hollywood and the intelligentsia, it was also coming to be viewed as the (interminable) treatment of the privileged by the privileged, and having little to do with the suffering of ordinary people in the ordinary world. The steadfast psychoanalytic preoccupation with the internal instinctual world made it seem increasingly remote from the concerns of ordinary folk struggling with life in the Great Depression as it came to be known. Treatments were costly and time consuming – meeting three to five times a week for ten or more years. At today's rates, a ten-year treatment using psychoanalysis in the UK would cost the patient something in the region of £140,000 at the rate of £70 per session. Rates in the US have always been more than double that of the UK. In this way psychoanalysis progressively came to be viewed as somewhat elitist and removed from the realities of ordinary everyday human existence. In some quarters, psychoanalysis was increasingly viewed as a form of faith healing and mystical thinking that exploited the vulnerable, and gullible, rich.

The psychoanalysts of course did not think of their profession and practice in this way. They presumed to have access to reality itself. The psychoanalyst's interpretation about what was 'really' going on in their patient's psyches were absolute and final. Questions, challenges and disagreements emanating from patients or commentators tended to be dismissed as defensive resistance to facing up to the truth named by the analyst. Analysts regularly construed the patient's disagreeing or questioning the analyst's pronouncements as being born of some kind of pathology, for example, born of innate envy of the analyst's capacity to think, and so forth. In this sort of way psychoanalysis made its world view impregnable with the psychoanalyst as the first and final arbiter of the nature of reality.

For these sorts of reasons, many people were becoming progressively disenchanted with the entire psychoanalytic enterprise. The imperial and imperious attitude of psychoanalysis and its preoccupations with the internal world *to the exclusion of all else*, prepared the ground for the advent of the cognitive revolution. In effect psychoanalysis was complicit in its own downfall.

The Behavioural challenge for the psychological throne

Whilst the psychoanalysts were rummaging about in the psyches of patients, a powerful new challenger was emerging on the psychological scene – Behaviourism – championed by proponents such as John B. Watson and B.F. Skinner in the US, Ivan Pavlov in Russia, and later by Hans Eysenck in the UK.

John. B. Watson started out as an animal behaviourist. As we might expect of a behaviourist, Watson focused entirely and only on behaviour. He thought animals were mindless, machine-like entities and, therefore, the need to engage with them was deemed unnecessary. He observed responses triggered by particular stimuli from a detached position as befitted a scientist. But then when he started to study human beings, he did that too in exactly this way: 'The behaviourist . . . recognizes no dividing line between man and brute. The behavior of man, with all of its refinement and complexity, forms only a part of the behaviorist's total scheme of investigation'

(Watson, 1913, p. 158). Although this statement was published in a paper called 'Psychology as the Behaviorist Views It', in Watson's psychology there was no room for psychology itself; notions of mind, thought and emotion were completely absent. Watson's psychology was not psychology as the term is commonly understood; it was an anti-psychology. He avoided consideration of mind entirely in order to focus on the outside of the body, on its visible *behaviour*. 'Psychology as the behaviorist views it is a purely objective experimental branch of natural science. Its theoretical goal is the prediction and control of behavior. *Introspection forms no essential part of its methods* . . .' (Watson, 1913, p. 158; italics added).

Behaviourism was a part of the same wave of scientification that was sweeping through economics, the social sciences and 'the humanities' in general. Large swathes of sociology, anthropology, psychology, economics and even ethics, were all recasting themselves as rational sciences by focusing entirely on the objective measurable and countable (facts) and distancing themselves from everything else; 'everything else' was consigned to the dustbin called 'values'.

Watson tells readers of his book *Psychology from the Standpoint of a Behaviourist* (1919),

> The reader will find no discussion of consciousness and no reference to terms such as sensation, perception, attention, will, image and the like. These terms are in good repute but I have found that I can get along without them . . . I frankly do not know what they mean.
>
> (Watson, 1919, p. xii)

In the 1930s, B.F. Skinner joined Watson's attack on 'mentalism'. Mentalism, according to Skinner was the mistaken belief that a person could understand their actions through introspection. Introspection of course was at the heart of psychoanalysis. This was a key feature used to define the identity of Behaviourism: it was not-psychoanalysis, it was the antithesis of psychoanalysis.

Skinner and his kin were anti-Kantian mechanists; according to them the experience of choosing, of reasoning, of will and the like, were all illusory '[consciousness] has never been seen, touched, smelled, tasted or moved. It is a plain assumption, just as unprovable as the old concept of the soul' (Watson and McDougall, 1929, p. 15). 'The behaviourist cannot find consciousness in the test-tube of his science. He finds no evidence anywhere for a stream of consciousness . . . We need nothing to explain behaviour but the ordinary laws of physics and chemistry' (ibid., pp. 27–8).

Human beings were simply animate *machines* to be studied from a detached scientific perspective, in order to learn how to control and manipulate behaviour by applying stimuli to generate required responses. Volition was an illusion. In this way the human subject became edited out of behaviourist investigations into human subjectivity.

Of course, if Watson and the behaviourists had allowed themselves even a modicum of introspection, they would have had to concede that their sense of autonomy was also illusory, and their seemingly rationalist scientific productions were simply mindless responses evoked by some previous stimuli. The stimuli being their hatred of psychoanalysis.

The cognitivist challenge for the psychological throne

It was on the back of behaviourism that some 30 years later in the 1960s, the psychiatrist Aaron Beck instigated the cognitivist revolution. Beck had trained as a psychoanalyst with the Philadelphia Institute in the 1950s. Although Beck completed his psychoanalytic training successfully, his application to become full member of the American Psychoanalytic Association was repeatedly turned down. This was because the treatment protocols that Beck started to introduce and promulgate (for example the use of questionnaires) ran counter to established psychoanalytic orthodoxy.

If you can't beat them, one strategy is to try to join them. If you can't do that either, then another strategy is to try to destroy them. Prohibited from joining the psychoanalysts, Beck was left with the second option, the destruction of psychoanalysis itself. Beck followed in the footsteps of his behaviourist forefathers. He stayed away from introspection and kept his focus firmly on visible, observable and measurable behaviour, that is, on the *outside of the body*.

During this time there was a growing tension within psychiatry between those who remained with the psychoanalytic orthodoxy and those who joined the ranks of the new behavioural and cognitivist 'science'. One territory in which this tension played out had to do with the politics of academic appointments. For example, when the time came to appoint a new Chair at Beck's very own psychiatric department, a battle broke out between the behaviourists and psychoanalysts as to whose champion should be appointed. Eventually, the behaviourists won the day when their man Albert Stunkard was elected. This was one of many such political victories which were taking place in academia all over the US. It was the culmination of these sorts of victories that led to a huge sea change that took place in psychiatry, away from introspection and towards measurement.

Aaron Beck's initiative was a corrective to the Skinnerian thesis. Beck's great insight was this: human beings were more than mechanical bodies; humans were more than machines mindlessly reacting to stimuli. Aaron Beck made the remarkable discovery that humans also had minds which contributed to *how* they responded to inputs and stimuli. While Beck allowed humans minds and the possibility of thought, it remained a mechanistic mind which produced thoughts that were hyper-rationalist. Beck thought that the difficulties of life were caused by logical errors in the thinking process, and so his cognitive treatments sought to correct them. Although in principle Beck had bolted cognition onto behaviourism, the focus of his treatments was almost entirely cognitive. This shift came to be known as the 'Second Wave', and Cognitive Behavioural Therapy was born.

The US: Psychiatrists *vs* medics, and the birth of the DSM

From its inception, psychiatry had been struggling to be taken seriously by the rest of the medical profession. Mainstream organic medicine dismissed psychiatry as non-scientific mumbo jumbo as it dealt with emotional and mental intangibles that could not be grasped by the positivist conventions that had become established norms within medicine. This was doubly the case in the US where during 'the late 1960s and early 1970s, most practicing psychiatrists had a psychoanalytic orientation' (Kutchins and Kirk, 1997, p. 62). The psychiatric profession was being continually embarrassed by the fact that there was no consistency or reliability to the diagnoses conducted by psychiatrists: 'a patient identified as a textbook hysteric by one psychiatrist might easily be classified as a hypochondriac depressive by another' (Spiegel, 2005: 57).

> In 1949, the psychologist Philip Ash published a study showing that three psychiatrists faced with a single patient, and given identical information at the same moment, were able to reach the same diagnostic conclusion only twenty per cent of the time. Aaron T. Beck, one of the founders of cognitive behavioral therapy, published a similar paper on reliability in 1962. His review of nine different studies found rates of agreement between thirty-two and forty-two per cent. These were not encouraging numbers, given that diagnostic reliability isn't merely an academic issue: if psychiatrists can't agree on a patient's condition, then they can't agree on the treatment of that condition, and, essentially, there's no relationship between diagnosis and cure.
>
> (Spiegel, 2005: 59)

The fact that psychiatric diagnoses were neither reliable nor reproducible constituted a methodological crisis and fatal problem for a profession that wanted to be a part of the scientific community. The nature of their problem was this: before research can even begin, there needs to be agreement as to what it is that is being researched. If psychiatrists could not even agree who was suffering from depression, how could they even begin to test whether a certain treatment was going to be beneficial to 'the depressed'? Psychiatry fell at this very first hurdle.

The birth of descriptive psychiatry

This is where a psychiatrist called Robert Spitzer comes in. According to Spiegel, Spitzer was 'without question, one of the most influential psychiatrists of the twentieth century' (Spiegel, 2005: 56).

Spitzer sought to improve the fortunes of psychiatry by jettisoning its affiliation to psychoanalysis as well as its focus on the internal psychological world. Spitzer was on a mission not only to follow in the footsteps of the behaviourists and cognitivists in focussing on the external and measurable, he was going to outdo them. He was going to make psychiatry a part of mainstream medicine, by turning it into an empirical evidence-based science.

He managed this extraordinary feat by transforming the *Diagnostic and Statistical Manual of Mental Disorders* (DSM) into the definitive diagnostic instrument utilized today not only by psychiatry and the 'mental health' industry, but also, among others, by courts, social services, schools, social scientists, insurance companies, and of course by IAPT and NICE. It is habitually used by governments and their agencies to design funding and treatment policies. The DSM has crucial significance for the subject of this book because all CBT research is pinned onto one or other of the diagnostic categories found in the DSM. So if the DSM is found to be wanting, then so will the claims of CBT researchers and clinicians.

Very quickly, the DSM became integrated into all aspects of scientific and public life. Today, there is almost no questioning of its validity in mainstream psychiatry and psychology. The prestige of the DSM is due in part to the fact that it is endorsed by prestigious psychiatrists (cf Elias), and in part by the general perception that its contents are the discoveries of science – empirical science. This perception was driven in large part by Spitzer himself (but also by prominent members of the psychiatric community) who blatantly stated in the 'Introduction' to the DSM-III, that the assertions found in the DSM had been rigorously scientifically 'tested': Spitzer claimed that drafts of the DSM were tested in field trials involving over 12,000 patients and 550 clinicians in 212 different facilities (Spitzer, 1980, p. 5). *There is no evidence for this momentous claim.* These sorts of claims are an instance of gossip – which if repeated often enough, come to take on the appearance of truth.

Spitzer's strategy closely follows that of Beck and the behaviourists. No more would psychiatry attend to aetiology, questions of *why* things have gone wrong. Imponderables of this kind – *explanations of difficulties* – were portrayed as the preoccupation of psychoanalysts. In lieu of *explanation*, psychiatry turned instead to *description*. Henceforth psychiatry would stay on the surface of things and construct its formulations only on the basis of what was visible, tangible and observable – symptoms, behaviours and traits – and in doing so, they would ensure that the psychiatric endeavour became objective. In this way, Descriptive Psychiatry was born.

Spitzer's DSM listed 265 'mental disorders', each allegedly discrete and differentiated from the others by virtue of the list of observable symptoms. The new diagnostic process consists of attending to a checklist of symptoms (do you have suicidal thoughts? No; yes, once a week; twice a week, etc.). Because the symptoms and behaviours are said to be observable, the diagnosis that followed out of it was claimed to be objective. Spitzer claimed that Descriptive Psychiatry had solved the reliability problem. Psychiatrists would now be able to agree diagnoses with each other because diagnoses were being based on objective criteria.

The advent of the DSM

But first, how did Spitzer and colleagues decide what was and was not a 'mental disorder'? And how did they come of formulate their checklist of symptoms or traits associated with each disorder?

In most people's minds the image of the process is likely to be one of dispassionate scientists laboriously and carefully sifting through data, testing, and retesting, to arrive at conclusions and assertions akin to objectivity. But what actually occurred was the polar opposite of that. According to the accounts of those *who actually participated in that process*, those meetings were entirely chaotic, and in no sense could they be said to be in any way scientific. David Shaffer, a British psychiatrist who worked on the DSM-III and the DSM-IIIR said:

> There would be these meetings of so-called experts or advisers and people would be standing and sitting and moving around . . . people would talk on top of each other. But Bob [Spitzer] would be too busy typing notes to chair the meeting in any orderly way.
>
> (Spiegel, 2005: 59)

One participant said that the haphazardness of the meetings he attended could be 'disquieting': 'Suddenly, these things would happen and there didn't seem to be much basis of it except that someone just decided all of a sudden to run with it' (Spiegel, 2005: 59). Allen Frances (who became editor of DSM-IV) agrees that the loudest voices usually won out . . .

> The way it worked was that after a period of erosion, with different opinions being condensed in his [Spitzer's] mind, a list of criteria would come up . . . It would usually be some combination of the accepted wisdom of the group, as interpreted by Bob, with a little added weight to the people he respected most, and a little bit to whoever got there last . . . Spitzer seems to have made many of the final decisions with minimal consultation.
>
> (Spiegel, 2005: 59)

> Someone would yell out the name of a potential new mental disorder and a checklist of its overt characteristics, there'd be a cacophony of voices in assent or dissent, and if Spitzer agreed, which he almost always did, he'd hammer it out then and there on an old typewriter, and there it would be, sealed in stone. It seemed a foolproof plan.
>
> (Ronson, 2011, p. 250).

Even so, it was not all plain sailing. There were many disputes and conflicts. For example, feminists and other activists objected to Spitzer's attempt to include three new diagnoses in the DSM-III, Masochistic Personality Disorder, Paraphilic Rapism, and Premenstrual Dysphoric Disorder, on grounds that they all unfairly blamed the female victim for the abuse suffered by them (women were 'asking for it', or they were genetically designed to desire violation). When asked, what happened to the Masochistic Personality Disorder by Jon Ronson, Spitzer replied: 'We changed the name to Self-Defeating Personality Disorder and put it into the appendix' (Ronson, 2011, p. 252). The Premenstrual Dysphoric Disorder was also put into storage in the appendix, where it languished until the production of the DSM-V. At which point it was dusted off and made its way back into the main body as a *real* disorder because of 'strong scientific evidence'. Quite what this evidence was remains a mystery.

Another of the disputes took place in regard to homosexuality. To begin with, in accordance with the psychoanalytic belief at that time, homosexuality was thought to be a perversion and an illness; for this reason, it was included in DSM-II under the classification *Sexual Deviation Disorder*. After much protest by gay right groups and argument within and without the APA, the next edition of the DSM-III downgraded the disorder to *Ego-dystonic Homosexuality*. This was a compromise solution to appease both camps – the ones who thought homosexuality was an illness and those that did not. The compromise was the tacit suggestion that those homosexuals who were not troubled by their sexual orientation could be thought of as 'well', but those who were troubled by their homosexual impulses were ill and suffered from this disorder. Further arguments developed following the publication of the DSM-III: activists argued that in a primarily heterosexual context, all homosexuals would inevitably be somewhat troubled by their impulses to a greater or lesser degree, and so DSM-III's definition pathologized *all* homosexuals. Their argument won the day and led to the removal of homosexuality entirely in DSM-IIIR. But in the DSM-IV it found its way back again, this time disguised as *Sexual Disorder Not Otherwise Specified*, one characteristic of which is 'Persistent and marked distress about sexual orientation'.

In their book *Making Us Crazy*, Kutchins and Kirk devote an entire chapter to 'The Fall and Rise of Homosexuality' because,

> The homosexuality controversy illustrates . . . that science is often not central to the decision to include or exclude a diagnosis from DSM. The dispute over the inclusion of homosexuality in DSM *was not about research findings*. It was a 20-year debate about beliefs and values. Although the professionals who formulated diagnoses couched their arguments in the language of science, the actual influence of empirical data was negligible. More often than not, the issues were settled by political compromises that promoted personal interests.
> (Kutchins and Kirk, 1997, p. 56)

The decision as to whether or not homosexuality is a disorder has repercussions not only for homosexuals, but for society as a whole in the most unlikely places. For example, when the definition of homosexuality was de-pathologized in the DSM,

> the APA president, Jack Weinberg, protested against the refusal of the United States government to naturalise homosexuals. Weinberg argued that the

deletion of homosexuality from the DSM necessitated a revision in immigration laws that excluded gays.

(Kutchins and Kirk, 1997, p. 85)

This is why the enormous scientific, political and cultural influence of the DSM cannot be overstated. Its iconic presence is everywhere; its authority is called on for all manner of things. The presence or absences of diagnostic categories are used to argue for and against social policy. It has become locked into, and is essential to, a range of formal decision-making processes in medicine, health, science and social policy. The DSM has become integral to the operation of health insurance companies, their policy on funding for treatment, and what they might pay out for. It affects university life: it is nigh on impossible to get funding for drug or psychological research that does not utilize categories developed by the DSM. Policy-making by governmental agencies regarding funding for psychological treatment is entirely reliant on the DSM.

The invention of PTSD

Lawyers belonging to the California Trial Lawyers Association wrote a paper 'The New DSM-IV: Is It Easier to Prove Damages?' (von Tagle, 1995) in which they celebrated the fact that the DSM-IV made it easier to prove damages because of the enormous number of confusing subcategories contained within the diagnosis of Post Traumatic Stress Disorder (PTSD).

PTSD did not exist as a diagnostic category in the early part of the twentieth century. It first started to come into prominence in the 1960s and 1970s, borne out of a specific need. Thousands of Vietnam War veterans could not settle back into ordinary life in the US because the war had damaged their emotional lives. To begin with, the government flatly denied that its soldiers had been severely traumatized by their experiences in Vietnam. The idea of trauma as a disorder did not exist. '[So] The first steps in obtaining treatment and other benefits for psychiatric disabilities were to identify the disorder from which the veterans suffered, to give it a name, and to have it included in the DSM' (Kutchins and Kirk, 1997, p. 108). The veterans militated for the inclusion of a category in the DSM, which Spitzer resisted because

the veteran's proposal violated basic guidelines about theory and research that had been established for DSM-III. Whereas *those involved in the creation of the new manual were attempting to eliminate etiology from their description of disorders*, the veterans' proposed a diagnosis *linked with a specific cause*, catastrophic trauma, to the disorder.

(Kutchins and Kirk, 1997, p. 114; italics added)

Nevertheless, despite this critical anomaly – allowing aetiology (explanation) into the diagnostic formulation rather than relying entirely on description – it was *political pressure* that overwhelmed the DSM's descriptive paradigm. This resulted in a new diagnosis being created, PTSD.

> Veterans fought hard for the inclusion of PTSD in the DSM not because they were enthusiastic about identifying their problems as a mental disorder, but because they needed recognition of the fact that war had seriously damaged them and that they needed help in overcoming its effects. *The price they paid was to be identified as mentally ill.*
>
> (Kutchins and Kirk, 1997, p. 125)

But this is not the end of this particular story. When PTSD was first introduced into the DSM-III, those who were deemed subject to this 'mental disorder' were traumatized soldiers. In other words, those who were traumatised primarily through being the *perpetrators* of violence. But in DSM-IV, PTSD shape-shifted and its focus became centred entirely on the *victims* of violence (accidents, domestic and sexual abuse and so forth). While this shift is not unreasonable in itself, it did not come about because of scientific research, but rather through the advocacy of various pressure groups.

In sum, the story of PTSD not only shows up the vacuity of the claim that its contents of the DSM are scientific but also reveals that the DSM is the gate through which all must pass before they will be given a hearing by the legislature and the authorities generally.

The creation of the mental disorder called depression

What I want to do next is to focus on the 'mental disorder' called depression, on how it came to be created, and how it continues to be sustained. I do this because the notion of depression played a key role not only in the 'psy' wars, but also in the production of CBT. In what follows, I draw heavily on the works of Kutchins and Kirk, Joanna Moncrieff, and Ben Goldacre.

I, like many, had taken it for granted that it is established scientific fact that depression is correlated with low levels of the neurotransmitter serotonin in the brain. Treating depression with SSRIs, that is, Selective Serotonin Reuptake *Inhibitors* seems perfectly reasonable as the drug helps *raise* the level of serotonin floating around in the brain. Rather bewilderingly, it turns out that another drug called Tianeptine which *lowers* the level of serotonin in the brain works as effectively as SSRIs on depression (Goldacre, 2012, p. 257). If only on this single piece of evidence, one would have expected reasonable scientists to abandon the serotonin hypothesis (the discovery of one black swan disproving the claim that 'all swans are white'). But it was not to be so. Despite the presence of this sort of evidence, the serotonin hypothesis, the 'chemical-imbalance-in-the-brain' theory, continues to hold sway within psychiatry. The serotonin hypothesis is psychiatric *folklore*, but enormously powerful nonetheless.

> It is somewhat bewildering to discover that despite SSRIs being around for several decades, that contrary to popular belief, it has *not* been demonstrated that depression is associated with an abnormality or imbalance of serotonin, or *any other* brain chemical, *or that drugs act by reversing such a problem.*
>
> (Moncrieff, 2011, p. 177)

The situation is even more extraordinary. There have been several meta-analyses of the data (for example, Kirsch et al., 2002, 2008), which unequivocally demonstrate that the advantage of SSRI's 'over placebo is small, and possibly clinically meaningless' (Moncrieff, 2011, 177). Yet substantial *scientific evidence* of this kind is unable to make a dent in the prevailing belief system. Which is somewhat ironic given that the rhetoric of the psychiatric profession deifies positivist scientific evidence. What on earth is going on and how has it come about? Moncrieff characterizes the thinking around psychiatric conditions prior to the 1950s as 'drug centred'. At that time psychiatric drugs were thought to be similar to recreational drugs in that both produced altered states of consciousness in the mind.

> According to this model, psychiatric drugs might well be helpful, not because they reverse an underlying brain abnormality, but because the psychoactive state they induce may suppress or mask the manifestations of emotional or behavioural problems . . . psychiatric drugs . . . work, or appear to work, when they do, by putting people in a drug-induced state which is preferable . . . to whatever state they are in when drug-free.
>
> (Moncrieff, 2011, p. 177)

Things changed with the arrival of the 'antipsychotic' chlorpromazine in the 1950s. Researchers claimed that chlorpromazine was not masking, but actually *treating* the underlying chemical causes of psychiatric conditions. Henceforth, medication was portrayed as 'disease specific' (in contrast to 'drug-centred'). Psychiatry was mimicking the course taken by organic medicine 'in developing disease-specific models of treatment, psychiatry was following a general trend within medicine . . . [in this task] drugs are often credited with revolutionizing psychiatry by bringing it in line with [the rest of] medical science' (Moncrieff, 2011, pp. 176–7).

With this in mind, let's get back to the story of the anti-depressant. Unsurprisingly, the first drugs used for the treatment of depression were stimulants (to counter depression), and they were thought to work because of the alternative states of mind that they produced – states of mind that *masked* the depression. But when depression started to be treated by a new class of drugs called tricyclics, the first of which was imipramine, things changed. Unlike the prior treatments (stimulants), these drugs were strongly *sedating*! Thus 'it was difficult to construct a drug-centred rationale for the usefulness of imipramine in depression . . . Its use could only be rationalized on the basis that it exerted its effects by acting on the pathological basis of a depressive illness' (Moncrieff, 2011, p. 180). This continued the shift in which drugs were presented as being disease-specific.

Imipramine was first proselytized by Swiss psychiatrist Roland Kuhn who promoted the *speculative* view with no basis in evidence of any kind 'that imipramine reverses the biochemical of physical substrate of depression' (Moncrieff, 2011, p. 181). With this unsubstantiated unscientific assertion, the idea of an antidepressant was born: a drug that allegedly targeted and *treated* the disease called depression (even whilst it sedated the patient). The idea was further promoted by the dissemination of propaganda by prominent psychiatrists who went on record making entirely fictitious claims with no basis in reality – positivist or otherwise. For example, '[these drugs have] clear-cut effects on pathological states and almost no effect on normals', and 'imipramine . . . is not merely sedative and symptomatic . . . but *curative*' (Deniker and Lemperiere, 1964, p. 230).

Despite dissenting voices (and evidence) challenging this increasingly prevalent belief, a consensus began to grow, so much so that by the 1960s, 'The overwhelming majority of research and other "official" information such as textbooks and formularies implicitly accepted the notion of a specific drug for depression . . . [and] contrasted the specificity of antidepressants to the implied non-specificity of stimulants' (Moncrieff, 2011, p. 183).

By the 1990s,

> the widespread use of antidepressants helped to strengthen the concept of depression as a common biological disorder and the idea that personal problems could be attributed to a chemical imbalance. That is, *the very concept of the antidepressant helped to fashion our modern notion of depression.*
>
> (Moncrieff, 2011, p. 184)

This whole way of thinking in the psychiatric profession was driven by the profession's concern 'to integrate with general medicine, to establish its scientific credentials . . . [in order to] improve its status' (Moncrieff, 2011, p. 184). To this end the DSM-III saw 'the deliberate restitution of medical diagnosis to the heart of psychiatric practice and research' (Moncrieff, 2011, p. 185). However, 'There was, and remains, *no evidence* to suggest that imipramine and other antidepressant drugs act in a disease-centred fashion on the biological basis of depressive symptoms' (Moncrieff, 2011, p. 187). This developing viewpoint suited the interests of the pharmaceutical industry for whom this became a lucrative commercial opportunity, and so it threw its weight behind the further medicalisation of human distress. Moncrieff concludes:

> Few people are aware that these [diagnostic] concepts have their origins, not in robust scientific research, but rather in the interests of a psychiatric profession desperate to cement its professional position, and in the marketing tactics of the pharmaceutical industry. Antidepressants have transformed a myriad of social and personal problems into a source of corporate profit and professional prestige.
>
> (Moncrieff, 2011, p. 188)

Depression and the depressing politics of science

As already mentioned, there have been a number of meta-analyses that unequiv-ocally show that anti-depressants hardly do any better than inert placebos. For example, Kirsch and Sapirstein (1998) drew on research that offered depressed patients anti-depressants, placebo, psychotherapy, or no treatment at all. While there was hardly any change in the group that received no treatment, it turned out that not only did those given anti-depressants improve, so did those that received psychotherapy as did those on placebo. What is more, is that 'the placebo effect . . . was twice as large as the drug effect' (Kirsch, 2011, p. 191). They rep-licated their study (Kirsch et al., 2002) using different sets of clinical trials – both published and unpublished. On combining the results from all the trials (published and unpublished) they found that the placebo response was almost as much (82 per cent) as the response to the anti-depressants. Kirsch continues:

> The mean difference between drug and placebo was less than *two points* on the HAM-D . . . [However], NICE which drafts treatment guidelines for the National Health Service in the United Kingdom has established a *three point* difference between drug and placebo on the HAM-D as a criterion of clinical significance (NICE, 2004). Thus when published and unpublished data are combined, *they show no clinically significant advantage for antidepressant medication over inert placebo.*
>
> (Kirsch, 2011, p. 193; italics added)

Given that these sorts of results have been replicated by many other groups of researchers (for example, Barbui et al., 2008), why is it that advice from NICE continues as before: there is a disease called depression, and it is to be cured by use of anti-depressants and CBT? The answer is money and politics.

Ben Goldacre argues that the pharmaceutical industry has played a significant role in the corruption of scientific research practices. Over the last few years it has increasingly become apparent that the research culture within evidence-based medicine and evidence-based psychology has largely been driven in directions that have served the fiscal interests of the pharmaceutical industry with the con-nivance of their champions bought and paid for within industry and academia. 'Ninety per cent of published clinical trials are sponsored by the pharmaceutical industry, [which means that they] . . . dominate this field, they set the tone, and *they create the norms*' (Goldacre, 2012, p. 174; italics added).

The (lack of) reliability of the DSM

Each CBT treatment is hitched onto a specific diagnostic category belonging to the DSM. Like psychiatric medication, each CBT treatment claims to be disease specific. They are obliged to do this for two reasons, the first is scientific and the second political. First, all scientific research is obliged to name and define a discreet entity that is being researched into. All the mental illnesses included in the DSM have already been defined descriptively, in the ways that we have just seen. So the DSM constitutes a ready-made list of approved categories requiring treatment. Second, it is nigh on impossible to get funding for research that is not hitched to one of the diagnostic categories contained in the DSM. So any doubt about the status of the DSM, will have an immediate impact on the status of any research that uses the categories provided by the DSM.

Key to the success of the DSM is its claim to reliability. Spitzer says emphatically in the introduction to the DSM-III, that the DSM has solved the reliability problem in psychiatry, and that that previous drafts of the DSM were tested in field trials involving over 12,000 patients and 550 clinicians in 212 different facilities (p. 5). This does make the whole enterprise sound very impressive: It 'was a momentous scientific and political claim . . . [However] All these recent claims about DSM-III's radical improvement in reliability were made *without citing a single study or source of evidence*' (Kirk et al., 2013, pp. 148–9).

Yet, the official position of the psychiatric profession remains that the reliability problem in psychiatry has been solved. In each new edition of the DSM is the claim that with this new edition, reliability has been even further improved. It is surprising then to discover that for a project that values evidence so highly, as yet there is no convincing evidence for this claim, and in actual fact what evidence there is, goes counter to this assertion.

> During the production of the DSM-IV the American Psychiatric Association received funding from the Macarthur Foundation to undertake a broad reliability study, and although the research phase of the project was completed, the findings were never published. The director of the project, Jim Thompson says that *the APA ran out of money.*
>
> (Spiegel, 2005: 63; italics added).

This seems to me to be highly implausible – in what sense would the American Psychiatric Association run out of money? After all, it had just sold 830,000 copies of DSM-III making many millions of dollars in the process. How much money would it take to employ a post-doctoral student to finish writing up research that has to do with the flagship enterprise of the profession? It seems to me more than likely that this is yet another case of researchers burying their unflattering negative results. I cannot believe that if the research showed any hint of an increase in the reliability of diagnosis, that it would not have been trumpeted from the rooftops. Another major study that was published was authored by Spitzer's wife, Janet Williams. The claim, in the way it was written up, was that the study unequivocally demonstrated the reliability of the DSM-III (Williams, 1992). But Kutchins and Kirk found otherwise:

> The study was conducted at six sites in the United States and one in Germany. Experienced mental health professionals . . . were given special

> training in how to make accurate DSM diagnoses . . . They were trained and supervised by a research team that was perhaps the most experienced in the world . . . Following this extensive training, pairs of clinicians interviewed nearly 600 prospective patients. The objective was to determine if the clinicians who saw the same client would agree on . . . [the] diagnosis.
>
> (Kutchins and Kirk, 1997, p. 52)

They continue:

> The findings of this elaborate reliability study were disappointing even to the investigators. The kappa values (the statistical measures of reliability) were not that different from those statistics achieved in the 1950s and 1960s – and in some cases were worse.
>
> (Kutchins and Kirk, 1997, p. 52)

But further, it turns out that the standard of agreement required by the study of those doing the diagnosis was that they should be in agreement merely about the general *class* of diagnosis, and not a specific diagnosis. In other words, all they were required to do was to agree that the patient had say, a Personality Disorder, not whether it was a Borderline Personality Disorder, or Avoidant Personality Disorder, or Schizoid Personality Disorder. So even if three researchers had separately arrived at a conclusion featuring a different personality disorder, this would have been counted as success according to the protocols of the study. So even with the bar set this low in these highly controlled laboratory conditions, the reliability of the DSM could not be demonstrated. What chance then for the beleaguered clinician in a busy clinic to produce accurate reliable and consistent diagnoses?

It hard not to agree with Kutchins and Kirk that 'The DSM revolution in reliability has been a revolution in rhetoric, not in reality' (Kutchins and Kirk, 1997, p. 53). Given that Spitzer had specifically set out to solve the reliability problem by replacing the variability in human judgement with objective lists of criteria, why has he and those who followed him not succeeded (although they continue to claim that they have)?

One reason is that the list of traits for any given disorders were (and are) by no means foolproof. Typically, for any 'mental disorder' the DSM will provide a list of symptoms and assert that if a specified number of them are present, then that individual is indeed suffering from that disorder.

For example, in the DSM-IV, the list for Major Depression has nine symptoms. We are told that if five out of the nine stated symptoms are present, then the person *is* suffering from Major Depression. Ironically, this à la carte menu from which one can pick and mix, does not help the question of reliability. This is particularly the case for PTSD, which in the DSM-IV has a menu of *175 possible symptoms*. The result?

> Ziskin . . . [shows that] patients who cannot be diagnosed with PTSD in one edition of DSM can be given this diagnosis in another one, even though the

symptoms remain the same . . . [he shows] it is possible for two people who have no symptoms in common to receive a diagnosis of PTSD, even if the same edition of DSM is used to make both diagnoses. [Further], many of the "defining" features of PTSD are shared with dozens of other diagnoses.

(Kutchins and Kirk, 1997, p. 124)

It is clear then that discrete lists of symptoms are neither necessary nor sufficient for the diagnosis of a disorder. Further, the basis of the 'scientific' decision making process remains mysterious as to why the requirement for one disorder is that five out of eight symptoms need to be present, and for another three out of five. But if the reports are anything to go by, the 'science' consists mainly of the capacity to shout louder than others.

Reliability is always going to be a problem when it comes to human beings, because the so-called objective diagnostic criteria are themselves ambiguous – and will always be so. For example, with the allegedly *objective* criteria 'poor appetite' or 'low energy'? How low is low, how poor is poor?

The claim to objectivity is further undermined by the fact that the psychiatric assessor is repeatedly required to make subjective judgements regarding the nature of the symptom. For example, the DSM-III cautions clinicians that Conduct Disorder should 'be applied only when the behaviour in question is symptomatic of an underlying dysfunction within the individual and *not simply a reaction to the immediate social context*' (p. 88; italics added). On what basis will the clinician decide that a behaviour is due to some internal malfunction in the patient (in which case they are ill), or whether it is a response to the social context. Having chastised the psychoanalysts for speculative reasoning about underlying psychological issues in internal worlds, descriptive psychiatrists are doing the very same thing when attributing behaviours and symptoms to underlying biological disorders.

They can't have it both ways, and yet they do. On the one hand they claim that the virtue of their method is that it stays with the tangible, visible and therefore describable, and on the other hand when it suits, they make speculative assertions about the existence of malfunctions in the realm of the underlying, the intangible and the invisible.

It is clear then, that however hard the DSM tries to edit human judgement out of the diagnostic process, it cannot do so. The DSM is the lynchpin on which all CBT research is hooked. And if the lynchpin cannot hold, then neither can anything hooked onto it.

The UK: psychologists *vs* medics

In the publicly-funded National Health Service in the UK, The medical doctor rules the roost. In part this came about with the deal that the politician and father of the NHS, Aneurin (Nye) Bevin, made with the medical profession at the inception of the NHS. The medical establishment had set itself against the idea of a state-run health service and fought it every step of the way. Bevin eventually won them over with money. He effectively bribed them, famously saying on one occasion, 'I stuffed their mouths with gold'. Not only did he agree to pay medical doctors prodigious amounts of money from the public purse for their work in the NHS, he agreed to them continuing to run their private practices alongside their NHS work. To this lucrative arrangement, the medical profession offered no resistance.

And so it has come to pass that 'the medical consultant' has come to have a demi-god-like status in the hospital environment, and often enough expects to be treated as such. Within this setting (the NHS) the profession of clinical psychology, was poor second to that of the medical doctor. They had less status, were paid less, and did not command the same authority as the medic. One reason that the medic was able to claim superiority over the psychologist (apart from the benefits gifted them by Bevin), was that medicine was a proper science that dealt with the tangible; it could be empirically tested and produced objective verifiable knowledge. Clinical psychology suffered from the same problem as psychiatry, that the mind and emotions were neither observable nor measurable. There was the material fact of the organic brain of course, which some clinical psychologists turned to with relief.

This then was the situation that clinical psychologists found themselves in for many a decade. Outgunned and dominated by the medics, the only way clinical psychologists could even begin to compete with the medic, was by producing empirical evidence. If they could do this, then they would be able to establish their credentials as respectable Scientists. It was a case of 'if you can't beat them, join them'.

For clinical psychologists to be able to do this, they had to draw on a mode of treatment that was amenable to this positivist paradigm – a methodology that generated data that could be counted, measured and tested. CBT made for the perfect entry ticket because its methodology fitted all these conditions. And so clinical psychology embraced and promoted CBT enthusiastically. In this way the fate of CBT became linked to that of clinical psychology, with the result that both came to prosper. By these means and over time clinical psychology entered the hallowed halls of Science and became a respectable member of the Academy. They have been spectacularly successful in their ambition to raise the status of psychology. These days clinical psychologists in private practice regularly charge the same hourly rates as medical consultants, as befits their grander professional status.

It has also come to pass that like the medics and the psychoanalysts before them, the profession of clinical psychology is busy creating its own closed cognitivist shop (despite the presence of very many dissenting voices within its ranks). Sections of the profession of clinical psychology have come to position themselves as the 'owners' of CBT – as *the* experts in this field, with the result that almost all CBT training is now delivered by clinical psychologists, and at the same time the therapy components of clinical psychology trainings are almost entirely CBT. Clinical psychologists have also become very powerful politically: psychologists (of a positivist persuasion) are in the majority on advisory and regulatory committees like those of NICE and so on.

In sum, my argument here is that in the British context, CBT has flourished not so much because of its merits as a treatment, but because it was useful to sections of the profession of Clinical Psychology in its battle for status within the medical profession.

***

It is an irony that even whilst sections of the clinical psychology profession are embracing and lauding the virtues of Cognitive *Therapy*, the discipline known as Cognitive *Psychology* (amongst a host of other disciplines) is increasingly disputing and problematizing many of the key ingredients of CBT that are currently mainstream. But these voices are falling on utterly deaf ears. The government, the funders, the commissioners, the researchers and the health practitioners, continue on their current merry way with hardly a pause. And when they do, it is only to take a potshot at the detractors as being anti-scientific and deluded by superstition.

It remains an extraordinary state of affairs, that a treatment modality, no better (and perhaps no worse) than others, has come to be conceived and positioned as the *only* rational viable treatment. The fact that this view is held and promulgated by a vast range of serious professionals is mystifying until one remembers Norbert Elias, and the vicissitudes of power relations.

Part III

Cognitivism

Chapter 6

Homo economicus

The hyper-rationalist conception of the human condition that is feted by CBT first took root in economics. This conception promotes the view that humans are essentially and primarily calculative rational beings. The histories of economics and psychology have been entangled from the first. This is not surprising because economics needs a model of human psychology prior to being able to anticipate how and why humans might react, interact and make decisions.

Over the centuries psychologists have written treatises on economics and economists have written on psychology. Perhaps the first and most well-known treatise on psychology was written in 1759 by the economist Adam Smith, *The Theory of Moral Sentiments*. Not long after in 1855, it was the psychologist Richard Jennings who wrote an influential book on economics, *The Natural Elements of Political Economy*. And most recently in 2005, we have the economist Richard Layard promoting the virtues of cognitivist psychology. In this sort of way over the last few centuries a positivist baton was passed back and forth between the two disciplines, and with each passing the conception of the human condition was further honed to become eventually the hyper-rationalist, cognitivist version that we find ensconced in both disciplines today.

But in earlier times, as Enlightenment philosophers cogitated about the complexities and anomalies of human existence, they made little distinction between the disciplines as we have come to know them. Psychology, economics, sociology, ethics, and science itself were all part and parcel of philosophy. For example, it is hard to tell from the title of Francis Edgeworth's (1881) book quite what it is about '*Mathematical Psychics: An Essay on the Application of Mathematics to the Moral Sciences*'. Is this a book on mathematics or psychology or ethics? It turns out to be a work on economics; but as the title indicates, on much else as well.

The rise of reason

The story of the interconnectedness of psychology and economics could begin in many places. I will start with the great Immanuel Kant, a contemporary of Adam Smith.

Kant sought to liberate humanity from the authoritarian grip of Church and State. He urged people to free themselves by thinking things out for themselves rather than unquestioningly accept the pronouncements of kings and priests as divine truths.

Kant divided the human realm from material universe on the grounds that the material universe was mechanistic; being mechanistic, it is explainable by cause/effect relations. The systematized study of cause/effect relations is called Science, a key feature of which is its predictive power. Prediction is possible because the material universe is deterministic. If we have understood that *p* causes *y*, then if we do *p*, we expect *y* to occur. In sum, *to understand the workings of the material universe, we look for causes.*

Now although humans were a part of the material universe, their behaviour was not determinable by prior causes. If it were, then humans would not have to take any moral responsibility for their actions which would simply be the reactions determined by what had occurred just before. Humans have the capacity to *choose* how to respond to whatever has impinged on them. This capacity is both moral and rational; it is the source of human free-will, and it is this that separates out humans from the mechanistic universe. In brief, *to understand human actions, we look not for causes, but reasons.*

David Hume (who Kant credited for having woken him up from his 'dogmatic slumbers') was also troubled by social conditions, and specifically the suffering caused by the religious wars that were tearing Europe apart at that time. Here too, populations blindly accepted the reasons given by the authorities for going to war: we are good, they should die.

Hume introduced the fact/value distinction partly in order to disrupt this state of affairs. He said that there were *real* things, objective truths called *facts*, and then there were opinions and other subjective phenomena that varied from person to person and people to people; these he called *values* and asserted that because they varied from person to person and peoples to peoples, they were not worth fighting over. This was particularly the case for the religious beliefs and 'values' that were the source of the wars taking place.

When these two dichotomies – cause/reason and fact/value – are put together, it gives rise to a conundrum. On the one hand humans are moral beings, and so they must be placed in the territory of values; in which case one is only able to understand their actions by looking for the *reasons* as to why they did what they did. On the other hand, humans are bodies made up of elements from the material universe and so they can also be placed in the territory of things, that is, the mechanistic universe; in which case one understands their actions by looking for their *causes*. This is the basis of the interminable free-will/determinism debate to be found in philosophy.

The picture is made further complicated by the fact that Kant believed that rules of morality were to be worked out by rational means, through a reasoning process. Kant supposed that the moral law was objective, and for this reason all rational humans were bound to agree as to what was moral. They would reason their way to *same* conclusions about the good, because the good was bound to be an objective *universal* truth (this belief is taken up by CBT and forms a key part of its rationale – as we will come to see a little later).

So even though Kant placed humans as moral beings on one side of the divide and the mechanical universe on the other side of the divide, both sides were (potentially) rational and logical. 'Potentially' because the nature and structure of the good life had first to be worked out through a rational thinking process, and then one had the harder task of living in accordance with it.

In this way Kant and the other Enlightenment philosophers came to privilege the individual's capacity to *reason* over all else. The Kantian division between cause and reason, between thing and person, should be kept in mind as it will be called on many times in what follows; it will play a crucial role to the critique of CBT, Managerialism, and of the excesses of positivism.

The psychology of *Homo economicus* (with ethics)

Despite Hume's fact/value distinction, early philosophising did not separate out the rational from the ethical when thinking about matters economic. After all Kant had said that the ethical was intrinsically rational. In the early days, before economics became a discreet discipline, its subject matter attended to broader and deeper ethical questions about the functioning of human societies in order to find rational ways of enabling societies do good rather than ill. In Amartya Sen's view, 'economics [was] largely an offshoot of ethics' (Sen, 1987, p. 2). This is clearly evident in the very title of Adam Smith's book *The Theory of Moral Sentiments* (1759) in which he put forward the view that human motivations were derived from the 'mutual sympathy of sentiments'.

Economic theories required a conception of human nature (psychology) in order to theorize how they might act and interact with each other in the market place. The conception of human psychology that started to take a hold in economics followed in the footsteps of Kant, Smith, Hume and others; a conception that presumed that humans were primarily rational, conscious, decision making beings. But in those early days ethics and psychology were part and parcel of the rational. By 'rational' what is meant here, are the *reasons* for pursuing one course of action rather than another, and critical to these *reasons* is the view that one should try to do good rather than ill. *Social responsibility was integral to early economic thinking.*

In his second great work, *The Wealth of Nations,* Adam Smith developed an alternative view of human nature; he came to think that humans were primarily self–interested beings. He supposed that self-interest was the principal motivating force that organized human interactions. He used this idea to develop his theory of the economics of a well-functioning society:

> It is not from the benevolence of the butcher, the brewer, or the baker, that we expect our dinner, but from their regard to their own interest. We address

ourselves, not to their humanity but to their self-love, and never talk to them
of our own necessities but of their advantages.

(Smith, 1776, Bk 1, Ch. 2: 26–7)

It is here that we find the beginnings of *Homo economicus* – a human whose
motivation is always to maximise his or her own financial interests. In this work
Smith also made passing mention of 'the invisible hand', which alluded to the
idea that the interactions of individuals, each pursuing their self-interest, 'naturally' worked in ways that benefited society as a whole without any intervention
from the authorities. This passing mention came to play a prodigious role in neoliberalist thinking. More on that anon.

The Utilitarians Jeremy Bentham and John Stuart Mill thought differently.
They thought that rather than keep out of things, the government should be doing
things to actively increase the happiness level of the nation. With this thought
a reversal took place in the arrangement between psychology and economics,
in that economic policy was made the servant of psychology. This became
enshrined as 'The Greatest Happiness Principle' according to which the function
of economic policies should be to achieve the greatest happiness for the greatest
number of people.

Now although Utilitarianist philosophy embraced economics, psychology as
well as ethics, it did so in ways that drove psychology further into the arms of the
positivists. It all hinges on the word 'increasing'. One can only speak of *increasing* happiness if it is a quantity; in other words, measurable. But how to measure an intangible subjective state? The answer that Bentham came up with was
'utility', thus 'utilitarianism'. Utility was (allegedly) a measure of the amount
of happiness any action would generate, an amount to be calculated by what he
called a *felicific calculus*. This calculated the amount of pleasure produced for
each individual by some action or policy decision. The quality and quantity of the
pleasure was to be calculated by looking at a range of elements which included
amongst other things, the intensity, duration and purity of the feelings. This was
to be done for every individual, and the results averaged out. The outcome of this
calculation determined whether a particular action or policy decision was to be
pursued or not.

So, while other 'harder' economists were measuring things to do with the
actual economy, (rates of unemployment and so forth), the Utilitarian measurements focussed on psychology, the state of the internal world.

In Utilitarianism, human psychology is a 'given' (which as we saw earlier, Layard
uncritically reproduced as though it were an obvious, uncontroversial and unproblematic given). Jeremy Bentham simply asserted that 'Nature has placed Mankind
under the governance of two sovereign masters, pain and pleasure'. Bentham did
not trouble himself to substantiate this assertion in any way, because it was so 'obviously' true. With this claim, the complexity of human existence was reduced into
a thin, one dimensional psychology, consisting of a single scale from unhappy to

happy. The 'science' as such involves measurement to determine where exactly one resides on the scale, and how to move from one end of the scale towards the other. In this way the focus on happiness renders Utilitarian moral philosophy curiously hedonistic and a–ethical. The right thing to do is that which makes you happiest, that which gives you greatest (measurable) pleasure.

But now, Utilitarianism hit a problem because pleasure and happiness were measurable only in principle, not in actual fact. Many thought (and think) that subjective feelings like pleasure were not measurable *even in principle*.

The psychology of *Homo economicus* (without ethics)

This put Benthamites and other 'psychological economists' at odds with the economists who harboured ambitions to transform economics into one of the objective sciences of the measurable, mathematical kind. One of the first to lead into this objectivist turn was W.S. Jevons who heralded the dawn of the new *science* of economics with his two books, *A General Mathematical Theory of Political Economy* (1862) and *The Theory of Political Economy* (1871 London: Macmillan). Although Jevons' philosophy was very close to that of the Utilitarians, he pulled economics away from psychology and ethics and towards mathematics: 'it is clear that economics, if it is to be a science at all, must be a mathematical science'.

In order to become a 'science', economics had to jettison all matters of 'value'. And because ethics were deemed to be values, they fell by the wayside and took Utilitarianism along with it. Apparently, later in his life Jevons regretted even using the term 'political' in the title of his books, because the term suggests that power and values play a role in the machinery of economics. Jevons and those that followed him wanted to purge all things human from economics, leaving only numbers and calculations in order that it be a pure science. John Maynard Keynes later formalized the distinction between fact and value in economics as a distinction between *positive economics* – matter-of-fact dealing with what 'is', and *normative economics* – matters of value dealing with 'ought'.

It is important to underscore the consequence of the way that *fact* is being privileged over *value* here. Enlightenment rationality had to do with *reasons*, reasons why we ought to do this rather than that. And these reasons were grounded in (amongst other things) ethics and necessarily involved persons. But now because ethics were decreed to be values, they were construed of as irrational 'noise' to be set aside and edited out of scientific inquiry. When people and ethics are removed from the picture, then all we are left with is the sterile version of fiscal efficiency.

Not everyone was convinced by this dichotomization. A number of prominent economists such as Amartya Sen fought back to say that ethics were integral to economics, and that economic policies should be designed to benefit society as a whole including the weak and needy. He argued that it was nonsensical to presume that ethics played no role in decision making and to believe that humans made their decisions primarily in the service of 'self-interest maximization'. Sen concluded 'The purely economic man is . . . close to being a social moron' (Sen, 1977, 336). The line that Sen and others like him were putting forward came to be known as 'welfare economics', the bête noire of Neoliberalists who dismissed it as misguided do-gooder nonsense.

***

While positivist economics did away with ethics, it could not entirely do away with 'psychology', because even highly abstract mathematical economic models required the presence of economic agents, that is, human beings; moreover, these humans needed to have motivations which would incline them to act in one way rather than another. Try as it might, economics just could not get away from the subjective ephemeral. Their solution to the problem was to ascribe to humans a psychology that was also positivist.

They declared humans to be rational calculating beings that functioned in accordance with three principles. First, these individuals were entirely rational; second, they acted in ways that would maximise their self-interests, and last, these individuals were unconstrained, autonomous and *free* to act as they desired. In ordinary parlance this becomes: humans are sensible beings, who being sensible, will naturally do sensible things, and the sensible thing to do is to look out for oneself. To do otherwise would be irrational.

Bizarre as this model of human psychology is, it has nevertheless become the ruling premise not only of mainstream economic theory today but also CBT. In one of its avatars it has come to be known as Rational Choice Theory.

But despite all its positivist manoeuvring, 'scientific' economics was not out of the subjective, value laden woods as yet. It was faced with two intractable problems: First, these premises about the human condition *remained assumptions* about the workings of the intangible internal worlds of individuals – their psychology. And second, it was obvious to one and all that *Homo economicus* as well as the premises he was generated by were patently and self–evidently unrealistic.

This predicament was dealt with in two very different ways.

One solution for some economists was to turn sharp right and follow in the footsteps previously taken by Watson and Skinner's behavioural psychology and forge out new territories soon to be named Behavioural Economics and Experimental Economics. Like the behavioural psychologists, behavioural economists would also simply ignore the human mind; they would not trouble themselves with speculations about internal motives and so forth; instead they would take account only of visible, tangible and (allegedly) measurable, *behaviour*.

Meanwhile, the Nobel Prize winning economist Milton Friedman, (the godfather of neoliberalism and austerity policy), dealt with the difficulty in a very different way.

The psychology of *Homo economicus* (with perverse ethics)

Friedman was totally unfazed by the unrealistic assumptions regarding human motivation in economic theory. In his 1953 essay 'The Methodology of Positive Economics', (which incidentally is generally regarded as the launching of the Neoliberalist manifesto) Friedman declared that a theory should not be judged on the basis of whether or not it was realistic in the way it represented the world. What mattered more than realism was how good the theory was at making predictions. So what if the assumptions about human motivation are utterly reductive, simplistic and fatuous? If the theory makes predictions that are useful, then that is all that matters. He even went so far as to suggest that there was an inverse correlation between predictability and realism: The better the theory at prediction the more unrealistic will be its assumptions!

> Truly important and significant hypotheses will be found to have 'assumptions' that are wildly inaccurate descriptive representations of reality, and, in general, *the more significant the theory, the more unrealistic the assumptions*.
> (Friedman, 1953, p. 14)

He did allow though that 'Of course descriptive unrealism by itself does not ensure a "significant theory"' (1953, pp. 14–15). Curiously, this was not the first time this sort of claim was made. A few hundred years previously, Andreas Osiander the editor of Copernicus' *De revolutionibus orbium coelestium* (*On the revolutions of the heavenly spheres*) defended Copernicus in the preface, saying 'these hypotheses need not be true nor even probable. [I]f they provide a calculus consistent with the observations, *that alone is enough*' (Sobel, 2011, p. 188 italics added). Sobel's intention was to assuage the wrath of the Catholic Church. In effect he was saying to the Church that it could continue hold onto its geocentric view of the universe as the real truth; Copernicus' heliocentric model merely gave better predictions, but this did not make his theory true. But while Copernicus's calculations did indeed turn out to be consistent with observations, this was not the case for Friedman's Neoliberalism.

Many years later this sort of belief was given some sort of philosophical legitimacy by

> a highly problematic tenet of Popper's (1959) philosophy of science . . . that the essence of science lies in hypothesis testing (the context of scientific justification) and that where one finds one's hypotheses (the context of discovery) is one's own business.
> (Westen et al, 2004, p. 641)

But let us leave all this aside for the moment. More important are the consequences of the idea that a theory's capacity to predict has little to do with the way that the theory models the problem. This is the claim: although economic theory bears no resemblance to the workings of the real world, by virtue of complicated mathematical calculations it will nevertheless somehow be able to make predictions about the workings of this world. This stance has become so normalized in economic thinking that it has become part and parcel of pretty much every positivist economic theory. For example, Dietz Vollrath (a professor of economics), throws cold water over the way that economic theories model the process of scientific discovery taking place in laboratories:

> The price-taking theory assumes that people just randomly walk around, bump into each other, and magically new ideas spring into existence. The market power theory assumes that people wander into a lab, and then magically new ideas just spring into existence, perhaps arriving in a Poisson-distributed process to make the math easier. . . . In the models, *they are both governed by arbitrary statistical processes that bear no resemblance to how research actually works.*
>
> (Vollrath, 2015; italics added)

It is worth pausing longer in order to highlight the significance of Friedman's claim about the 'science' of economics, by contrasting it with the science of physics which it is trying to ape. The predictability found in physics is grounded in its explanations, explanations that constitute the theorization of *why* things are happening in the ways that they do. Apples fall *because* of the gravitational attraction between the earth and the apple (Einstein would demur of course).

Friedman is advocating a form of prediction devoid of explanation. In which case all this kind of 'knowledge' would be able to say, and *all it would need to say*, is: there is a strong correlation between the letting go of an apple, and it falling to the ground. This prediction works well enough when it comes to Newtonian apples, but as many learnt to their cost in 2008, economic theories in general are not particularly good at predicting outcomes.

The decoupling of prediction from explanation, gives licence to misrepresent all kinds of crimes and misdemeanours as science. In effect, they do away with the caution that 'correlation is not causation' by saying that the only thing that is important is correlation. This notion became the ruling ethos in sections of sociology as well as psychology research. This is also the ethos behind CBT's rationale for the distinction it makes between 'cause' and 'maintenance'. This is also the same rationale that drives the logic of questionnaires called psychological diagnostic instruments. It is believed that the questions themselves within the questionnaire don't necessarily have to have any direct bearing on what the instrument is allegedly 'measuring'. For example, while researching for a book on positivity, the author Barbara Ehrenreich completed Seligman's questionnaire the 'Authentic Happiness Inventory'. While interviewing him, she said that some of the questions in the Inventory seemed somewhat arbitrary. He snapped back:

> That's a cheap shot and shows your failure to understand test development. *It doesn't matter what the questions are so long as they have predictive value.*

It could be a question about butterscotch ice cream and whether you like it. The issue is how well it predicts.

(Seligman in Ehrenreich, 2009, p. 156; italics added)

But I have digressed. Let me get back to Friedman's neoliberalist agenda.

The bones of neoliberalism as put forward by Friedman and the 'Chicago School' rests on the premise that when businesses are left alone to get on with making money for themselves, then not only will the businesses flourish, so will the economy, and this will be of benefit to society as a whole. This is nothing other than Adam Smith's notion of the 'Invisible Hand' writ large and deified.

Why doing good is bad

But even while Friedman and the Chicago School economists positioned themselves as hard headed scientists who only dealt in, and faced up to hard facts and only facts, they nevertheless smuggle ethics into their justifications. In effect, they used 'values' to support the legitimacy of their 'facts'. They did this by using the notion of the invisible hand to turn moral sensibility on its head.

They begin with their axiomatic assertion that when businesses are left alone to get on with making money, then the economy is at its most efficient because it is in its *natural state*. In other words, not only is it *right* (fact) but also *good* (value) that individuals and businesses should be left alone to pursue their own interests.

This is swiftly followed by the assertion that if self-interest is good, then other-interest must be bad. Friedman thought that it was not only wrong but actually harmful to society, when governments put in checks and balances that powerful organizations were answerable to; it was also harmful when economists produced policies that tried to help the needy. They both constituted 'interference' in the natural working of things.

The title of Friedman's article published in 1970 in the *New York Times Magazine* makes this crystal clear: 'The Social Responsibility of Business is to Increase its Profits'. This article sounded the charge: the coming of neoliberalism; and very soon it took over main stream economics almost entirely – a positon it continues to enjoy even today. Friedman voices the central dogma of neoliberalism 'There is one and only one social responsibility of business – to use it resources and engage in activities designed to increase its profits' (Friedman, 1970).

But this statement is not 'fact'; rather it is 'value' presented as fact. And when values are disseminated as self-evident facts, then it is clear that what is being disseminated is not science, but ideology masquerading as science. For example, when Friedman famously said when being interviewed on *The Phil Donahue Show* in 1979:

When government in pursuit of good intentions tries to rearrange the economy, legislate morality, or help special interests, the cost come in inefficiency, lack of motivation, and loss of freedom. Government should be a referee, not an active player.

> (Friedman, 1979, TV interview with Phil Donahue)

Friedman portrays himself as a champion of freedom and says that those that do not agree with him are attacking the idea of freedom itself. 'Underlying most arguments against the free market is a lack of belief in freedom itself' (Friedman, 1962, p. 21). The invisible hand has become a hallowed God that will ensure that everyone will get what they deserve: 'A society that puts equality before freedom will get neither. A society that puts freedom before equality will get a high degree of both' (Friedman, 1979).

There were many other economists who also believed this kind of thing, for example Arthur Okun. His influential book *Equality and Efficiency: The Big Tradeoff* (1973) argued that increasing equality reduced efficiency in three ways: because it cost money to administer a welfare state; that helping the less well-off demotivated them looking for work; and that taxing the rich was punishing them for being successful and so demotivated them too.

Friedman's influence on the world has been prodigious. In the 1980s Friedman acted as advisor to the governments of both Ronald Reagan and Margaret Thatcher, promoting his neoliberalist agenda with missionary zeal. He soon had two passionate converts to his cause, two fundamentalist zealots who set about deregulating the business sector and radically reducing state provision in almost every facet of life.

In this 'brave new world', greed was nothing to be embarrassed about; greed was no longer a deadly sin, it was a virtue; greed became good. With the help of Reagan and Thatcher, neoliberalism fostered a deeply corrosive conception of the individual and atomist individualism, conceptions that did away with Kant's vision of social responsibility and replaced it with a hard-hearted vision of each-one-for-himself self-sufficiency. Each person should stand on their own two feet and pay their own way, as should each institution. It is *morally* wrong to support the weak and vulnerable, and to subsidise public services, because it breeds a culture of dependency and entitlement. Today, dependency is become a dirty word. This view has crept into CBT theology, wherein to be dependent on another (even your therapist), is a sin.

The central organizing principle of this discourse is the god called 'efficiency', a god that knows the cost of everything and the value of nothing. Because the free market is the instrument that is thought to produce efficiency, the neoliberalists think that all state-run services, health, transport, utilities, etc., are by definition inefficient as they do not have to earn their own living. Therefore, they should all be privatized. Market forces and competition will ensure that privately owned organizations will be as efficient as possible. They claim that privatized institutions will provide a better service at a lower cost to the citizen, as they will not need to pay tax to support those institutions.

To this end all public services, even if they were being funded and run by the state – transport, education, health, etc. – were recast as 'businesses'. This is where managerialism makes its entry. As soon as they were viewed as businesses, then it was demanded that they should comply with Friedman's injunction which we met earlier, this being, 'There is one and only one social responsibility of business – to use its resources and engage in activities designed to increase its profits' (Friedman, 1970).

It is for this reason that today institutions like universities and hospitals providing public services are required to be efficient, in other words make profits, and if not, then at least pay their way. This sort of principle is at the heart of managerialism. There are other principles too, which we come to later. Anyhow, believing this to be true, Thatcher sold off the nationalized utilities, industries and services to the private sector for a song, and the monies used to cut taxes and so seduce the people into thinking this to be a good thing.

In this way, through the 1980s and 1990s, Adam Smith's 'self-interest' was ramped up to selfish-interest. If self-interest benefited society, then even more self-interest (selfish-interest) would benefit society even more. In this war of all against all in the deregulated economic Hobbesian jungle, it was better to let nature take its course and the weak go to the wall.

To recapitulate the point: the perverse ethic promulgated by neoliberalism is that it is both mistaken and morally wrong to design economic policies that look out for the interests of the vulnerable, the needy and the weak. All services, from health provision to education to care to transport to utilities should be privatized. There should be no government 'interference' in the economy. The task of the government is to ensure that businesses are allowed to be as free as possible to conduct their business.

Social carnage

In the UK and US this state of affairs prevailed for almost two decades. As the rich got richer and became more complacent, the poor became poorer and suffered increasing hardship. The streets of British and American cities started to fill up with those made homeless by changes instigated by the Reagan and Thatcher governments.

It was in this harsh and brutal social context that Tony Blair's Labour government won its famous victory over the Tories (Conservatives) in 1997 in the UK. A change in a similar direction had just taken place in the US when Bill Clinton won the Presidential election in 1993 to become the first Democrat to hold that office in 14 years. There was a sense of hope that a Blair/Clinton partnership would undo some of the harm inflicted by the Thatcher/Reagan partnership.

Over the previous two decades, during the time of Thatcher and Reagan, large swathes of the population had become deeply despairing having lost jobs, homes, families and status. These were the casualties Layard and Clark promised to help with CBT. In the midst of the carnage wrought by neoliberalist policies, Layard's Utilitarian voice came across as the voice of compassion and reason: money is not everything, he said; more important than money is the wellbeing of its citizens. In this brutal and brutalizing social context, Layard's CBT and Happiness agenda came across as a benevolent salve capable of healing the hurts caused by the excesses of neoliberalism.

But it turned out that the euphoria and hope that greeted the victory of the Democrats in the US and the Labour Party in the UK, did not last very long. It soon became apparent that Tony Blair's government – *New* Labour – was actually intent on continuing to pursue the same neoliberalist agenda as the Tories. Meanwhile across the Atlantic, Bill Clinton having swallowed wholesale the neoliberalist myth fed to him by Alan Greenspan, recanted on his electoral promises. Greenspan, a staunch Republican, was first appointed by Reagan as Chairman of the Federal Reserve Board. For reasons hard to fathom, Clinton reappointed him knowing full well that Greenspan was an ultra-conservative devotee of the Social Darwinist, Ayn Rand.

Not only did the promised change of government policy not manifest, the help promised by CBT also turned out to be untrue for two reasons. First, the ointment proffered by Layard and Clark was a positivist Utilitarian one. Second, rather than challenge the social iniquities that had produced so much human misery, Layard and Clark effectively joined hands with those that produced the misery. *They too medicalized suffering and pathologized the sufferers*, in effect saying: 'the world is fine; the problem is you and your way of thinking'. And so CBT set about adjusting the psychological state of the casualties by asking them to change their responses to the situation they found themselves in.

CBT would teach the unhappy how to have happy thoughts in unhappy circumstances.

Earlier, we encountered the claim of CBT that it is unnecessary to look into the *causes* of distress. It is rationalized as being borne out by scientific evidence. However, to my mind the *real* reason why CBT avoids thinking about the *reasons* why people are suffering, is because if they did think about them, they would find themselves faced with the unpalatable fact that to a large degree, the suffering was caused by the excesses of neoliberalism. This would immediately set CBT at odds not only with its paymasters, those who actually caused the suffering, but also the ways of thinking which the paymasters used to legitimate the actions that caused the suffering.

Neoliberalism: austerian ethics

The consequences of governments being seduced by the neoliberalist agenda and deregulating the world of finance are well known: the financial crisis, followed by austerity, because supposedly austerity was the solution to the crisis. It is no coincidence that CBT has come to prosper in the time of neoliberalist austerity; not only is CBT's understanding of the human condition closely aligned with the ideology of neoliberalist individualism and the managerialist fetish for imaginary measurement, the economic argument was integral to CBT's very conception, and is a part of its DNA. In some ways what follows – a short gloss on the austerity agenda – might seem to be a digression from the developing critique of CBT. However, it is relevant for two reasons. Austerity has produced vast amounts of human distress, distress which is to be treated by CBT. And second, the austerity agenda helped foster the flourishing of CBT.

A significant moment in the austerity story took place in 2008 when the world's financial institutions went into meltdown, caused by the build-up of a number of corrupt and questionable banking practices, one of which was the fact that banks lent out eye-watering sums of money to those who had little or no chance of paying back the debt.

Why were they so keen to do this? When the bank lends you money, for your mortgage for example, it is very different from the situation in which I might lend you money. When I lend you money, I have to give you money that I actually possess; I will end up with less money in my pocket, while you will have more. However, when the bank lends you money, it is literally creating it out of thin air. The £100,000 that the bank puts into your account, did not exist in the moment before it appeared in your account.

When I first learnt of this, I was flabbergasted both, by the degree of my ignorance and by the fact that I was taking so much for granted. I had thought that it was only the Bank of England that could create money; but this has not been the case for many a decade.

This is from The Bank of England's 2014 Quaterly Bulletin, 'Money Creation in the Modern Economy'

> Commercial [i.e. high-street] banks create money, in the form of bank deposits, by making new loans. When a bank makes a loan, for example to someone taking out a mortgage to buy a house, it does not typically do so by giving them thousands of pounds worth of banknotes. Instead, it credits their bank account with a bank deposit of the size of the mortgage. **At that moment, new money is created**.
>
> (Bank of England, 2014, p. 16)

It turns out that, '97% of the money in the economy today is created by [commercial] banks, while just 3% is created by the government' (Positive Money, 2017). In other words, the creation of debt is the engine that drives our economy; debt of this kind is *necessary* to a capitalist economy. The banks create money for us to borrow. We borrow, we spend, we pay back money to the bank that they did not have in the first place, the banks end up with more money, our money; the 'economy' flourishes. The banks need us, *wants us*, to borrow from them. But borrowing is the wrong word here because borrowing suggests that they are in possession of the thing that they are going to 'lend' me. What happens in fact is a kind of magic. They lend me something that does not exist and therefore they don't have. In the very same moment I am lent this, it comes into existence and at the same time a space magically appears in their ledgers that makes it seem that it was always there in the first place. Now I have to return this thing to its proper owners and express my gratitude by giving more back in interest.

Despite the fact that deregulated banks had the ability to create limitless amounts of money, they managed to contrive a situation in which they needed to be bailed out.

This is where the Exchequer stepped in with our money to the tune of hundreds of billions. How did the State manage to lay its hands on these hundreds of billions to save the banks, given the fact that the Exchequer had been pleading poverty when it came to paying teachers and nurses a proper wage? They simply created it in exactly the same way as the commercial banks, out of thin air, and then passed it onto the commercial banks. They called it Quantitative Easing.

Cameron's Conservative Party perpetuated the narrative that the rocky economy had nothing to do with the banking crisis, and entirely to do with the previous Labour government being profligate. Labour is supposed to have spent vast amounts of money that they did not have on health, education and welfare, thus creating huge amounts of unsustainable public debt; and this is why the economy was suffering. If this were the case, then cutting back on spending would make sense. Thus, austerity.

There are several falsehoods with this rationale for austerity. First, they are misrepresenting the way that the macro-economy works by making it seem that the macro-economy works on the same principles as household accounts. But as we have seen, in the household account, debt is a bad thing and creates terrible consequences for those in debt. To the capitalist macro-economy, debt is essential, debt is necessary.

The austerity agenda was bolstered by accruing academic respectability with the publication of scientific papers by a number of well-regarded economists. Particularly influential were two studies, one by the highly influential Harvard economists Alesina and Ardagna (2009), and the other being Reinhart and Rogoff's paper *Growth in the Time of Debt* (2010). According to their empirical evidence, spending cuts somehow stimulated depressed economies.

The academic stature of the authors and the presence of graphs, numbers and statistics immediately gave their claims the stamp of scientific credibility. But the idea itself was counterintuitive and did not make sense. 'Expansionary austerity' claimed that in times of hardship, when the economy was struggling, the state should impose harsh spending cuts rather than put money into the economy.

The idea does not make sense; it is akin to saying that to further deprive a starving person of food will make them healthier. Nevertheless, the scientific *evidence* put forward in these prestigious publications said that this was so. In order to explain why it worked, they came up with the following psychological theory, which goes like this:

I know that sometime in the future, the state will be smaller, and so apparently, *I know* that the government at that time will demand less tax from me. For this reason, I will not feel the need to save right now. Apparently because I know that

I will pay less tax in twenty years' time, I will rationally *decide* that I don't need to be so cautious right now with what I have; and so I will spend it now. This spending will stimulate the economy, which is how it will recover. Apparently, I will rationally decide to spend more today, despite the fact that I might be out of work or struggling to feed my family.

Most people would think such action folly on my part because the only way that I could spend money when I don't have it, is by putting myself further into debt. And yet the economists would claim that not only is this a rational choice, this is the choice we should rationally make in this sort of situation. If this were indeed so, then it would not just be folly, but stupidity.

Stupidity or folly, it was on this basis, around 2010, that many world governments were sufficiently convinced by the idea to put their nations through austerity informed social policies. But then, a couple of years later it was discovered that the statistical manipulations in each of these highly influential studies were deeply and critically flawed. A proper reading of the data suggested the reverse: that in times when the economy was struggling, what was required was stimulus not cuts. This was the astonishing discovery: one should feed a starving person, not starve them further.

Even the International Monetary Fund (IMF) eventually came to the same conclusion in an official report – that what was required in the time of recession was stimulation through investment, not cuts. The economist Krugman tells us that 'Since the global turn to austerity in 2010, every country that introduced significant austerity has seen its economy suffer, with the depth of the suffering closely related to the harshness of the austerity' (Krugman, 2015).

Notice what was happening: what was believed was the data – even though it flew in the face of common sense. Recall the episode of the Neem tree. Once again it was documentation – numbers – that prevailed over common sense and reality. The austerity idea is utterly stupid: that starving a malnourished person will make them stronger. Yet it was believed to be so by the great and the good because of the numbers saying that this was the case. The reason that the data was so readily believed was because it fitted with the ruling ideology of the time – a hyper-rationalist, neoliberalist ideology.

Krugman tells us that three years later, by 2013,

> the entire edifice of austerian economics had crumbled. Events had utterly failed to play out as the austerians predicted, while the academic research that allegedly supported the doctrine had withered under scrutiny . . . The doctrine that ruled the world in 2010 has more or less vanished from the scene. Except in Britain.
>
> (Krugman, 2015)

Lucky us.

Despite the fact that there is now an established international consensus amongst economists that in a depressed economy austerity does more harm than good,

Cameron's government continued to pursue the discredited austerity agenda. The reason for this is entirely ideological and is that of Neoliberalism. Austerity is the pretext being utilized by Cameron and the Conservatives to pursue their ideological agenda of dismantling and privatizing many of the functions of the state, from health to education to welfare.

> The 'primary purpose' of austerity, the *Telegraph* admitted in 2013, 'is to shrink the size of government spending' – or, as Cameron put it in a speech later that year, to make the state 'leaner . . . not just now, but permanently.
>
> Krugman, 2015

This then is what we are forced to conclude: the medicine called austerity is iatrogenic. Not only is it needlessly increasing the suffering of vulnerable individuals, it is also harming the economy; both are being made to suffer needlessly. But perhaps this does not matter because the real work of the austerity agenda is privatization. The austerity rationale is used to starve public institutions of funds and made to look inefficient. In this weakened state, they are easy game for the private sector to step in and take over.

Austerity, unemployment, psychological suffering, and the alleged treatment for that suffering (CBT), are all decoupled to make it seem that they have nothing to do with each other. But each is integral to the other. One consequence of this is that in many ways austerity increases the burden on the Exchequer rather than reducing it. As austerity bites, businesses close and public services are cut back to the bone and then into the bone itself. More and more people find themselves unemployed, consequently they suffer from increasing stress, depression and anxiety. And so they end up costing the Exchequer money; money for treatments, money in benefits.

Entrenched worklessness

While government ministers blind themselves to the fact that it is the austerity agenda itself that has increased the burden on the Exchequer, they remain very alert to the promises made by Layard and Clark in their *Depression Report*. The promise being that their treatments would get people off benefits and into gainful employment. It was no surprise then to discover that in 2014 senior ministers sought to put in place *mandatory* CBT in job centres, as a *condition* of receiving benefit.

Layard and Clark's CBT thesis holds that people are unable to work because they are ill with depression, anxiety, or some other mental disorder. Treat the illness and they will get back to work. On the back of this, new diagnostic categories have appeared in speeches and papers emanating from the Department for Work and Pensions (DWP), for example 'psychological resistance to work' and 'entrenched worklessness'. The DWP is offering lucrative contracts for providers of treatments for 'mental illness' of this kind. One such invitation to tender for a contract states:

> The Cumbria and Lancashire Jobcentre Plus identified a need for provision that uses innovative methods to inspire entrenched worklessness. Claimants to address the barriers and issues preventing them from entering the work arena. The programme will change the 'hearts and minds' of Claimants by empowering them to take responsibility for improving their lives. The key objectives for the programme are to: challenge Claimants benefit dependency; increase Claimants self-esteem; and inspire Claimants to make lifestyle changes.
>
> (DWP, 2014, p. 4)

This is where the medicalized, individualized accounts of neoliberalism and CBT come together to form a powerful unholy alliance. The blame for an individual's suffering is within the individual. Either they suffer from a chemical imbalance, or they suffer from some form of cognitive malfunction, or they are suffering from excessive dependency, or they are feckless and workshy. There is a bespoke, tailor-made treatment for each and all of these.

Chapter 7

Managerialism

New Public Management

The previous chapter approached cognitivism through economics, history and philosophy, and also gave a brief account of neoliberalism – its ideology and rationales. This chapter looks at the other side of the coin, at the implementation of this ideology. The execution of this task has been delegated to Managerialists. New Public Managers are the shock troops unleased by neoliberalism on the Public Sector; their task: to put neoliberalist theory into practice. The ethos of CBT fits closely with that of Managerialism in very many ways. They both subscribe to a cognitivist and hyper-rationalist world view. Both claim to be evidence–based sciences. Both imagine that people can be controlled in predictable ways. And in the British context at least, both managerialism and the cognitivist tsunami were unleashed at pretty much the same time by Tony Blair's New Labour. It has suited Managerialism to promote and push CBT into its dominant position, and in return CBT provides Managerialism with a rationale and technology for perpetuating its practices.

But what is Managerialism? Its key feature is that it is 'top down', in that it subscribes to the belief that organizations are knowable, and that processes and procedures can be designed to control organizations in predictable ways. Managerialism is a science after all. Managerialist environments are highly planned with goals and targets set out for those lower down on the echelon by those higher up. In effect managerialist institutions tend to be rigidly hierarchical.

> managerialism relies on a central elite which believes that it, and it alone, has the skill and know-how to devise policies to cope with the inexorable forces of economic change. And this skill allows apparently conflicting objectives, such as equality and efficiency, to be reconciled through the design of clever policies.
>
> (Dillow, 2007, p. 11)

Recall also the neoliberalist view that private sector organizations are necessarily efficient, because if they were not, then competition would ensure that they would fail. By implication, public service organizations are bound to be wasteful and inefficient because they are state funded and do not have to pay their way. This belief triggered the bonfire of state-owned industries and services in the UK in the 1980s and 1990s; they were sold off in the belief that the private sector would run these services more efficiently.

As for the services that are still funded by the state (but only just), such as health, education and social care, the neoliberalist mentality decreed that they too should be run along the same lines as for-profit institutions in order to ensure that they would operate as efficiently as possible.

So public, charity and other not-for-profit institutions started to be run as though they were businesses, and the people to do it were the new managerial caste – New Public Managers. Managerialism then is the 'art' of running public services efficiently, that is, as cheaply as possible.

We now come to an anomaly. The rationale for a business is to make profits, to 'do well'. Meanwhile, the rationale for not-for-profit institutions is mostly to 'do good' in some way – to educate, to care, and so on. We saw in the last chapter how mainstream economics made a sharp distinction between doing good and doing well, saying that it was not the business of businesses to try to do good; they should limit themselves to doing well – to make profit. Friedman and the neoliberalists had gone even further to claim that it was unethical and even harmful for businesses or the State to try to do good.

But now, when it came to the running of publicly funded services – the function of which was to do good, neoliberalist New Public Managers suddenly changed their Friedmanesque tune to say that it is in fact possible to do well and do good at the same time. They would use established business practices learnt from the private sector to ensure that for a given amount of money, the amount of good would be maximized. This was to be New Labour's project – to marry equality with efficiency. It was going to be a win-win situation – doing good and doing well. And this task was to be accomplished by the new managerial caste – New Public Managers.

And so today the phrases, 'business model' and 'business case', have become necessary and commonplace in all kinds of unlikely institutions such as charities that cater to the homeless. All this resulted in a very quiet, yet very powerful revolution in organizational life. The effect of which was a radical power-shift from the professional – the one who actually does the work, to the manager – the one who is supposed to enable and facilitate the professional do the work. In this way, the (public) servant had become master. In the new world order, the old servants tell their previous masters what they are to do and how they are to do it. And if they do not they will be punished in some way. Managerialists distanced themselves from old school 'mere' administrators; managerialists would 'think' and 'determine' and not just 'serve', and so it has come to pass that the 'public servant' is servant no more.

Empowered by the state, the activity of management became increasingly professionalized and management proclaimed itself to be a science. As befits a science, managerialism asserts that its knowledge base is generalizable; it is of the opinion that 'management' is a 'skill' which once learnt, is universally applicable to all fields, whether or not a manager has any experience in it. The CEO of a homeless charity moves on to become the CEO of an art gallery, to Chief Executive of a local authority, and then to become the Chancellor of a university. My own professional organization, The Institute of Group Analysis, London, appointed two Chief Executives, neither of whom had any prior experience or knowledge of the practice or philosophy of group analytic psychotherapy. One was by profession a lawyer and the other a psychologist. On substantial salaries as befits Chief Executives, what they accomplished remains a mystery to me. They eventually moved on, no doubt to bigger and better things.

This point is important in regard to the proliferation of CBT. Given that commissioners of services in the NHS and those managing services mostly have no knowledge of the field that they are managing – psychotherapy and psychology – we have to ask on what basis are they making their decisions about which modalities should be promoted, and on what basis have they made decisions about the kind and duration of therapy? A question I will return to later, but the short answer for now is – money and targets.

Managerialist practice, the art of delivering more bang for less buck, throws up a curious contradiction. When it comes to the 'market-place', the neo-liberals want it unfettered by regulations so that organizations are free to maximize their own interests. But within organizations a very different culture has come to prevail, a culture that is the opposite of freedom, a culture that is highly regulated, highly controlled, very rigid, and often very punitive.

This is somewhat odd because the rationale for implementing managerialist practices was to free up the stodgy old systems by cutting out bureaucratic red tape and streamlining process to make them more efficient. What has happened though is that the red tape that has been cut from the 'outside' of organizations, has ended up being used on the 'inside' of the organizations to entangle the workforce in other bureaucratic protocols and procedures so much so that they find it more difficult to do their jobs. The resulting inefficiencies have been caused by two instruments found in the neoliberalist Managerialist's 'toolbox': measurement and marketization.

Measurement

Managerialism claims to operate on scientific evidence-based principles. The focus of New Public Managers is to ensure that employees are doing what they have been told to do, in the way that they have been told to do it. To this end managers create reams of protocols and procedures to monitor and control their employees. In pursuit of this end some end up micro-managing the workforce giving them targets, checking performance in relation to the targets, and adjusting rewards accordingly. Employees are required to spend more and more time accounting to their masters, leaving less and less time for the actual work, increasing the chances of stress-related illness and consequent absenteeism. The NPM way of dealing with this is to require the employee to account for their illness too.

To this mentality employees are means to ends, objects rather than subjects, resources rather than persons, and most importantly, resources to be managed rather than related to. In its initial conception, Human Resource (HR) Departments acted in the interests of employees. But today the Head of HR sits in the boardroom as a member of the Senior Management Team, which is where their allegiance has come to lie.

The various kinds of data that are collected are put through algorithms to produce 'scores' and performance indicators, by which means individuals, departments and entire institutions are evaluated.

This has resulted in a hyper-rationalist reversal. Because data becomes the measure of success, data collection is become more important than the work itself, leaving the professional less and less time to actually perform, to do the actual work. In this way the tail has come to wag the dog. Managerialists are finding it difficult to wake up from their 'dogmatic slumbers' to the fact that the processes for collecting this so-called evidence about the work, gets in the way of the doing of the work itself. In effect, managerialism has simply replaced the old-fashioned blockages in bureaucratic systems with new blockages, this time in the name of science.

When employees fall short of expectations or fail to comply with decreed targets, the managerialist solution is do one or all three of the following. First, the employees are put through further trainings to train them about how to better do what is expected of them. Second, even more procedures are drawn up, to ensure that the initial procedures are implemented in the correct way. And third, the monitoring processes are increased to ensure that everyone is staying on track. The burden for the monitoring process of the employee is placed entirely on the employee themselves, leaving them even less time to do the work. Stress levels increase dramatically.

This is the individualistic, rationalist, cognitivist, 'command and control' ethos that is the norm in contemporary organizational life, and as we will shortly see, the norm that prevails in NICE and IAPT. More recently, managerialism has started to take the emotions into account. However, it approaches emotional life with the same individualistic, cognitivist ethos. It is presumed that the emotions too can be, and ought to be, controlled by techniques and procedures, to produce the correct emotions – the productive ones.

Symptom focused CBT is perfectly at home in this managerialist culture as they both speak the same hyper-rationalist language consisting of numbers, manuals and inflexible procedures. The commissioners are specific in their demands: we will give you so much money for salaries and sundries, for which we expect you to see so many patients for these sorts of symptoms; we expect this many of them to be cured. Not only does CBT claim to be able to say how many patients have been treated, but also to what degree the symptom has been reduced for each patient. It seems that everything is copacetic. Until we look a little more closely into the actual research and actual practice.

Marketization

Managerialism's second 'tool' marketization, is simply the embodiment of the neo-liberalist belief that efficiencies are generated through competition in unfettered market places. While this notion might make some sense in actual marketplaces with vendors selling goods (but even this is to be disputed), when it comes to institutions like hospitals and universities, it makes no sense whatsoever. To make public institutions more efficient, they were turned into internal markets consisting of 'purchasers' buying services from 'providers'. For example, a local doctor 'buying' an operation for one of her patients from the local hospital.

Managerialism treats the components of an organization as elements of an internal market economy. To this end it fosters competition between these components, in the belief that competition will force each of them to become more efficient, and so reduce overall costs for the institution. Each department is decreed to be a separate unit; its task becomes to compete against the others in order to maximize its self-interest, with little or no regard to the interests of other departments. In this way one part of the body attacks and undermines other parts of the same body. But because all are parts of the same body, any victory is a pyrrhic victory. What has happened to the idea of cooperation, of working together?

In the tension between doing good and doing well, money is given the final say. The final arbiter becomes not whether something is worth doing, but whether it will make money, or at the very least, not lose money. Thus, 'business model'.

Although the combination of measurement and marketization has actually resulted in a dramatic decrease in efficiency, this is not readily apparent.

In the UK, to ensure that public bodies such as schools, health services, dental practices, psychiatric services, universities and the like are working efficiently to the required degree, they are subject to being reviewed by the Quality Care Commission (CQC), the National Audit Office (NAO), and so on. In the main, the reports emanating from these bodies, seem to find that organizations are more or less meeting their targets and outcomes, suggesting that the culture of managerialism has indeed made public bodies more efficient.

On the other hand, it is become a commonplace to hear all kinds of professionals from academics to police to teachers to social workers to psychiatrists complain that they spend more time doing paper work than the actual work. This has come about because of the command and control mentality of managerialism, and their wish to continually scrutinize and monitor the work of the professional.

These self-same professionals also spend inordinate amounts of time in 'the market place', fighting for funding, applying for grants, putting out or/and responding to tenders; in effect they spend a lot of time either promoting and 'selling' their services or doing the paper work to 'buy' services from others (more on this in the IAPT chapter).

In sum, according to the accounts of professionals managerialism has made the workplace much more inefficient. But the official reports say otherwise. How to account for the difference?

The contradiction is not really a contradiction because *what the review bodies are checking on is the paper work, not the actual work.* They check on record keeping and whether compliance requirements are being met; they check on the calculations being used to calculate the scores for Performance Indicators, and so on. If these numbers are satisfactory, then the institution is deemed to have met its targets and done its work appropriately. Being constituted out of numbers, this must be science.

Meantime, the frustrated experiences of the professionals are merely experiences not numbers. We can see here how hyper-rationalist accounting processes manage to transmute increasing inefficiencies into seeming efficiencies.

Managerialist rhetoric makes many claims about being able to increase the quality of service being provided, and also about giving customers more 'choice'. But how to do this without additional resources? The answer as we have seen is by increasing efficiency. It is undoubtedly possible to make organizational processes more efficient to some degree. But when the resources really are insufficient for the tasks required of the organization, then managerialists find the so called 'savings' and make 'efficiencies' in one of three ways. The first is by reducing the service being offered, in other words by reducing the quality; the second is to require the employee to do more for less; the third is by massaging the numbers to make it appear that the same quality or even higher quality of service is being delivered. This kind of deceit can be thought of as gamesmanship.

The fetishization of measurement

Gamesmanship is rife in organizational life because of the requirements of NPM and the imposition of targets. In this game, numbers rule. Not only do the numbers define reality, they replace reality. And so there is a lot of pressure to make the numbers sing the kind of song it is supposed to sing. Examples are rife and to be found everywhere. In the newspaper today (29 September 2017) we read about a chicken supplier changing the actual dates that chicken were slaughtered in order to extend their shelf life (Goodley, 2017). Meanwhile, we discover that three former executives on the Board of the supermarket chain Tesco, are to go on trial for 'pressuring employees to massage profits and mislead the stock market' (Butler, 2017). The arithmetic of targets and the logic of internal markets is such that one side's gain is another's loss.

For example, to help save lives, the ambulance services were given a target of eight minutes for reaching emergency calls. And for Accident and Emergency departments in hospitals, the Government introduced a target of no more than four hours between registration and treatment. Some beleaguered A&E departments, short of resources, unable to meet the four-hour target, resorted to the strategy of delaying registering those coming for treatment by the device of leaving them in the ambulances, thereby delaying starting the clock. This gave rise to situations in which ambulances were left waiting on the forecourt of hospitals for lengthy periods. While this strategy enabled the A&E department to meet its target, the ambulance service's performance suffered, as the shortage of available ambulances meant that they could not meet their eight-minute target. To solve this situation the government introduced yet another target – no more than 15 minutes to transfer the patient from ambulance to registration desk. The way things are set up, each part of the service is actually working against the other, it becomes a competition, it becomes a game, and so inevitably there will be gamesmanship. In some mad way this actually fits with the market paradigm. What works for the benefit of one, is to the detriment of the other. In effect each of the targets is in conflict with the others. In this mad, Social Darwinist world that has been created, it makes sense to kill or be killed.

But targets are meaningless when there are insufficient funds to provide the service. The situation in regard to hospitals, ambulances and waiting times is become dire. During 2017, 'Almost 59,000 patients in England have endured long ambulance waits before being admitted to A&E departments this winter . . . Hospitals are struggling to stick to stringent rules that demand no patient waits more than 15 minutes' (Marsh, 2017)

IAPT targets and statistics are similarly compromised. The success of one part of the service undermines the functioning of another part; the casualties remain consistent: the already suffering patient (customer) and the made-to-suffer practitioner.

Marketization walks hand in hand with its close cousin, marketing; a preoccupation with appearance – marketing to the market. Often much more money and energy is spent developing and promoting an appealing image of company (the 'brand'), rather than on the work itself. The pharmaceutical industry spends twice as much on marketing as it does on research.

The central dogma in practice

In making its pact with CBT, managerialism has also made a pact with the prophets of happiness. The friend of my friend is my friend after all. It is these prophets that are called on to help staff deal with the hardships of living in a managerialist milieu.

When there are insufficient funds to meet targets, but the workforce is nevertheless required to meet them, then the workforce is put under intolerable amounts of stress. This is so particularly in milieus where the governing authorities deny the reality of the situation and put the blame on inefficient staff. In these situations, targets are turned into instruments of coercion and control.

This is the situation in a beleaguered NHS mental health day hospital in Devon, UK. It is afflicted by staff absences generated by a mix of extraordinary high levels of stress caused by working with very damaged patients, short of resources, in shabby working conditions, staff shortages and persecutory managerialism. On the staff notice board is pinned a pamphlet 'Happiness at Work' (HAW) produced by an Employee Assistance Programme called CiC. Their website tells us that they are here to offer emotional support, counselling and advice to the staff of the institution (www.cic-eap.co.uk).

The cover has a picture of a group of laughing, smiling people. In its first paragraph it asks, 'How do we find happiness at work when we are facing unrealistic deadlines . . . [and] feel underappreciated? And how do we create happiness at work?' (CiC, p. 1).

In its second paragraph it answers, 'Fortunately a recent boom in happiness research has prompted scientists and psychologists to ask what happiness is and extrapolate steps to achieve it' (HAW, p. 1). Good fortune indeed. Next, comes the central dogma in its most succinct form: 'Happiness is related to our internal wellbeing rather than external factors' (CiC, p. 1).

The dogma is bolstered in the very next sentence by the notion of adaptation we met earlier – that the pleasure in new things pall quickly:

> Being awarded a pay rise can raise happiness levels temporarily but once we adjust to having more money the happiness fades . . . Additional wealth makes little difference to our happiness levels after our basic financial needs have been met and we have comfortable housing, clothing and enough to eat.
>
> (CiC, p. 1)

Happiness ideologists corrupt the truth that 'money is not everything' by collapsing into 'money is of no relevance whatsoever to your level of happiness'. Apparently 'Research has shown that we are more motivated by praise rather than remuneration' (CiC, p. 2). So better to praise your workers rather than pay them more – because ultimately that is what will make them happier. Strangely, senior managers are not inclined to follow the same advice that they are showering their workers with. This presumably is why in 2014 the pay rise offered to nurses was just 1 per cent (Johnson, 2014), and in the same year senior managers awarded themselves over 6 per cent (Campbell, 2014) and Members of Parliament awarded themselves over 11 per cent (Boffey, 2013).

What are we to make of this? First, it is hard not to read the injunctions emanating from the Happiness agenda as propaganda in the service of making and keeping the workforce compliant by telling them why they should be satisfied with their lot. The advice to the workforce is, or as they like to say 'research has shown' that '[Happiness] is an attitude. We either make ourselves miserable, or happy and strong' (Francesca Riegler, quoted CiC, p. 1; italics added).

The choice is YOURS: that is, it is up to you whether you are happy or not, and it has little to do with your material conditions, your boss or your colleagues; happiness is a state of mind, an attitude. All tracts on Happiness echo Layard, Seligman and others, to make these sorts of pronouncements:

> [1] One way to improve happiness at work is to feel in control of your destiny. [2] When things don't go your way it is all too easy to blame others. You may think that life would be better if your manager were more supportive or your client was less demanding. Having a good moan can feel very satisfying

but is very unlikely to change the situation. [3] Most people are focussed on satisfying their own needs rather than thinking about those of others. [4] In the organization the person who cares most about your development and wellbeing is you.

(CiC, p. 3; italics added)

At first glance, these seem to be benign homilies. It is worth going through this paragraph step by step. Notice the use of the word 'feel' in the first sentence [1], which privileges the internal psychological world: you need to find a way to feel in control of your destiny. Whether you are or not actually in control seems to be of less importance. The next sentences [2] are saying: if things are not going well at work, then don't whinge, don't blame others. You may think that life would be better if your manager was more supportive, but you would be wrong. How foolish of you. The penultimate sentence [3] is entirely moralistic: You really are self-centred – all you do is think about you, you, you. Think about the welfare of others instead. However [4] even though you need to be thinking about others, don't expect anyone else to be thinking about you. The only one who cares about your wellbeing is you.

In this way the problem is located firmly in the suffering individual. The context is let off the hook. This throws light on the fundamental contradiction at the heart of the CBT and Happiness thesis: while these individuals are being asked to focus on the wellbeing of others, but there seems to be no requirement on these 'others' to keep in mind the wellbeing of this individual. An important additional issue needs to be noted: the reason that individuals are being told to think about others, is because it is the means of making their own selves happier. This is what the Science of Happiness has done. It has taken the noble ideal of 'good will to others' and instrumentalized it, by putting it in the service of selfish ends – my happiness.

So, although Layard has made much of wanting to promote a change in social policy in order to make the nation happier, the policy change that Layard has actually unleashed is a very different one. The policy change has been one of training practitioners of CBT and its promotion in the NHS through IAPT, and the annihilation of all the other forms of psychotherapy. And rather than fostering sincere happiness, what is being perpetuated is the training of individuals in the art of mind control, so that they can think themselves happy in unhappy circumstances. Ultimately Layard and the cognitivists are purveyors of a kind of cognitive Soma, which in Aldous Huxley's words has 'all the advantages of Christianity and alcohol . . . [and] none of their defects' (Huxley, 1932, p. 37).

Part IV

Dispensing CBT

Chapter 8

NICE

The Bureaucratization of Science

Happy Feet

It is really quite extraordinary that in the current economic climate of austerity, the State continues to fund the IAPT project rather than cutting it back along with everything else. In actual fact, the government has actually increased its spending on the project by hundreds of millions of pounds over the years. This has been the case since 2004 (Labour under Blair then Brown, the Conservative/Liberal Democrat coalition, followed by the Conservatives under Cameron and May); and they have each done so claiming that this is because they are concerned about the wellbeing of its citizens; that they really truly care about us and our 'mental health'.

This is their rhetoric. They care, they say, and yet they continue to inflict deep and vicious cuts to other public services that are necessary and critical to the 'wellbeing' of citizens, from the National Health Service to education to social care to housing, and so on. When making these cuts, their rationale is the austerity one. On this matter they appear to be completely indifferent to the fact that the cuts are raising the stress levels of the workforce to intolerable levels, as they are being required to do more and more with less and less. In these ways the State clearly demonstrates that it does not really care about the wellbeing of those providing these services, nor with the wellbeing of those who are supposed to benefit from these services.

In short, the favoured status of IAPT appears to be an anomaly. But when viewed in another light, a fiscal light, it becomes apparent that this is no anomaly because the rationale for supporting the IAPT services is the same one that is dismantling the NHS, education, and every other public service. This being the neoliberalist intention to make the State as small as possible and its insistence that each individual should stand on their own two feet. There are many though, who are not on their feet by virtue of being the unemployed. According to Layard and Clark unemployment has little to do with the state of the job market. The unemployed are unemployed because they are suffering from some 'mental disorder' which is preventing them from working. CBT treatments will help them to get back on their feet – back on their happy feet.

This will result in the benefits bill going down and the tax income going up. In effect, CBT is a money-making venture. It was this promise that convinced the Exchequer to spend more today in order to save much more tomorrow. The figures in the original Depression Report claimed that half a billion pounds invested now, would eventually save the State seven billion a year, and the economy itself would benefit by twelve billion a year.

This is the real reason, the 'bottom line' reason that the State is so enthusiastic about CBT. If the governments were truly concerned with the wellbeing of its citizens, then it would be putting more money, not less, into the public services that it is busy decimating. The usual response, that there is not enough money does not hold water, because they regularly find the funding for their ideological projects to the tune of hundreds of billions of pounds a year; the official cost of the Trident missiles is around 20 billion a year; Greenpeace's estimate is much higher at 130 billion a year (Norton-Taylor, 2009); the estimate of the subsidy to the arms industry is something between 420 million to 700 hundred million a year, the subsidising of private schools is estimated to cost the Exchequer around a hundred million pounds a year, and let us not forget the sudden capacity to print money to the tune of hundreds of billions to bail out the banking industry, and so on. This then, is the economic context that surrounds and supports IAPT.

IAPT was designed by Managerialists and it is Managerialism writ large. This is the chain of command: at the top of the edifice reside the policy-making 'Legislators' who decree things. It becomes the task of New Public Managers to put these decrees into practice. And it is the task of the workforce to follow the dictats of the Managers. However, the Legislators can only make their decisions and produce their decrees on the basis of information supplied to them by Experts. But which of the experts should they listen to? There is no consensus between Experts when it comes to human suffering – neither its causes nor what is to be done about it.

Layard convinced government ministers (who, it should be remembered are ignorant about matters psychological) that the experts they should listen to are the ones who claim to be scientific and evidence-based, the positivist cognitivist psychologists. The point needs underlining: the 'experts' that the government is seeking advice from are partisan and invested in promoting their world view and their kinds of treatment models over others. The circle is closed. The cognitivists advise the legislators, and the legislators based on this advice, create policies that decree that the cognitivists are best suited to provide the kinds of treatment they provide. And once the circle closed, it becomes very hard for the other voices to break in and be heard. This is politics; not science.

The reliability of the whole system is premised on the belief that that the data being generated is trustworthy, and the presumption that the advice from the Experts is genuinely neutral and value free. The whole endeavour will fall if just one of these turns out to be problematic; in fact, both of them do.

NICE

The Legislators look to its scientific committees for the scientific facts, advice and guidance on the subject matters they are creating policies on. In our case, this committee is The National Institute for Health and Care Excellence (NICE), which is supposed to be 'an independent public body that provides national guidance and advice to improve health and social care in England. NICE guidance offers evidence-based recommendations made by independent Committees on a broad range of topics' (NICE, 2017a). The key word here is 'independent'; it will become clear very quickly that NICE is not independent in that the membership of its committees as well as its methods are designed to favour the cognitivists and their supporters.

NICE produces guidelines for all manner of things from cancer treatments, to antibiotics to surgery and 'mental health'. It goes about its business in the following way.

First it decides on a medical 'condition' that it is going to examine. For psychological matters, the 'condition' has to be one of the 'mental illnesses' that feature in the latest edition of the DSM – currently the fifth edition. Second, it puts together a team of experts and other interested parties to form what is called a Guideline Development Group (GDG) to examine the evidence for that condition. The GDG is then supposed to critically collate the research on treatments for that for mental illness in an unbiased way. It is on this basis that it draws up its guidelines of best practice. Various interested 'stake holders' can also apply to be a part of the GDG.

Each of these steps is highly problematic. The first being the status and reliability of the DSM, which as was previously noted, is problematic and highly contested; also contested is its whole ethos and the medicalization of human suffering that it perpetuates. Most importantly, to date there has been no evidence produced to substantiate the 'chemical-imbalance-in-the-brain' thesis. The diagnostic categories in the DSM have been generated by committees, and unruly committees at that.

Also problematic is the fact that the membership of the 'mental health' GDGs is made up almost entirely of clinical psychologists of the cognitivist persuasion; the other members are drawn mainly from the medical profession, and with 'psychotherapists being notable by their absence' (Guy et al., 2011, p. 8). Given that these GDGs are primarily made up of clinical psychologists with a declared commitment and allegiance to research on CBT lines, then it is unsurprising that the guidelines that they produce favour CBT. This is tantamount to poachers writing out rules of good practice for gamekeepers, rules that favour the poachers.

The final issue to be addressed has to do with the way that GDGs gather information, make decisions and deliver their advice.

Despite the legions of 'scientific' studies, there is a paucity of robust empirical evidence for the efficacy of CBT, and what there is, is very often equivocal. When evidence is absent then the GDG produces its advice through a consensus that is supposedly arrived at dispassionately through discussions between the experts that constitute the GDG. How is the consensus arrived at?

In a rather disturbing paper, Moncrieff and Timimi (2013) describe the machinations that took place to manufacture an illusory impression of consensus. Timimi, a member of the Critical Psychiatry Network, was invited by the GDG for Attention Deficit Hyperactivity Disorder (ADHD) to participate in their 'conference of experts'. Timimi was reluctant to participate as he feared that he would be used as 'the token critic to enable NICE to state that they had represented a cross-section of professional opinion' (Moncrieff and Timimi, 2013, p. 63). Despite his reservations he attended and presented empirical evidence which challenged the mainstream neurodevelopmental model of ADHD and its treatment through medication. The GDG did not address his evidence and instead grilled him about whether or not he had ever prescribed medication for the condition. He said that he had done so early in his career but had not prescribed medication for many years. The GDG latched onto this.

> the Full Guidelines described the meeting as a 'consensus conference' and the report emphasises repeatedly the agreement and 'unanimity' between participants, particularly with regard to the Guideline recommendation for the drug treatment of children with severe symptoms . . . the admission that he [Timimi] had in the past prescribed stimulants appears to be the basis for this claim of consensus. The conference report . . . misrepresents his views on stimulant treatment, claiming consensus and unanimity where there was none.
>
> (Moncrieff and Timimi, 2013: 63)

'This strategy enabled NICE to employ the rhetoric of consultation, while effectively marginalizing dissenting views, in order to produce an impression of consensus' (Moncrieff and Timimi, 2013: 67). In general, this is how GDGs are able to regularly magic away evidence that contradicts the official narrative to give the impression of robust scientific consensus and certainty.

Evidence of the wrong kind

The GDGs regularly utilize two strategies to sideline annoying evidence that contradicts their ruling paradigm. The first strategy is to say that it is the wrong kind of evidence. For example, in a highly respected study Shedler (2010), compared outcome claims of CBT with those of psychodynamic psychotherapy. He reached his conclusions having conducted an extensive review of psychological research; his verdict: the effect sizes of psychodynamic psychotherapy were at least as large as those reported for the so-called evidence-based therapies. In other words, here is evidence for psychodynamic psychotherapy. However, NICE took no notice of this work and did not even trouble itself to refute it or even make mention of it. When questioned about why they ignored it, they replied that the paper fell outside the parameters laid out by NICE. For a study to be considered legitimate by NICE, it has to study one specific 'mental disorder'. All other forms of research fall outside its remit.

This point is really important. Before NICE will even deign to consider a piece of research, that research has to buy into a very narrow way of looking at things, in other words, the results obtained by one treatment treating one specific mental disorder. Anything outside these narrow parameters, for example, a study comparing two treatments for one disorder, is simply not considered, however valid and robust that research might be. In other words, NICE only speaks to those who speak its language; it does not entertain any questioning about the nature and status of that language.

On these grounds NICE took no notice of Shedler's study as the structure of his research was the comparison of two methodologies. NICE does not dismiss Shedler and others like him, they simply ignore them. They simply do not exist in NICE's positivist chopstick world. They ignored Shedler despite him having argued his case in their own language, that of statistics and the medical model. In this way NICE simply ignores the reams of research. For example, the work of Weston and colleagues who have investigated the statistical claims made by CBT trials, and finds them seriously wanting. NICE blinds itself to empirical evidence of the uncomfortable kind in the same kind of way that the patent office blinded itself to existing evidence about the uses of the Neem tree over centuries and millennia.

Evidence of the right kind

But NICE also manages to dismiss the right kinds of research when findings do not accord with its ideological agenda. Here too, they use their self-same practised strategy of simply ignoring it. Here is an instance.

The submissions made by the Critical Psychiatry Network questioned the credibility of the bio-medical chemical imbalance assumptions about the sources of depression. Their submission had put forward a number of rigorous meta-analyses which all showed that the efficacy of SSRIs was hardly any better than placebo. NICE agreed with this, admitting 'Although [the difference was] statistically significant, the differences were so small that they were 'unlikely to be of clinical significance (NICE, 2004, 169)', (Moncrieff and Timimi, 2013, p. 62)

But then NICE found a way of chopping up the data and analysing it in a way that generated results that made it look like anti-depressant treatments worked. And it was this latter version of things that the GDG used to make its recommendations for antidepressants. The GDG simply ignored the critical submission and all of its arguments.

This strategy is habitually and openly employed. For example, this is how the GDG for ADHD dealt with the critical submission from Critical Psychiatry Network:

> Thank you very much for your comprehensive and detailed critique of the concept, diagnosis, classification and treatment of ADHD and related categories. Unfortunately, we are unable to dismiss the diagnosis as we would be left without a guideline to undertake.
>
> (NICE, 2006, p. 34, quoted in Midlands Psychology Group 2010)

But that surely is the point. This is akin to the evidence showing that the emperor does not wear clothes, and the response being but if we accepted that then the tailors and designers won't have any work to do. It is in these sorts of ways that the GDGs and NICE do away with scientific evidence that conflicts with their paradigm and agenda; and when they can't disappear the evidence, they find ways to spin things to make them appear to be more positive than they actually are.

Two faces of NICE: not so nice and not nice

NICE produces and publishes Full Guidelines but also other more condensed versions such as a 'Quick Reference Guide', a 'Short Version' and also a version giving guidance to the general public. NICE presents its 'nice(ish)' face in the Full Guidelines in the sense that this is where we find some gestures towards scientific integrity – remarks that acknowledge the limitations of the claims. But then, having made tokenistic mention of these matters, they play no further role in the Full Guideline for Depression. Remarks of this kind function in the same way that the disclaimers hidden in small print function; the point of which is to be able to say one thing loudly and clearly, and say the other, truer thing, so quietly that no one even hears it; it is a way of covering your back without anyone noticing. The Full Guideline on Depression is over 700 pages long – too long for a busy professional to delve into. Having ticked the scientific credibility box, the cautions get buried within the 700 pages of the Full Guideline; they fail to raise any questions about the integrity of cognitivist treatments. As a busy professional, if you only read the passages on treatments, you would gain no hint of the limitations and doubts that were mentioned earlier. This is the not-so-nice face.

All this is even more the case in the condensed versions of the guidelines in which the cautions do not feature at all. They are completely absent. It is here, in the shorter versions we find the not-nice face of NICE. The language in these versions is that of the instruction manual delivered in the imperative: if 'this', then do 'that'. It brooks no alternatives. For example,

> Lower intensity psychological interventions
> 1.5.1 Offer group-based cognitive behavioural therapy (CBT) specific to depression as the initial treatment for people with less severe depression.

1.5.2 Deliver group-based CBT that is:

- based on a cognitive behavioural model
- delivered by 2 competent practitioners
- consists of up to 9 sessions of 90 minutes each, for up to 12 participants
- takes place over 12–16 weeks, including follow-up.

(NICE, 2017b, p. 16)

Over time, statements emerging from NICE have become increasingly closed and dogmatic. The shift in tone in the Full Guideline on Depression in the years between 2004 and 2009 is instructive. The 2004 Guideline concedes that not only is it hard to 'measure' depression with any conviction, it also concedes that the very concept of depression as an illness is suspect and difficult to pin down.

> it is doubtful whether the severity of the depressive illness can realistically be captured in a single symptom count . . . there are some significant limitations to the current evidence base [which] include very limited data on both long-term outcomes . . . these limitations arise from the problems associated with the randomised control trial methodology . . . for psychological and service interventions . . . However, the most significant limitation is with the concept of depression itself. The view of the Guideline Development Group is that it is too broad and heterogeneous a category, and has limited validity as a basis for effective treatment plans. A focus on symptoms alone is not sufficient because a wide range of biological, psychological and social factors have a significant impact on response to treatment and are not captured by the current diagnostic systems.
>
> (NICE, 2004, pp. 8–9)

All this disappears in the 2009 version in which depression is spoken of as established scientific fact: '2.1 Depression refers to a wide range of mental health problems characterised by the absence of a positive affect . . . low mood and a range of associated emotional, cognitive, physical and behavioural symptoms' (NICE, 2009, p, 17).

***

NICE guidelines are hugely important because they have consequences for individuals not only in the UK, but across the world. They have become the international benchmark and used by many countries to formulate their treatment policies and strategies. They determine the kind of psychological treatment a suffering individual is likely to receive. This is particularly the case in situations where the treatment is to be funded through insurance as insurance companies will only fund psychological treatments that have been validated by NICE.

The next chapter asks, what exactly does this fabled CBT treatment look like? And the chapter after that looks at how the treatment is implemented by IAPT.

Chapter 9

CBT treatment

John and Martin were both unexpectedly made redundant at the same time. A few weeks later John was out there looking for jobs, whilst Martin had slipped into a state of lassitude. He found it hard to get out of bed and hardly went out. His GP diagnosed him as suffering from depression.

What's going on? Why are they having such different responses to the *same* situation? CBT explains the difference between the two of them in this way: Events produce emotional responses in people. The fact that John and Martin are having different emotional responses to the *same* situation shows that something else is going on; a something which sits *between* the event and the emotional response. This something is a mechanism called 'cognition'. Cognitions are the beliefs and assumptions that are used to process events. Martin's cognitions are more prone than John's to experience events in a more negative way creating a sense of help-lessness in him. This is how the '2nd wave' of CBT formulates the predicament. This is the 'pure' research-based version of CBT; it is mainly this version that is 'dispensed' to the suffering public. I will have more to say about the 'third waves' in the final chapter.

Pretty much every CBT book, technical or self-help, contains this kind of picture:

Event $\rightarrow$ Cognition $\rightarrow$ Emotion

First, the event, then cognition, then the emotional response.

> If an event automatically gave rise to an emotion . . . it would follow that the same event would have to result in the same emotion for anyone who experienced that event . . . [therefore] there must be something else . . . CBT says that this 'something else' is cognition
>
> (Westbrook et al., 2008, p. 3)

The entire CBT thesis is encapsulated in these few sentences: because thoughts are said to cause emotions, if you change what you think, then you will be able to change how you feel. CBT will teach you how to change what you think. Once you have learnt how to change what you think, you have a *choice* about whether or not you will decide to change your thoughts. The notion bears repeating: you can choose what to think. You can choose to think that you are likeable rather than unlikeable. If you *choose* to think you are likeable (because there is rational objective evidence for this) then you will not be anxious in social situations.

This conception of the human condition found in cognitive psychology is akin to that of Rational Choice Theory which we met earlier in the chapter on economics. But whilst economists are aware that their model of human functioning is reductive and unrealistic (but think that this not matter), cognitive psychologists seem to think that this is how things actually are and how human beings actually function.

This improbable account of human suffering has come to flourish in cognitivist circles as established science. There are a number of different versions of CBT, all claiming to be scientific, with slightly differing technical terminologies and technologies. But they all more or less follow the same template. For example, Albert Ellis's Rational Emotive Behavioural Therapy is based on the acronym ABC. 'A' being the activating event, 'B' being the beliefs about these events, and 'C' being the consequences that follow – emotional and behavioural.

Cognition itself is broken down into different levels. At the top are NATs, *Negative Automatic Thoughts*, for example 'I am no good' or 'nobody likes me'. We are informed that these sorts of 'thoughts are opinions not facts' (Westbrook et al., 2008, p. 7). These sorts of automatic thoughts are expressions of deeper structures. There are conflicting reports as to what these deeper structures are in the CBT literature; sometimes they are referred to as *Core Beliefs*, sometimes as *Dysfunctional Assumptions*, sometimes as *Schemas*. In some accounts Core Beliefs are linked to Schemas and in others one is a subset of the other. The main thing about them though is that unlike NATs which are conscious, *schemas and the like are unconscious and shaped by early life experiences*.

CBT presumes that depressed individuals get depressed for three reasons: first, that they tend to have a negative view of themselves; second, that they tend to interpret their life experiences negatively; and third, that they wrongly presume that that the future will follow the same pattern as the past and the present. All this creates a sense of helplessness in the person. And it is this helplessness that is the cause of depression. (Recall Seligman's dogs who 'learnt' helplessness).

The purpose of CBT treatments is to question and undermine each of these beliefs. The treatments themselves are delivered one to one, in groups (because that's cheaper), and now increasingly through online computerized self-help programmes (because that's even cheaper).

The last thing to keep in mind before we get to the treatment itself, is the fact that CBT treatments focus on the present and are designed to disrupt the cognitive habits that 'maintain' the symptom. CBT repeatedly asserts that it has no interest in looking for causes, because that is a waste of time, and the preoccupation of misguided psychoanalysts.

CBT treatment

Let's come back to Martin who has been diagnosed with depression by his GP. The GP will refer him to the IAPT service. His first contact with the service is likely to be a 'telephone screening' at which the details of his problem will be noted. Martin will also be required to complete a number of questionnaires pertaining to his state of mind (How anxious do you feel? from 1 to 4; how many times a day do you feel anxious? And so on). All this data will be amalgamated into some kind of 'score' which will be entered into a computerized system.

There are a number of different ways of testing, and this varies from service to service. The prospective patient is habitually required to fill out three tests, the GAD 7 (General Anxiety Disorder which has seven questions), the PHQ 9 (Patient Health Questionnaire consisting of nine questions), and WSOS (the Work and Social Adjustment Scale consisting of five questions). Then depending on the 'score' at the end of each test, the patient will be declared to have, or have not, 'caseness'. This rather peculiar term is said to denote whether or not the person is suffering from a mental disorder. If the score on the PHQ 9 is more than ten, then the person is said to be suffering from the mental disorder called depression, and this constitutes 'caseness'. Meanwhile if they score more than eight on the GAD 7 test, then they are suffering from a generalized anxiety disorder, and this too constitutes 'caseness', and so on.

In the next chapter we will see how these scores are used and misused; but for now, all we need to know is that the score determines whether or not the person is thought to be suffering from a mental disorder (caseness). The patient is required to complete these forms and tests each and every session, in the expectation that there will be a steady improvement in the scores. And finally, if and when the score moves below the threshold, then the patient is deemed to be in 'recovery', cured of their mental disorder.

You might expect these tests to be fearfully complex and sophisticated, as they are able to look deep into the mind. Here they are:

General Anxiety Disorder 7

Over the last 2 weeks, how often have you been bothered by the following problems?
Not at all (0), several days (1), More than half the days (2), Nearly every day (3).
Feeling nervous, anxious or on edge
Not being able to stop or control worrying
Worrying too much about different things

Trouble relaxing
Being so restless that it is hard to sit still
Becoming easily annoyed or irritable
Feeling afraid as if something awful might happen

Add up the numbers to arrive at your score. If it is more than eight, then you are suffering from the mental disorder called 'Anxiety'.

Patient Health Questionnaire 9

Over the last 2 weeks, how often have you been bothered by any of the following problems?
Not at all (0), several days (1), More than half the days (2), Nearly every day (3).
Little interest or pleasure in doing things
Feeling down, depressed, or hopeless
Trouble falling or staying asleep, or sleeping too much
Feeling tired or having little energy
Poor appetite or overeating
Feeling bad about yourself — or that you are a failure or have let yourself or your family down
Trouble concentrating on things, such as reading the newspaper or watching television
Moving or speaking so slowly that other people could have noticed? Or the opposite — being so fidgety or restless that you have been moving around a lot more than usual
Thoughts that you would be better off dead or of hurting yourself in some way

If your total score comes to more than ten, then you are suffering from the mental disorder depression.

Then there is the Work and Social Adjustment Scale, which NHS England informs us is, 'a simple, reliable and valid measure of impaired functioning'.

Work and Social Adjustment Scale

Score from 0 – Not at all, to 8 Very severely
My problem affects my . . .
ability to work
home life – cleaning etc
social leisure activities (with other people – outings etc.)
private leisure activities (done alone – reading etc.)
relationships

Some services elect to use alternative diagnostic instruments. For example, according to the DSM if a person experiences at least 5 out of a list of 9 symptoms found below, then they are suffering from the mental disorder called Depression:

1   **Depressed mood or irritable** most of the day, nearly every day, as indicated by either subjective report
2   **Decreased interest or pleasure** in most activities, most of each day
3   **Significant weight change (5%) or change in appetite**
4   **Change in sleep**: Insomnia or hypersomnia
5   **Change in activity**: Psychomotor agitation or retardation
6   **Fatigue or loss of energy**
7   **Guilt/worthlessness:** Feelings of worthlessness or excessive or inappropriate guilt
8   **Concentration**: diminished ability to think or concentrate, or more indecisiveness
9   **Suicidality:** Thoughts of death or suicide, or has suicide plan

Another diagnostic tool provided by the DSM consists of two columns, A and B.

A	B
Depressed Mood	Reduced self-esteem and confidence
Loss of interest and enjoyment in usual activities	Ideas of guilt and unworthiness
Reduced energy and decreased activity	Pessimistic thoughts
	Disturbed sleep
	Diminished appetite
	Ideas of self-harm

The diagnostic method consists of mixing and matching answers from each of the columns. To count as having Mild Depression, the person has to have one symptom from A and one or two from B. For Moderate Depression, the person has to have one symptom from A and two or three from B. And for Severe Depression the person has to have all the symptoms listed in A and B. But the person might also be diagnosed as having subthreshold depression. By which they mean that they have two or fewer symptoms for a duration of two weeks.

This is the diagnostic 'science' that CBT is based on. Anyone, with or without training, will be able to administer these diagnostic tests, armed simply with paper and pencil. Also note (and this is critically important) the list of questions make no effort to ask the sufferer anything about why they might be depressed or anxious. In accordance with the ethos of CBT, the tests are totally uninterested to find out what the causes of the distress might be.

Once Martin has been through this battery of tests, his scores will place him on one or other of the 'steps' in the Stepped Care Programme which is set out below in its entirety.

Step 3: High-intensity interventions	Depression Moderate to Severe	Cognitive Behavioural Therapy or Interpersonal Therapy, each with medication.
	Depression: Mild to Moderate with individuals	CBT or IPT Behavioural Activation (BA), a variant of CBT Couple Therapy (if the patient has a partner, the relationship is considered to be a contributing to the maintenance of the depression, and both parties with to work together in the therapy) Counselling or brief dynamic, interpersonal therapy (consider if patient has declined CBT, IPT, BA or couple therapy)
	Panic disorder	CBT
	Post-traumatic stress disorder (PTSD)	CBT or eye movement desensitisation and reprocessing (EMDR) therapy
	Generalized anxiety disorder (GAD)	CBT
	Obsessive compulsive disorder (OCD)	CBT
	Social Phobia	CBT
Step 2: Low-intensity interventions	Depression	Guided self-help based on CBT, BA, structured physical activity
	Panic disorder	Self-help based on CBT, computerised CBT
	PTSD	None
	GAD	Self-help based on CBT, psycho-educational groups, computerised CBT
	OCD	Guided self-help based on CBT
	Social phobia	None
Step 1: Primary care/ IAPT service	Recognition of problem Moderate to severe depression with a chronic health problem	Assessment/referral/active monitoring to include careful monitoring of symptoms, psychoeducation about the disorder and sleep hygiene advice Collaborative care (consider in light of specialist assessment if depression has not responded to initial course of high-intensity intervention and/or medication)

If Martin's 'score' is low, he will be offered one of the lower 'stepped' interventions, from psychoeducational web links that give advice, to self-help workbooks, to online self-administered CBT treatments, and so on. If his score is higher, then he will be stepped up to a manualized IAPT treatment, occasionally counselling, sometimes IPT, but mostly CBT. Let us suppose that Martin's score was high enough for him to be offered 16 weeks of CBT treatment in a one-to-one setting.

Martin's CBT therapist will be using a designated manual in which the steps and stages that the treatment will follow are already laid out. The manual itself is simply a record of the actions followed by the original researchers.

Martin's CBT treatment will typically proceed in this kind of way: In the initial sessions the therapist will educate Martin into the principles of CBT as well as the rationales behind the method of treatment that is about to be implemented. This rationalist conception of human life is the first thing that the client has to buy into in order to begin the 'treatment'. Given that this reading of human psychology is presented as established verified science, it would be pretty hard to resist. With facts, there is nothing to be argued about; they are not matters to be debated. If you are of the opinion that 6 is a prime number, then I would *educate* you about why you are wrong, and why it is not just my opinion that this is so. In this way, the patient is obliged to swallow a whole tranche of so-called objective facts about the nature of human existence as decreed by CBT, before the treatment can even begin. This initial stage, the 'educative' process, is already a form of indoctrination and coercion and not the collaborative one it claims to be. Many drop out at this stage; presumably some of those do so because they are not convinced by the facile picture of the human condition that is being presented to them.

After having been educated, the patient and therapist agree the symptoms the treatment will target for modification. Once this agenda is set, the patient is not allowed to deviate from it without resetting the contract in a semi-formalized way. Martin will be required to fill in one or more of the questionnaires each and every session to check his 'progress'. If his scores are do not show regular improvement, then the therapist is likely to be micromanaged through a supervision process.

The treatment itself consists of catching hold of the 'Negative Automatic Thoughts' (for example, no one likes me) and subjecting them to empirical testing followed by a rational analysis of the data. The idea is to demonstrate *rationally* to the patient that their cognitions are distorted. The forms of these distortions are catastrophizing, over generalizing, and so on. The idea of questioning process is to produce evidence that 'clearly *some* people *do* like you; therefore, you must be likeable'. Faced with this truth, the patient is bound to agree that their emotional responses are illogical and irrational. They will then be able to stop having these illogical and unhelpful emotional reactions in social situations. The treatment should also make the suffering person aware of their core beliefs and schemas (I am unworthy) that underlie their negative automatic thoughts.

But for many, these revelations are insufficient in themselves to shift the symptoms. For this to take place, the patient is taught various practical techniques to monitor and record their behaviours and thoughts. For example, to go out for a walk every day; to make a note every time they felt anxious; they might be asked to constantly 'test' their cognitions to check if they are distorted by looking for evidence (that shopkeeper does not like me). If no evidence is found, then the thoughts are distorted; in which case they should be replaced with objective thoughts that correspond with reality (there is no evidence that he does not like me). When cognitions are no longer distorted, then the patient will feel better about themselves and their lives; they will feel 'happier' and no longer depressed. CBT claims that if the habit of replacing negative thoughts with positive ones is practiced long enough, then it will eventually become 'natural', and the patient will no longer be depressed (or anxious or whatever).

That's it. That's CBT treatment in its entirety.

Emotions in thought cages

There are any number of difficulties that can be raised with the treatment protocols and the belief systems they are based on; for example, with the fundamental sequence that CBT treatment is based on: event, cognition, emotion.

CBT texts take this 'map' for granted and assume that two (rational) persons ought to have the *same* response to an event. They think this is because rational beings, being rational, are bound to agree with each other about the nature of objective reality. Therefore, they will necessarily have the same emotional response to the same thing. If someone has a different emotional response, then that is because there is something wrong with their rational capacity, that is, their cognition.

However, it is one thing to say that all rational beings will agree that when two is added to eight, the answer is ten. It is quite another thing to say that they should have the same emotional response to some event; this is because the response will depend, in part at least, to the meaning that the event has for each person, and that in turn depends, in part at least, with the context and life circumstance of that person.

To the CBT mind set, 'thought' is distinguishable and separable from 'emotion' in a neat and tidy way; both are decontextualized, made out to be floating in a sociological vacuum. Further, the emotions *per se* are conceived of as problems unless they are of the positive happy kind. Other, so-called 'negative' emotions such as despair, sorrow, guilt, fear, shame and anxiety, being troublesome, are viewed as problematic symptoms to be done away with. In an earlier chapter we came across Layard's view that these sorts of emotions were an unfortunate legacy from primitive times, emotions that are unnecessary in today's rational civilized world. This division between thought and emotion not only fits well with the Cartesian blight that shapes the modern condition, it actually constitutes it.

In CBT discourse 'thought', (cognition), serves two functions. First, it determines the kinds of emotions that arise in a person – happy or troubled feelings. Second, thought is a kind of rationalist cage that corrals the emotions and holds them in check: thought 'says' to an emotion that it deems unnecessary, 'you are unreasonable. So cease to exist. And if you can't disappear, then at the very least don't express yourself'. This capacity constitutes mental health.

So, when some 'negative' emotion manages to break out of its rationalist analytic cage by virtue of its power and intensity, it manifests as a person becoming distressed and troubled. The problem is made out to be the very presence of the emotion, not the reason for it. As we have noted, CBT by its own account, is not interested in *why* the person is distressed, and only on how the person is maintaining their experience of distress. Remember, the DSM V tells us that desperate grief should last no more than two weeks. If you are still distressed a month or so after a profound loss, then you are doing something to keep the distress going, (you are 'maintaining' it), and you must be doing this because you are suffering from a mental disorder; why else would you cause yourself so much pain? So what CBT treatment protocols try to do is to get those pesky emotions back under control, back into the rationalist cage that they had just escaped from. We have just seen that the way that CBT tries to do this is by using hyper-rationalist arguments to coax the emotions back into a rationalist cage.

Even so, these sorts of CBT treatments do work to some degree in certain sorts of situation. These being when the issues are simple and discreet: such as a spider phobia or a fear of flying, or agoraphobia or compulsive hand washing, and so on. It is clear then that the way that CBT works, when it works, is as a form of symptom control. That in itself is not to be scoffed at. If someone is helped to leave their flat for the first time in many years, walk to the corner shop and buy a pint of milk, that is a great thing and to be celebrated. Also, to be celebrated are the occasions when someone is helped to manage their anxiety sufficiently to be able to step onto an aeroplane. These are all good and worthy accomplishments, for the patient as well as the therapy. No irony intended.

But the thing is that this in itself is insufficient to privilege CBT over the other therapies. Because counsellors and therapists of all kinds of persuasions habitually help patients manage these sorts of tasks at least as well as CBT practitioners.

The point I want to end this discussion on is the observation that most people do not come for therapy because of suffering from tidy symptoms that lend themselves to be placed in discreet symptomatic categories. People mostly come because of being troubled by deeper existential themes that they are hard put to name. Perhaps all they can describe is being inexplicably overcome by ennui. The CBT therapist will look no further than this. The therapist will think of the ennui itself as the problem, and use rational argument to try to convince the patient that they will feel better for taking more exercise. If the patient is able to do this, they would undoubtedly feel the better for it. For some, this is enough and it is all they need. But for many others, not only is this thin hyper-rationalist gruel, it misses the point entirely in relation to the existential complexities that many people struggle with; in my view, *most* people struggle with.

Chapter 10

IAPT

Managerialism and the privatization of 'mental health'

Having prepared the Clinical Guidelines, NICE passes them onto the statutory agency called Increasing Access to Psychological Therapies (IAPT), whose job it is to deliver these treatments in NICE approved ways.

Here is a quick recap of the official line so far: There are large numbers of mental disorders, which large numbers of the general population are suffering from. NHS England tells us that 'Around one in six adults in England have a common mental health disorder, such as depression or anxiety' (NHS England 2016, p. 11). CBT has been scientifically tested and found to be an effective treatment for a number of these mental disorders. This evidence has been checked and verified by NICE, who have ratified the delivery of this therapy by IAPT.

The way that IAPT works is like this: the State gives IAPT monies on condition that it *will* deliver treatments to 15 per cent of the general population (said to rise to 25 per cent by 2021) and it will ensure that 50 per cent of them *will recover* from their mental illness. Once this bargain is struck between State and the IAPT Service, then the situation is changed. Now, the emphasis of the whole IAPT enterprise shifts from that of helping suffering human beings (their rhetoric) to one of producing data that matches the targets – 'meeting the tariff' as it is called. In one stroke, the scientific method is reversed. Rather than empirical evidence (numbers), being used to shed light on the nature of reality, reality is distorted to ensure that it fits with predetermined numbers. We are about to witness a version of hyper-rationality in action.

In what follows, I draw heavily on the research published by the Centre for Psychological Therapies in Primary Care at the University of Chester, UK (Griffiths et al., 2013). Their report is an analysis of extensive interviews with managers, commissioners and practitioners in the world of IAPT. I also draw on material from interviews that I conducted.

Top-down design

IAPT has been designed 'top-down' by the managerialists who reside at the 'top'. Consequently, IAPT's structure and processes are designed to suit the needs of the 'top' rather than the 'bottom': practitioners and the suffering patient.

When you factor in the fact that most of those at the 'top' – commissioners and managers – are not clinicians, it helps explain why the structures and requirements of IAPT are data friendly and treatment unfriendly. So much so, that the already shabby treatment is further distorted and diluted in the service of generating the correct kind of data.

The principles underpinning IAPT are reminiscent of those behind many a privately-run corporation. Like them, IAPT uses the rhetoric of customer care and customer choice to camouflage its neoliberalist ideations. It is not much of an exaggeration to say that the reason that IAPT is structured in the way it is, is entirely to do with money. But of course, it is never put like that; the closest it comes to acknowledging that is through the notion of efficiency.

IAPT uses the usual rationales and language of efficiency to squeeze as much as possible out of as little as possible. The repercussions that follow out of this way of proceeding are treated as though they were 'externalities'. 'Externalities' is a term used in economic theory to describe what happens when a company or industry does not take responsibility for the ramifications of its activities, for example, atmospheric pollution caused by coal-fired industries, or health problems caused by smoking. These consequences are made out to be 'external' to the company, not a part of its ethical responsibilities, and most importantly, external to its balance sheet. The dirty work of clearing up is paid for by the State (that is, you and me). As will shortly become clear, in the IAPT case, the 'externalities' are carried by the providers, the practitioners, and most importantly, the patients.

IAPT has embraced the neoliberalist's veneration of the marketplace combined with that of 'Customer Choice'. Customer Choice has become a requirement for all kinds of organizations that declare themselves dedicated to serving the best interests of each individual customer. IAPT is no exception. The IAPT rationale for providing customer choice draws on a belief that

> when patients are given a choice in provider they are more likely to engage with the treatment . . . Advocates of the choice rationale argue that when a person chooses their provider, they gain a sense of control and become an integral part of their journey to recovery.
>
> (Griffiths et al., 2013, p. 8)

Customer choice: privatization by another name

In 2011 the Department of Health (DoH), published a document (Talking Therapies: A Four-Year Plan of Action) in support of the government strategy called 'No Health without Mental Health'. They initiated a consultation entitled 'Liberating the NHS: Greater choice and control'. (Notice by the way the presence of the weasel word 'liberating'). They tell us in paragraph 43, that intention of the consultation is to offer 'customers' the possibility of 'greater choice and control over their care and treatment' (DoH, 2011). But then in the very next paragraph (44), having just offered up the idea of greater choice and control, the Department of Health cautions its 'customers' not to get too excited by the consultation process:

> 44. It is important not to pre-judge the outcome of this consultation, but it should be recognised that NICE has *approved* a number of evidence-based therapies for treating depression (some in particular circumstances). *This requires IAPT services to invest in training in approved therapy modalities*, putting in place delivery arrangements that offer choice. This needs to take account of the commitment by the Government to create a presumption that *all patients will be able to choose from any willing provider.*
>
> (DoH, 2011, p. 12; italics added)

In other words the so-called consultation is yet another empty tokenistic gesture; there is to be no consultation and *no choice* about the *kind* of therapy one is able to receive. Only IAPT approved stalls will be allowed to into this marketplace; stalls delivering the manualized therapies – primarily CBT. The only choices that are being offered have to do with 'delivery arrangements'.

Suffering individuals, that is, customers, are thought to wander around the mental-health market place examining the contents of different stalls; and then eventually, having weighed up what each of the stalls has to offer, the customer is thought to *freely* choose which of the stalls to give their custom to. This is pure Milton Friedman and it is where the Any Qualified Provider (AQP) gambit comes into play. In order to increase customer choice, the DoH puts out a tender inviting 'providers' to *deliver* IAPT approved therapies, in IAPT approved ways. These applications are vetted by commissioners who give their blessing (or not) to institutions deemed to meet the criteria required of Qualified Providers. After that it is a free-for-all in the kind of way envisaged by Milton Friedman. The idea is that referrers or self-referrals will now be able to freely choose between a range of providers delivering IAPT compliant therapies in the market place.

In order to 'qualify' the provider has to comply with a large number of onerous managerialist requirements to do with new administrative systems, compliance, as well as investing in new IT systems that 'speak' to the national IT systems. Because of the prodigious amounts of financial investment involved, the system favours large organizations who are able to risk investment over smaller enterprises. In effect, AQP is a way of 'outsourcing' psychological services.

Outsourcing is another name for privatization, privatization which is camouflaged as 'Customer Choice'. This is what the 'Any Qualified Provider' protocol is really about. Outsourcing is a way of reducing costs and at the same time keeping one's ethical hands clean. Not only is the task outsourced to another organization, so are the ethical responsibilities the original company has to the wellbeing of its workforce. The original institution makes an arrangement with those who will manage the outsourced work, and it is *they* – the new managers – who become ethically responsible for the working conditions of *their* employees.

If they happen to erode the workforce's conditions of service (in order to cut costs), then that is nothing to do with the original institution; it is become the responsibility of the company that the work has been outsourced to.

The NHS is being sold off at an alarming rate. In 2017, Virgin Care 'won' contracts worth *one billion pounds*. 'Overall, private firms scooped 267 – almost 70% – of the 386 clinical contracts that were put out to tender in England during 2016–17. They included the seven highest-value contracts worth £2.43bn between them, and 13 of the 20 most lucrative tenders' (Campbell 2017, p. 5). In December 2017 it came to light that Virgin Care had successfully sued Surrey NHS, after they gave a contract to an NHS provider rather than to Virgin. The contract itself was to provide around £82 million pounds' worth of children's services. Virgin is set to receive around £2 million pounds of taxpayer's money in damages (Taylor, 2017).

The ideological rhetoric behind outsourcing is that of choice and efficiency. However, the outsourced service costs less not because it is more efficient, but because the service forces its employees to do more for less. It is just good business sense apparently, as one mental health commissioner complacently says,

> The new provider only takes on the people that they need . . . the existing bigger providers are struggling because their working model, they're employing staff on paid contracts with holidays – da-de-da-de-da – it's lovely for the staff – but it's very difficult to run an AQP model like that.
> (Griffiths et al., 2013, p. 36)

As we will shortly see, the business model also requires the 'customer' to make do with less. So yes, the outsourced service is cheaper, and in this sense (but only this sense) more efficient; however, there are costs nevertheless – which are paid for by others. These costs are not accounted for because IAPT treats them as the afore mentioned externalities. The language used in this world is Social Darwinist: the law of the jungle, survival of the fittest and all that. For example, a commissioner:

> [it is] the brave [provider] who invest[s], who will have a far greater chance of becoming more viable and *mopping up the market share, the timid won't*. I think it goes right back to the question of why the decision was made to introduce the market to this pathway. . .once the decision is made, it's almost, *"live by the sword, die by the sword"*. It is to a great extent a market driven service.
> (Griffiths et al., 2013, p. 41; italics added)

But the market place is not bursting with providers as you might expect it; very often there are just one or two stalls: the NHS and one other AQP. As one provider said: 'It has certainly enhanced patient choice: clients have a choice between us and long NHS waiting lists' (Griffiths et al., 2013, p. 39).

Not only are there very few stalls in this market, the stalls are all selling the same thing, because that is the only thing they are allowed to sell. Customer choice is a 'Hobson's choice' when faced with a monopoly. Given that there are hardly any stalls in the market, long lines of customers inevitably start to form outside the few stalls that there are, as there is nowhere else to go. Reality is now perverted to make this out to be a good thing. The long queue for treatment is made out to be simply an expression of *customer demand* and evidence for the popularity of CBT. 'Demand for evidence-based psychological therapies services remains high across all communities' (DoH, 2011, para. 45).

This is a little like claiming that long queues for food in the time of famine are due to the high quality of the food; or that before the fall of the Berlin Wall, the cars that East Germans loved most were the Trabant and Wartburg preferring them over BMW and Mercedes Benz. What the research actually shows, as does ordinary common sense surely, is that meaningful choice is not just about where to receive treatment, but more importantly, choice about the *kind of treatment*.

Even so, even the limited choices the patient has are only meaningful if they have some understanding about the different treatments and treatment settings they are supposed to be choosing between. Not many people understand what IAPT is, nor what the differences are between gestalt therapy, psychodynamic psycho-therapy and counselling, and whether these differences matter. The desperately depressed person is not likely to be in any position to make a meaningful choice between IAPT and Primary Care Counselling; all they are likely to know is that they want and need help, and they will look to experts to guide them. In the main the first of these experts are likely to be GPs, who in turn will act in accordance with the advice disseminated by the Department of Health. This advice being: fol-low NICE Guidelines – give them prescription drugs or send them for CBT. The whole mythology about customer choice falls apart as soon as we realize that it is not the 'customer' who will be allowed to make choices. The choices about what is to happen and where it is to happen will be made by the 'experts'.

But it is often the case that the waiting list times for treatment from AQPs is much shorter than for the NHS. Is this because the AQPs are much more efficient than the clunky old NHS? Let us look more closely into the contracting process between AQPs and commissioners.

Zero hour contracts and payment by results (PbR)

Quite astonishingly, the contract between commissioners and AQPs is a zero hour contract. Payment to providers is directly linked to results and outcomes – Payment by Results (PbR) – as it is called. Providers will only get paid for works completed. In this way, allegedly, there will be no 'waste'. Com-missioners calculate what they call a 'tariff' based on a service specification. The financial arrangements between commissioners and providers varies across the country. Typically, providers get paid according to how many people are seen (throughput), and whether or not they 'recover'.

On the whole organizations are only likely go through the onerous effort of applying to become an AQP, if they think that they will make money out of it.

They are businesses after all; businesses in the business of making money. But even so, they are obliged to take a considerable financial risk. They have to invest large amounts of money into their infrastructure in order to comply with the requirements of IAPT commissioners. Having invested this money, there is no guarantee that they will get patients to treat, and nor is there any guarantee that they will get sufficient numbers of patients or even the right kind of patients. And finally, there is no guarantee that the patients will 'recover' following treatment. In other words, there is no guarantee that the business will even get its investment back, let alone make money. This then is an IAPT 'externality'; the financial risk involved in providing treatment is externalized by IAPT and divested onto the provider who has to suffer the risk. But that's business. In order to make money one has to risk money; but you have to have money you can afford to risk. This is why the system favours large providers like Virgin Care, and this is also why so few companies are keen to get into this 'market place'. As one potential provider put it '[the requirements] put a lot of small groups off, they didn't have the resources to take a gamble; and then there's a zero value contract, [and] no guarantee of any work at the end' (Griffiths et al., 2013, p. 20). But the low tariff has turned out to be problematic for larger AQPs too, many of whom are withdrawing because they found that it was not financially viable for them to continue (Griffiths et al., 2013, p. 26).

AQPs in turn pass on the financial pressures landed on them by commissioners, onto the practitioners in their employ. For financial reasons AQPs are unwilling to employ sufficient numbers of practitioners to cope with the ups and downs of referral streams. Said one, 'obviously, if we don't get sufficient referrals we can't have staff waiting around and expecting to be paid' (Griffiths et al., 2013, p. 29). Obviously. The low staffing levels mean that practitioners employed by AQPs are put under huge amounts of stress. But this too is an 'externality' and not of import to the masters and paymasters of IAPT.

It becomes progressively evident that AQP protocols are driven primarily by the profit motive: the wish to do (financially) well rather than to do (psychological) good.

Tariff

The Depression Report claimed that the cost of 'recovery' for each suffering patient was £750. But a number of independent studies since then have shown that this figure is wildly out. According to The Artemis Trust's calculations, the actual cost was in a range between £833 and £3,176. And a more recent study (Radhakrishnan et al., 2013), calculated the cost for each recovered patient to be £1,766.

The government used the unrealistically low estimates given by Layard in the Depression Report to the fund the IAPT service, which they determined to be about £400 million over a four-year period to 2014/15. IAPT commissioners used this money to buy services from AQPs on the basis of an agreed tariff. The tariff is made up of several components – numbers of people being seen, how quickly they are seen, the level of treatment delivered, and whether or not they can be shown to have recovered at the end of treatment.

Because there is not enough money in the pot, the tariff has been set at levels that are unrealistically low. According to many providers it barely covers the fee paid to the therapist and room rental, and little else. 'They just assume you are working out of a shoebox for no cost' (Griffiths et al., 2013, p. 22). The tariff takes no account of the time and money needed to comply with all the onerous administrative tasks and data requirements of IAPT.

An independent study into the financing of IAPT revealed just how wildly optimistic the official tariff is: 'The analysis suggests a cost per IAPT session of £102.38 for low intensity therapy, and £173.88 for high intensity therapy, compared to DH Impact Assessment estimates of £32.50 and £55.20 respectively' (Griffiths and Steen, 2013, p. 142). As one provider said:

> We will need to employ the services of an administrator to maintain a database. No administration time has been included in the tariff, which means that the counsellors are having to collate data in their own time. There is no paid time allocated for administrative, managerial and supervisory input. The tariff is £40 per session, there's no DNA [Did not Attend] paid, no cancellation fee paid, no holiday fee paid, of that £40 each counsellor's paid £35, and £5 is paid into the company. These are negative consequences, that we are working under far more pressure with more paperwork, PHQ9, CORE and GAD 7, we have to fill in monthly activity sheets, listing everything about a patient, their NHS number, their age, every time we see them has to be recorded, it's a very big undertaking doing that, in unpaid time. It makes us feel undervalued.
>
> (Griffiths et al., 2013, p. 23)

Yet another externality.

Cutting cloth . . .

With such impossible margins, providers are forced to cut their cloth to fit within the agreed tariff. But managerialists have become masters at making it seem that a cut to the service is magically an enhancement of that service. For example, in order to cut costs, replacing face to face meetings between patient and practitioner with telephone contact and then claiming that this is in the interest of, and for the convenience of, the patient. In IAPT teaching materials called Reach Out, we find that,

> Low Intensity treatment is *more convenient to patients,* in that it can be seen as a lower dose of treatment techniques, often represents less

> support from a mental health worker in terms of duration or frequency of contact, and is often delivered *in non-traditional ways such as by telephone or using the internet.*
>
> (Richards and Whyte, 2011, p. 7; italics added)

Notice the presence of the weasel words, convenient and non-traditional. Another place cuts are made are to the fees paid to practitioners:

> Does the tariff reflect the input of time by our organisation to each patient, including administrative, managerial and supervisory input? No. It's £40 an hour, *we're going to be paying counsellors £20 an hour,* because there's admin, reports, we don't know how busy we will be, so at the moment we're going to really struggle to break even and pay overheads.
>
> (Griffiths et al., 2013, p. 24)

The consequence of this is that lower fees will draw practitioners who are less experienced, and therefore cheaper, 'There's an assumption I think, that the cost is what a cheaper-end therapist will charge' (Griffiths et al., 2013, p. 23). Because AQPs are unwilling for financial reasons to employ sufficient numbers of practitioners to cope with the ups and downs of referral streams, the practitioners that are employed are required to do more than they can cope with and are put under huge amounts of stress.

> Psychological wellbeing practitioners delivering low intensity interventions are expected to operate in a stepped-care, high-volume environment carrying as many as 45 active cases at any one time, with workers completing treatment of between 175 and 250 patients per year. Workers must be able to manage case loads, operate safely and to high standards and use supervision to aid their clinical decision making.
>
> (Richards and Whyte, 2011, p. 84)

However, practitioners cannot manage these workloads, safely or otherwise. But they are afraid to speak out. I contacted a colleague, a senior manager in a psychology service in a health trust in the UK, asking whether any of his colleagues might be willing to be interviewed about their experiences delivering IAPT – anonymously and 'off the record' of course. He replied:

> I doubt they will . . . fear of losing their jobs but I will ask. Turnover rates are very high amongst staff, it may be possible to find people who are no longer reliant on IAPT to pay the bills.
> [I] Spoke to two more colleagues . . . one said not . . . would put her in a difficult position. The other is agreeable . . . She is going to give me her

personal e-mail for me to pass on to you. This Trust has a 'reputation' for going through whistleblower's work e-mails.

(Personal email communications, 2017)

IAPT It is a highly regulated set-up – a version of the Panopticon – in which everyone from the bottom up is constantly being scrutinized and relentlessly required to produce data to show that within IAPT all is copacetic. But it is clear to many of those who are actually delivering these IAPT services that it is mostly not doable, even though the official rhetoric presents a reality in which not only is it doable, *but that it is being done*. Those in the field are very reluctant to speak out for fear of being censured, of being disciplined, and ultimately a fear of losing their jobs. IAPT culture is akin to that of a totalitarian regime.

Because IAPT imposes a regime that is both coercive and tyrannical, people only feel safe to speak out when they can do so anonymously. The internet platform *ClinPsy* is one such place for those working in IAPT services (www.clinpsy. org.uk, strapline: 'For aspiring and qualified clinical psychologists'). In a post called 'surviving targets' found on this site, 'redheadgingerbread' bemoans his/ her workload:

we used to carry a manageable caseload of 18 clients per week . . . However, we were not meeting clinical targets (set at 20 contact hours per week) . . . As a consequence, HI [high intensity] therapists (and PWPs also) have been asked to compensate for this by booking in 30% more clients . . . But . . . then there is no time to get everything done . . . I find the business model, targets etc really take away my enjoyment of the job and the recovery rates have been affected by this change in working, which I feel reflects a reduction in the quality of the therapy.

(redheadgingerbread, 2015)

A year later, redheadgingerbread is still beleaguered:

our recovery targets set by the CCG have increased from 50% to 60% . . . I've not had proper clinical supervision for months, only micromanagement supervision which looks at client improvement and throughput, so am finding it to be continued high stress and low satisfaction because *I'm not learning anything other than how to meet targets and am looking to move away from IAPT*. In April there was a league table of each therapist's recovery rates (no names, just numbers) but all those with less than 50% felt anxious about getting a grilling from management. It felt really awful . . . it feels very much that the therapist is blamed, rather than the system.

(redheadgingerbread, 2016; italics added)

On the same post 'bluegoat' commiserated with 'redheadgingerbread' and wondered

> whether setting up a support group of some sort might be helpful? I heard that some IAPT services run groups such as mindfulness and CFT [Compassion Focussed Therapy] specifically for staff.
>
> (bluegoat 2015)

Notice the irony: Practitioners who are becoming demotivated, burnt out and stressed by their attempts to deliver manualized CBT treatments to inappropriately complex patients, are in turn being offered the very same manualized CBT treatments to deal with the stress that this work is generating in them.

In effect what is occurring here is that the AQP is generating its own sets of externalities. It passes on the pressures that it was landed with by IAPT, onto the practitioners who end up suffering from increased stress suffering and a deteriorating sense of wellbeing.

Gaming the tariff

The way the system is structured, it is imperative for the provider to 'meet the tariff' else they won't be paid. Consequently, the managerialists in charge of AQPs become entirely fixed on 'meeting the tariff' rather than that of helping the suffering patient. But what meeting the tariff has actually come to mean is to *produce numbers that meet the targets* having to do with how many people have been seen, how quickly, and the recovery rate. This then becomes the main preoccupation of the institution.

However, the tariff can only be met by a number of subterfuges, in part because the service is seriously underfunded; in part because of the shortage of personnel; and in part because CBT does not actually heal people in the way and to the degree that the research claims. The only way that AQPs are able to meet the tariff is by distorting the evidence to make it appear that they are doing what they are supposed to be doing. In other words, by cheating.

This is a consequence of the way that the IAPT system is structured. You can only succeed by cheating whilst making it appear that you are not. This perverse incentive is not only true at the level of provider, it is also true at the 'lower' level of practitioner, and also true at the 'higher' level of IAPT itself. In the IAPT/NICE Panopticon, everyone is watching everyone else to make sure that they find a way of saying the right thing.

In order to make the statistics sing the song they want it to sing, AQPs and IAPT itself engage in gamesmanship. Gamesmanship occurs when one uses the rules of a game for strategies that the rules were not intended for. For example, in a circumstance in which a tennis player is losing, players have been known to take an unnecessary toilet break in order to disrupt the concentration of their opponent and interrupt their winning streak. All perfectly legal; bending a rule as much as possible without actually breaking it, in order to put it to a use that it was not intended for. The point of the IAPT/AQP game is to 'meet the tariff' by any means possible.

Games IAPT plays

Earlier we saw that one of the places that the 'cloth was cut' had to do with practitioners; with AQPs employing fewer than the required number of practitioners and asking the ones that were employed to do more, faster, and for less money. This creates high levels of stress and burnout, resulting in practitioners leaving the service in droves.

Crucially, the actual treatment itself is also cut back. Said one provider: 'we were forced to cut the service spec "cloth" to meet the tariff' (Griffiths et al., 2013, p. 23). This then is another externality. This time the price is paid by the very persons that the service is supposed to be helping – the suffering patient – who gets a much reduced service.

Typically, the service specification is cut in two ways. First, the duration of each session with patients is reduced to give the counsellor time to do the outcome measures, paper work, data entry and so on – from 60 minutes to 45 and in some instances even down to 30 minutes. And second, the number of sessions offered for the full treatment package is dramatically reduced from 20 to 12 to 6 or even less.

This is somewhat bizarre for a treatment that is supposed to replicate scientific research. This is a bit like arbitrarily reducing the dosage of an antibiotic that is known to cure an infection if taken three times a day for seven consecutive days. Imagine being told that we are only going to give you enough for five days at the reduced rate of half a tablet a day. In any other branch of medicine this would be unthinkable. Yet it seems perfectly acceptable to play fast and loose when it comes to 'mental health'.

But the situation turns out to be even more outlandish. IAPT has developed a bizarre view of what 'completed treatment' means. *If a person attends just two sessions* and then does not return for whatever reason, that is counted as a *completed treatment*. And if the 'scores' on the questionnaire of the second treatment are sufficiently high (compared to the initial scores), then it is decreed to be a successful treatment that has led to 'recovery'. This is one of the extraordinary devices by which the tariff is 'met'. The outcome measures will show that a person has been treated and that they have recovered. On this basis full payment will be made to the provider. We have now reached the situation which is akin to saying that a person need take just two half antibiotic tablets to complete their treatment and recover.

> In stepped care, if a client has only one session it is considered as no therapy and no payment. If it is two sessions, the therapy is considered completed and

therefore the provider can claim a flat rate. It makes a slightly perverse model where some rogue organisation might be able to get a sizeable fee just by offering two sessions and claiming a flat fee. There's a bit of a joke in some circles that 'oh all I need to do is deliver my two sessions.'

(Griffiths et al., 2013, p. 24–5)

But this is no joke as this kind of practice is commonplace within IAPT because of the open goal generated by the hyper-rationalist ethos beloved by New Public Managers. NHS England blithely sets it up in this way:

Finished treatment: This is a count of all those who have left treatment within the reporting quarter having attended at least two treatment contacts, *for any reason* including: planned completion; deceased; dropped out (unscheduled discontinuation); referred to another service or unknown.

(NHS England 2016, p. 11. italics added)

The reason for this has to do with ease of data collection, rather than anything to do with the therapy. A successful therapy has little to do with what happens in the session. All that is required for the therapy to be 'complete', is for two sessions to have taken place. The reason that NICE is not challenged about this outrageous assertion is because this sort of practice is commonplace within CBT research. For example Clark et al's (1994) study took the view that if a person attended just four out of fifteen sessions then they had completed treatment. However, even this laughably minimal condition of two sessions equalling completed treatment is not sufficient to make the statistics sing the song that the managerialists want it to sing.

'Serioussham' describes how waiting list and treatment targets are being further distorted. The government targets for IAPT services are that 75 per cent of those referred should be seen within six weeks of referral, and 95 per cent should be seen within 18 weeks.

In the service in which I work, all assessments are marked as 'assessment and treatment' [which makes it look like more people have been treated than is the case] . . . When I discussed this concern with management, I was told that 'NHS England have told us to do it this way' *which would indicate either that the service is wilfully lying or the NHS England are actually aware of this and are allowing the data to be manipulated.*

(Serioussham, 2016; italics added)

The practice is not a one off. 'Jim' (anonymized, interviewed 2017), has just been made redundant shortly after he blew the whistle on the same statistical malpractices taking place in his service. He and the other practitioners in his service were also *required* by senior managers to mark all assessments as treatments. Jim wrote to the National Audit Office (NAO) about the malpractice. The NAO initially declined to look into this saying that as their budget was so small (ironically due to more managerialist cuts and 'efficiencies'), they did not have the funds to launch an investigation. Jim persisted, informing them that the numbers in the Accessed Services column were exactly the same as those in the received treatment column. Therefore, it was blindingly obvious that all assessments were being marked as treatments. This mobilised the NAO who recently informed him that they would be making a report on the matter; but for mysterious reasons the report will not be made public.

During the telephone interview, Jim described some of the other kinds of gaming behaviour and statistical scams taking place at his old place of work. Therapists were being required by managers to use the simpler General Anxiety Disorder 7 (GAD7) questionnaire to measure treatment benefit, and not the deeper Anxiety Disorder Specific Measures (ADSM) questionnaire. This was because the GAD7 measure showed symptomatic improvement more readily than the ADSM.

According to Jim, another trick is to shift patients that do not improve onto a non-IAPT list during or after treatment. Having done this, the data will show the service as having met two targets: the accessing services target and the waiting list time target. Two parts of the tariff will be 'met' for which the AQP will collect payment. The non-IAPT data is of no interest and so not counted, and so the recovery statistic will look better than it actually is.

Jim had even more to say. The computer software being used to record the data is crude and inflexible, and so it regularly *requires* practitioners to go into the database to change and overwrite things *manually*. According to Jim, when practitioners are under continual pressure to show results, and particularly when they are being 'performance managed', then many find themselves manually adjusting the data to make their own performance look better. In doing so, the patient is also declared as having improved by the required amount, and IAPT is made to look like it is providing the service it is being paid to provide.

Jim then told me that IAPT workers are being 'trained' in the use of these questionnaires in a very particular way. They are being required to use the last session or two focusing in on the questionnaires. The hope is that the patient will be invited (coerced?) to consider the possibility that they might have actually improved more than they think they have. In this and other ways, the numbers are being regularly tweaked in more positive directions. The fact that we hear about versions of this kind of practice from a number of different sources indicates that the practice is widespread.

> [PbR] introduces a potential for providers to jiggle the data, or to lean on clients to fill in their recovery forms – you can easily do it: 'Oh, you're much better now aren't you – I'm sure that's a six. . . . I think you've been doing much better this week, don't you think that's a two?'.
>
> (Griffiths et al., 2013, p. 28)

> some providers . . . take the measures until . . . [the patients] go into recovery, and they continue to see them, but don't do the measures in case they relapse.
>
> (Griffiths et al., 2013, p. 49)

> There's an onus for providers to demonstrate some form of recovery. The pitfalls are that recovery might not be real, and then it might be just to get the payment, to put pressure on the client to say that they're well when they're not. Then the patient is at risk: please say you're well or I won't get paid. I can see people doing that. You want to please the therapist.
>
> (Griffiths et al., 2013, p. 32)

The end result? One commissioner concluded: 'I don't trust the data that I get' (Griffiths et al., 2013, p. 28).

Another of the corrupt gaming practices described by Alice (pseudonym, interviewed 2017) echoes the one described earlier by Serioussham. If during treatment it became apparent to the CBT therapist that the patient was not 'improving' on the test scores each week, then they were *required by managers* to send the patient elsewhere and to record the contact as an 'assessment'. It is important to note that this is an officially sanctioned procedure – open and not shamefully hidden. In this way, by virtue of the person simply having been seen by a practitioner, the Waiting List target is met, and so is the Accessing Services target; most importantly, the Treatment target is preserved and not degraded by any record of the lack of improvement.

The institution that employs Jane (anonymized, interviewed 2017) has an official policy that when a 'recovered' patient returns to the service having 'relapsed', the returning patient *has to be seen by another therapist*, even though the patient might wish to see their original therapist, and even though the original therapist might think this to be desirable therapeutically. The reason for this is a statistical one. When this person is seen by a new therapist, it will count as a new 'treatment episode' in the overall statistics. In other words, it will look like two people have been seen rather than one person twice. The side issue that the patient has not 'recovered' following the initial set of sessions is conveniently obscured by the glittering statistics which will show two recoveries rather than one failure.

LIWY's response to Serioussham's post provides further evidence that these sorts of malpractices are not uncommon.

> This practice [of manipulating data] is certainly rife in the South East where I know services. The one service that I know that was honest got absolutely slated in their local press for their wait times but they were no worse than anywhere else, they were just honest.
>
> It sickens me because we all know that IAPT services are horribly short staffed, full of staff suffering burnout and patients not being offered full courses of treatment according to NICE guidelines recommended number of sessions yet, because wait times are reported as being met, it gives the government a get out to not up budgets. Put this together with the services that up their apparent numbers accessing by starting new treatment episodes and you've another reason for the government to not up budget.

I have written to various government officers/offices about it and not received a single reply. Everyone just seems to want to keep a lid on it as the truth means more money to be spent.

It has made me wonder if any government figures can be trusted, the Audit Office themselves recently said "Nationally, the access and waiting times for IAPT are already being met" - https://www.nao.org.uk/report/mental-health-services-preparations-for-improving-access/ - how can the Audit office put out a statement that includes IAPT services *when no one audits IAPT numbers that are sent in from services?!*

(LIWY, 2016; italics added)

The way that the figures published by IAPT are able to make it seem that all targets are being met, is by massaging *the way* that data is collected, *when* it is collected, and modifying the way that the service is delivered. One target is called 'Accessing Services'. IAPT services currently are obliged to see 15 per cent of the local population, because apparently it is a scientific fact that 15 per cent of the population suffer from a 'mental disorder'. CBT practitioner 'Alice' described what happens in reality:

you actually *have to* get those people through the door [to meet the 15% target] . . . which leads to some very funny skulduggery . . . So, if the figures aren't going to hit 15%, oh, we'll open up the flood gates a bit and have some people who are completely inappropriate come through the doors . . . Basically the system starts working towards the numbers rather than working towards the individuals and helping the individuals, and in fact, sometimes works against the individuals . . . So, you're working towards numbers. You're not working towards people being better.

(Alice, interview, 2017)

Another target that IAPT services are obliged to hit is that 50 per cent of those seen *have to 'recover'* at the end of treatment; this is 'measured' via answers to a range of questionnaire that the patient has to fill out at the end of each and every session. But when

people finish their . . . sessions [but are not showing measurable improvement according to these questionnaires] . . . They just sit on the case load until they recover because we know that some people spontaneously recover. [After some weeks or months] you call them up. And you say, 'Oh, how are you feeling? Can we run through these questions?'

(Alice, interview, 2017)

If the answers given during the phone call show improvement, then the case is marked as a successful treatment and closed; if not, the patient continues to languish for a few more weeks or months, until they are telephoned in the same way again.

Waiting lists and sausage factories

Success is deemed to have occurred when certain numbers are hit. One of these is the number 2; if the person attends two sessions then this constitutes a completed treatment. Another number has to do with waiting list times. Short waiting list times are proclaimed as proof for the success for the AQP/IAPT/PbR system. Said one commissioner, 'The question of competition through AQP improving the experience of patients is about waiting lists.' (Griffiths et al., 2013, p. 42). But neither number has much to do with what goes on in the treatment itself. The improvement in waiting list times are taken to be a validation of the market system and competition.

If one AQP had 'big waiting list pressures, you'd hope that a GP would notice that and start sending patients to a competitor who has no waiting list. And similarly, that would drive provider A to drive their waiting list down. To improve quality, that's the idea behind it' (Griffiths et al., 2013, p. 42). Another commissioner praised one particular AQP because it had 'no waiting lists and all [referrals were] very quickly seen or signposted' (Griffiths et al., 2013, p. 14).

According to the hype and rhetoric, the AQP system is deemed to be an outstanding success: 'How does the AQP regime compare? Far more people being seen for broadly the same financial envelope, far shorter waiting time. More people getting more interventions in a shorter time scale.' (Griffiths et al., 2013, p. 41).

It is all about throughput; but throughput is no measure of success. Throughput has no bearing on the quality of treatment, nor its duration. In fact, and as we have seen, the situation is quite the reverse. The higher the throughput, the lower the quality of treatment. Waiting lists are cut and throughput increased by giving patients shorter and fewer sessions. In effect, IAPT and AQPs have become sausage factories in which the important thing is to increase the number of sausages being produced by reducing their size and quality.

And remember too, that there is in fact very little competition between AQPs because there are not very many of them.

Problems, problems, problems (with outcome measures)

But perhaps the number that is most important to the IAPT endeavour, is that of the outcome measure, because it gets hitched to payment. For this reason, gamesmanship is particularly rife when it comes to outcome measures and the production of the impression of 'recovery'. It is a requirement that the patient completes a number of questionnaires each and every session, for example like that for General Anxiety Disorder (GAD7) – which comprises of seven questions having to do with anxiety. The answers are scored, and the score ostensibly reveals whether or not the person is suffering from General Anxiety Disorder. If they are suffering from the said disorder, then the questionnaire 'measures' the degree of mental illness the patient is suffering from. In effect these tests are said to be clinical diagnostic tools, capable of revealing the state of one's being and one's mind. This is what these 'tests' were designed for.

There are several critical problems not only with the outcome measures themselves, but more particularly with how they come to be used. The first of the problems has to do with whether these tests are meaningful at all, let alone whether or not they are accurate scientific diagnostic instruments. Even if it were true that the GAD gives some indication about the person's state of mind, in no way could it be said to 'measure' anything. The presence of numbers and decimal points generates the illusion that a measuring process has taken place and gives succour to the more fundamental illusion that the thing being measured is actually measurable.

Clinicians often find that there is a mismatch between what the score says and the experience of the practitioner and that of the patient. One provider said:

> We . . . find with CORE that there's . . . a disconnect between CORE figures, and (a) presentation, (b) the therapist's experience, so we might have a CORE-10 that the counselling co-ordinator brings to me and says, I don't get this, CORE-10 says this person is doing really well, but in the room, they were in huge distress, it doesn't match the presentation.
>
> (Griffiths et al., 2013, p. 47–8)

Another made the point that

> The OCD form gives you an idea whether they've got OCD, it's not a diagnosis. They could just score four on hand washing as a maximum but they could be hand washing 24 hours a day and score nothing on the rest of the form. So technically they haven't got OCD – I know they have OCD, they know they've got OCD, but the form says they haven't!
>
> (Griffiths et al., 2013, p. 48)

Even more importantly, these sorts of measures are unable to capture large swathes of lived human experience. Recall the metaphor of the difficulty of grasping soup with chopsticks. Said one practitioner

> what about all those people who are not reflected in the measures? . . . there is no outcome measure for [people with Irritable Bowel Syndrome] . . . a lady [who] . . . couldn't leave the house . . . [After treatment] she went across the Sahara on her first holiday [in thirty years] . . . No outcome measure for that – one of the best pieces of work I ever did.
>
> (Griffiths et al., 2013, p. 48)

In sum, not only is much missed by these 'instruments', there are also real questions about the meaningfulness of what it does not miss.

The second problem has to do with the fact that clinicians are obliged by IAPT to implement these tests each and every session. Whose need is this serving? Certainly not that of the patients, who resent the repetitive and relentless form filling that it involves. These so-called measures are there primarily to serve the needs of auditors, not patients, not therapists. Form filling takes time, time which reduces the actual contact time between therapist and patient. According to one provider, 'Practitioners complete data collection at the start of each session. This can take up to 15 minutes in exceptional circumstances, out of an already brief session (35–45 minutes)' (Griffiths et al., 2013, p. 45).

Another practitioner described the relentless testing to be 'intrusive and insensitive, treating people like robots, not recognising that this deals with deep thoughts and feelings and you're expected to do it in five minutes' (Griffiths et al., 2013, p. 45). In sum, many practitioners are very sceptical about the usefulness of this kind of measurement process and find that it gets in the way and degrades the quality of treatment.

The third and more critical problem with these outcome measures is that they are put to uses that the diagnostic scores were never intended or designed for. The diagnostic score is being used to calculate the *performance* of the provider (Performance Indicators), and most crucially, they are also used to trigger payments (PbR) to the provider.

But what this means is that the data collectors (providers and practitioners) are no longer neutral objective data collectors; they are invested in their data showing one thing rather than another. This goes against the protocols of good scientific practice which make it a point of distancing the researcher from the researched. Without this there is no chance of neutrality and objectivity. IAPT's arrangements with AQPs go in the opposite direction – enmeshing the researcher with the researched, and so compromising the integrity of the data. By linking outcome measures with payment, the treatment outcome measure is entangled with the wellbeing of the provider (income and profit), and also entangled with the wellbeing of the practitioner (wages), as well as entangled with the wellbeing of the patient (mental health). But the interests of the first two are in conflict with the interests of the third. In effect, this perverse incentive is an incentive to distort, in order to pay the mortgage. Earlier we saw instances of this perverse incentive in action – pressuring practitioners into 'talking up' the outcome measures to make it seem that 'recovery' has occurred. Gaming the tariff.

But even worse is to follow. The fourth, and perhaps most important perverse incentive generated by linking outcome measures with payments is that it ends up *restricting patient choice* rather than increasing it. So much so, that it generates perverse incentives *not to provide treatment* to suffering patients.

The idea of this game is to 'win' the bonus paid out for the recovery of each patient, and to achieve this with as little input as possible. '[there are] providers who will be cherry-picking the easy ones, to get *the quick win*' because 'more complex cases work out at less per session . . . So they'll do the easy work, the ones that take three sessions, and send the other ones elsewhere, where you'd have to put in a lot of work' (Griffiths et al., 2013, p. 22).

AQPs avoid taking on the more complex cases because they 'aren't going to be your quick *win*, these are going to be 20+ sessions who are going to cost them. It probably costs the provider more than they are going to get back'. (Griffiths et al., 2013, p. 38). Notice by the way the use of gaming language such as winning and losing.

> '[if] they didn't get well before – do I want to be the one that takes that risk - or give them the number of the other provider down the road, tell them we're full up at the moment?'. . . I'll be brutally frank, if I see a person on AQP who's presented to me . . . [with complexities], I'll get them closed down enough to discharge them from AQP, and refer them to our main counselling service.
>
> (Griffiths et al., 2013, p. 36)

In other words, for many of those suffering from complex issues, 'customer choice' ends up becoming not only 'no choice', but 'no treatment'.

> [this system has] given . . . [patients] a choice of places to try, but if all those providers become risk averse, that's a choice [only] for those that would get well with a minimum of support – *it's not a choice for those that would require NICE guidance 20 sessions* . . . [These patients will end up saying] I've got four people to choose from, none of which would accept me – that's not a choice [that's no treatment].
>
> (Griffiths et al., 2013, p. 36)

It becomes clearer and clearer that the reasons that patients are given one thing and not another has more to do with the needs of the provider and the data rather than the needs of the suffering person. In reality, patients have no choice as to what they receive, nor its duration, nor from whom. It is the need of the provider to 'meet the tariff' that drives decisions about what is to happen to the suffering person.

Recovery that is harmful

The final, and perhaps most abhorrent consequence of linking PbR to Key Indicators that trigger payments have to do with the perverse incentives generated by Layard's claim that many of the unemployed are unemployed because they are mentally ill; and his promise that CBT treatment is able to cure them of their mental illness and so enable them to start working, earning money and paying taxes. This assertion is a key component of the economic argument that convinced the government that their investment in CBT would pay for itself. And so IAPT has to deliver on it come what may.

In this context, whether or not a person is deemed to have a mental illness becomes the marker of whether or not a person is entitled to receive benefits. If a person is deemed to have recovered from their mental illness then by definition, they have regained the capacity to work, and so benefits are withdrawn. There are two linkages here. First, recovery from mental illness leading to disqualification from benefits. And second, recovery from mental illness triggering payment to the provider, PbR. Consequently, 'recovery' will put more money into the pocket of the provider and remove money from the pocket of the patient.

This would work well if the recovery were a genuine recovery rather than something that is simply made to look like a recovery. But it is in the interest of the providers to make it seem that as many people as possible have achieved 'recovery' whether or not they actually have. The consequences of this perverse incentive for some of the suffering are dire.

> In the past three years, the efficacy of the Department for Work and Pensions' (DWP) Work Capability Assessment, on which IAPT's 'reduced benefit dependency' key performance indicator (KPI 7) depends, has been the subject of severe criticism from many sources including the BMA (British Medical Association, 2013) and leading mental health organisations (Mind, 2013) with one conservative estimate positing more than half a million benefit claimants with limiting illness or disability being *wrongly disqualified from benefit*, many of them with mental health problems (Griffiths, 2011).
>
> (Griffiths et al., 2013, p. 143–4; italics added).

So much for outcome measures; measures that always seem to match the pre-decreed outcomes. All the games, tricks and statistical scams we have just encountered are generated by the perverse incentives born out of the neoliberalist ideations about efficiencies which are supposedly delivered by payment by results being linked in with outsourcing and privatization. PbR not only undermines 'science' it also compromises the therapy and the wellbeing of suffering persons.

To end this chapter, I draw on Rosemary Rizq's (2011) description of her experiences whilst working with an IAPT service, as her narrative captures all this and more in a compelling tale.

Managers and clinicians

A small *part time* primary care psychotherapy service was absorbed into the new IAPT service which was staffed by 38 *full time* low and high intensity workers. The service was inundated by referrals. Initially the team worked well and worked cooperatively. They initiated a weekly clinical team meeting at which they all discussed the best treatment for each person assessed. It shortly became evident that the all the more complex cases were being referred to the psychotherapists. This was because the *consensual view* of the referral meetings was that the Low Intensity workers were not sufficiently experienced nor adequately trained to deal with these emotional complexities. But these same cases were also thought to be inappropriate for the High Intensity workers. This was because the High Intensity workers were obliged to follow the manual and which mirrored the strictures in the original CBT research, this being that they were only allowed to treat those suffering from a single ailment – say depression. However, on being assessed, most of the patients being referred to the service were deemed to have 'comorbidities' – that is, they were thought to be suffering from more than one thing – say depression and another 'mental disorder'. What this meant was that the only place left that these more complex cases could be allocated to, was psychotherapy. (For 'more complex' read real persons with real life issues). Consequently, the waiting list for psychotherapy became bloated.

This situation had two negative repercussions on the service's performance indicators. First, following assessment, these patients were languishing for a long time on the waiting list for psychotherapy. This was because there were insufficient numbers of psychotherapists to deal with the deluge of referrals they received – and they were part-time to boot. This meant that the IAPT service as a whole was seen to be falling short of IAPT waiting list time targets. Second, the Low Intensity workers were also falling short of their IAPT targets. Low Intensity workers (later called Psychological Wellbeing Practitioners – PWPs) are trained to deal those suffering with mild difficulties who are allegedly amenable to being 'treated' with a bit of education, telephone support, online self-help, and so on. What the assessment process was revealing was that there were fewer people of this kind approaching the IAPT service, fewer than the policy makers and commissioners had assumed to be the case. This resulted in the PWPs also falling short of their targets for 'numbers of persons to be seen'.

In short, the entire IAPT service was thought to be 'failing'. But the blame was placed on the psychotherapists in the following way. Given the situation, the reasonable thing to do here would be to employ more psychotherapists because this was where the need appeared to be. But this would be anathema to the IAPT mentality. Their entire belief system is that whatever psychotherapy can do (and it can't do much) CBT can do better, quicker and cheaper. Psychotherapy is redundant. On this basis the commissioners decided not only not to employ more psychotherapists, they also decided not to replace two psychotherapists who had just retired, thus reducing the capacity for psychotherapists to work effectively even further.

But the managerialist classes also focused their ire on Low Intensity IAPT staff for not meeting their targets of numbers of persons to be seen. They started to be micro-line-managed which led a lowering of morale. This in turn led to many IAPT staff abruptly leaving the service, and this no doubt further reduced morale.

IAPT managers then decided that the psychotherapists should no longer attend the referral meetings, on the grounds that their time was better spent reducing their waiting list. In effect they were cut out of the clinical loop. Very quickly, the referral meeting itself faded away. With no referral meeting and the team fractured, managerialists took charge of the referral process. They issued an edict which decreed that *by default* most of the referrals were to be passed onto the Low Intensity workers. This was their way of boosting throughput numbers to meet their targets. This resulted in the PWPs becoming more anxious and stressed because they did not have the experience or training to deal with the more complex cases that they were being asked to deal with. Many left the profession. Meanwhile the length of the waiting list for psychotherapy was taken as evidence of poor time management on the part of the psychotherapists and their inability to meet targets. They were deemed to be inefficient. The final managerialist master stroke was this:

> Low intensity workers . . . unable to manage, were persuaded by managers either to offer brief treatment, or to assess and quickly 'signpost' clients on to community or voluntary sector services . . . [which] resulted in dissatisfaction and increasing levels of complaint expressed by both clients and GPs referring to the service.
>
> (Rizq, 2011, p. 49)

We can see here clearly the consequences of clinical decisions being made by managers rather than clinicians. The focus of (these kinds of) managerialists is to manipulate the system in every which way in order that it produces the right kind of data. As the scenario above shows, concern for the actual suffering patients does not feature much in their considerations. What matters is that the figures should show that targets are being met. The fact that the suffering are not actually being helped with their difficulties is just an incidental annoyance.

***

IAPT reports regularly claim that their data shows that the moving to recovery rates are around 50 per cent and are therefore on target. in 2103 were around 45 per cent, and so in line with expectations. However, this figure is calculated on the basis of those who 'complete' treatment, not for all those referred for treatment. The real calculation ought to have been based on *all those referred for treatment*; in which case it is just 12 per cent who are 'moving to recovery' (Griffiths and Steen, 2013). One year later, the figure had dropped even lower, to 6 per cent (Atkinson, 2014). If just 6 per cent recovered, then '94% of referrals to IAPT failed to receive a successful course of therapy, and 86% failed to complete any course of therapy at all. What happened to 757,000 referrals who never completed a course of therapy?' (Atkinson, 2014, p. 18). When we also take into account the fact that it requires just two sessions for the treatment to be 'completed', the entire evidence base about numbers recovered is either bad arithmetic, or wishful thinking, or simply institutionalized (and therefore normalized) lying.

Part V

CBT research

Chapter 11

Good science

I have heard it said on many an occasion that: 'You can prove anything with science'. That's a pretty strange thing to say, given that science is supposedly a quest for truth. Many parents, having heard of Andrew Wakefield's study assert that the MMR (measles, mumps, rubella) vaccine can cause autism in children, have not allowed their children to have the vaccine. They believe this despite the large number of other scientific studies that dispute Andrew Wakefield's claim. On the other hand, Wakefield says that these studies are a form of disinformation produced by those with vested interests who want to cover up the uncomfortable truth that his research has exposed. We then discover that Wakefield's research had been funded by the litigants who were suing the company producing the vaccine. Who is speaking the truth? Contradictory scientific claims of this kind regularly follow one upon the other. A respected scientific study in 2012 contradicted established wisdom to say that saturated fats were not a health risk. Five years later, in 2017, the American Heart Association issued advice reversing this, saying that saturated fats remained a health risk. What are we to believe? Who are we to believe? And why should we believe it?

Newspapers and the internet are replete with claims that research has discovered this or that. An assertion that coffee rots the brain is countered by another, that it is an antidote to dementia. A warning that coconut oil is lethal is followed by that claim that it is the solution to all kinds of health problems. For decades, the tobacco industry produced evidence that had all the appearances of respectable science declaring that there was no correlation between smoking and lung cancer. Even today, the scientific studies that show climate change is accelerating are being undermined by many other scientific-looking studies claiming that it is not.

Which of these claims is an honest but mistaken claim? Which of these is bad, lazy science, and which is deliberately corrupt science? Persons who say 'you can prove anything with science' have stopped trusting science.

In order to understand why this has come about, and also understand the nature of corrupt science, we first need to have a grasp of what good science looks like, or ought to look like.

It is completely reasonable . . .

The Exchequer has a responsibility not to squander public funds and to spend our money sensibly in ways that benefit us. When it comes to the issue of the psychological suffering and the emotional wellbeing of its citizens, it is completely reasonable that the Exchequer should ask: 'what is most beneficial?'. And being the Exchequer, it is also completely reasonable that it should add – 'for the least expenditure'.

In this sort of situation, there will be a range and number of candidates each claiming to offer something that they think beneficial. And so, it is completely reasonable that the exchequer asks each of them: Why should we (the Exchequer) believe you? Demonstrate to us that your suggestions and methods do what you claim they will do. Show us evidence that people feel better after they have gone through your treatment.

Hard science: Empiricism

The questioning process that began during the Enlightenment eventually evolved into what we have come to know as the scientific method. To this end, anything – everything – ought to be and should be, relentlessly questioned and questionable. Nothing is to be exempt from scrutiny, not even the claims of science about itself.

Science sets out to produce objective facts which are 'out there' independent of observer, facts that are consistently true. Its methods are empirical in that its claims and hypotheses are tested in experiments to see if they hold up to scrutiny. The experimenters themselves are, however, problematic. It turns out that scientists are no less prone to wishful thinking than the princes and priests that they sought to replace as purveyors of knowledge. Despite their best efforts, they too are unconsciously inclined to find a world of evidence that mysteriously accords with their beliefs and desires. The strong correlation between expectation and outcome is in itself established 'scientific fact'.

In order to screen out the wishful thinking of the scientists, a number of scientific protocols have evolved to facilitate this; for example, randomized control trials, placebos and double blind protocols.

Even physicists, involved in the 'hard' sciences are prone to unconscious drift, in that they are unconsciously inclined to read data in ways that fit their expectations and desires. I use the term 'hard' to underline the point that for our purposes, 'hard' scientific facts are not pliable; they are unchanging, verifiable, predictable and repeatable. For example, the fact that two plus two is always four; that the mass of a ball remains the same wherever it happens to be in the universe and whoever measures it. Here we have something akin to objectivity and certainty, but never complete certainty.

This was brought home to me very early in my undergraduate studies in physics. We were asked to do something very simple. To repeatedly put a table tennis ball on a sensitive spring balance and record its weight each time. Surely here is a concrete fact. But each time, the reading was subtly different. We had to plot the results on a graph and then infer its weight by taking an average of the readings in various ways. But then there was the further question of which kind of average? Each kind, graphical, mode, median or mean, gave up different answers. We learnt that all we could reliably say was that the weight of *this* table tennis ball was accurate to so many decimal points when measured in this sort of way.

Induction and deduction

This simple experiment captures the activity and method of empirical science – experience and experimentation. But as we have seen, even here, in the realm of the everyday concrete, my knowledge is limited. All I can say with certainty is that the weight of *this* table tennis ball is 2.7 grams accurate to one decimal place. Of course, a more sensitive scale will be able to be definitive to a more refined degree – to four decimal places, and so on. But before this finding can properly be called a scientific fact, it needs to be verified (someone else should repeat the experiment to arrive at the same result), and it needs to be repeatable (we arrive at the same result each and every time the experiment is conducted).

So far, the only fact that has been established is that the objective weight of *this particular* table tennis ball is such and such. If we were to repeat the experiment with many more table tennis balls, say 357 of them, and the weight turns out to be the same each and every time, then we can venture the claim that the result is likely to be true of *all* table tennis balls.

But wait. I have not weighed *all* the table tennis balls in the world, so I cannot know for certain that this will always be the case for each and every table tennis ball. But having weighed 357 balls, I might reasonably *infer* that the 358th ball will weigh the same as the other 357. This form of inference is called *induction*. We have used induction to say *all* table tennis balls weigh 2.7 grams. We have now fulfilled all three of the conditions necessary before a claim can be called scientific: that it is verifiable, repeatable and generalizable. Things are looking good. Now, when we next come across another table tennis ball, we can use *deduction* to assert that this table tennis ball weighs 2.7 grams, *without weighing it*. The argument goes like this:

- All table tennis balls weigh 2.7 grams;
- This is a table-tennis ball;
- Therefore it will weigh 2.7 grams.

Deduction is a kind of short cut that saves us the effort of reinventing the wheel over and over again. In effect, we have used a mix of induction and deduction to make *predictions* about the weight of all future table tennis balls. This is the virtue of empirical science: its *predictive power*. In the main, the empirical method is used to discover and generalize relationships between causes and effects, in order to manipulate the world in *predictable* ways. If you do this, then that will always happen. Science of this kind is determinism writ large. Here we find Kant's inanimate mechanistic universe and it is sufficiently trustworthy to fly us to the moon and back again.

'Hard' truths

For the sake of argument, let me call these sorts of facts and truths, *hard* facts and truths. The key characteristics of 'hard facts' that I want to underline, are their consistency and reproducibility – but always within certain limits (remember the object I was asked to weigh as an undergraduate). Hard facts reside in a predictable, deterministic universe constituted by relationships of cause and effect.

But what if we now came across a table tennis ball and discover that it weighs 2.6 grams? We have three options. We can either say that it is not a table tennis ball because by definition table tennis balls weigh 2.7 grams, or we can say that it is a deviant or distorted table tennis ball. Or, we can rethink our assumptions about the nature of table tennis balls.

This is how empirical science works using a mix of experiment, induction and deduction. The version of empirical science utilised by the natural sciences is called positivism. Positivist science limits itself to what can be observed and measured.

Harder science: the Logical Positivists

In the 1920s a highly influential group of intellectuals belonging to the Viennese Circle developed a narrower understanding of positivism, called Logical Positivism.

They went much further than the old positivist assertion that only the observable and measurable could count as science. They insisted that if something could not be observed and measured then there was no evidence that it existed, *therefore it simply did not exist.* Any and all allusions to intangibles such as the notion of virtue or the inner psychological life were consigned to the dustbins called superstition, fantasy and wishful thinking. In effect, logical positivists solved the tension between fact and value, by dispensing with value altogether.

> All statements belonging to Metaphysics, [and] regulative Ethics,. . . are in fact unverifiable and, therefore, unscientific. In the Viennese Circle, we . . . describe such statements as nonsense.
>
> (Carnap, 2012 [1934], 26)

Although the proper logical stance towards untestable assertions (untestable by the decreed methods and protocols) ought to be agnostic (that is, we don't know whether they are correct or not), in practice they tend to be dismissed and ignored as fictions, as hearsay, superstition, wishful thinking, and so on.

In taking this step, the logical positivists created a version of science that was fundamentalist, and it is exactly here that we find the roots of the hyper-rationality with which our world is infected. This fundamentalist and hyper-rationalist vision of science has come to be the dominant perspective not only in scientific research, but in all areas of public life from social policy to the fashion industry.

Even harder science: Karl Popper

But not everyone was in agreement with logical positivists because of the problem of induction. For example, for many centuries the principle of induction led Europeans to believe that 'all swans are white' because that had been the totality of their experience for thousands of years. But then, in the 18th century the discovery of black swans in Australia showed that belief to be false.

For this sort of reason, Karl Popper thought that science should occupy itself with trying to falsify claims rather than verify them. Verification can never be absolute and final: despite the prevalence of untold white swans and only white swans, there is always the possibility that the next swan one stumbles over will not be white. Meanwhile falsification can be absolute and final. The presence of just one black swan is sufficiently powerful to overturn the evidence accrued over thousands of years of tens of thousands of white swans. On this basis Popper insisted that only the factual statements that were in principle falsifiable, could be called scientific facts.

Statistical science

However, not all kinds of knowledge that count as scientific are 'hard' in this sort of way. Empirical science is mostly used to produce statistical truths of the more-or-less kind, rather than 'hard' truths of the true or false kind.

I have a small bowl of apples. Having counted the apples in the bowl (experiment), I find that there are more green apples (8) than red ones (2). I now know (prediction) that if I pick an apple at random then it is likely to be green on about eight out of ten occasions. Note the words 'likely' and 'about'.

But if the container were so large that it held thousands of apples which I could not reasonably count, then I would have to proceed differently. One way would be to repeatedly fill a bucket with apples from different parts of the container and count the colours of apples in the bucket each time (experiment). Eventually, through averaging the numbers of red and green found in each bucket load, I would be able to infer that (say) 80 per cent of the apples in the container are green and 20 per cent are red.

In either case (small bowl or large container), we can say with some confidence that if you picked an apple at random, it is much more likely to be green than red. But note: some of the data (red apples) 'contradicts' the statistical truth (most of the apples are green). The red apples are not 'wrong' or obdurate for not being green. If it turns out that the apple you picked happens to be red, you are not wrong for having done so and there is nothing wrong with the apple for being red; and nor have you 'failed' because the apple you picked turned out to be red rather than green. (This last point will be very important to us later on when we come to examine CBT research in more detail).

We can see that 'statistical truths' are very different to 'hard truths'. The opposite of a 'hard truth' is 'false'. A hard fact has to be consistent with *all the evidence*, not just some of it. The claim that 'all the apples in the bowl are green' requires the presence of just one red apple to falsify it. Whereas the statistical truth that 'most of the apples are green' can accommodate the presence of 'conflicting' evidence (red apples) without being rendered false. In the realm of statistical knowledge, there is no truth/falsehood dichotomy; rather, notions of 'most probably', 'more or less likely', 'more or less often' and 'more often than not', better describe the situation. Most importantly, in this kind of data set, some of the data (red apples) will always go against the generalized claim (most of the apples are green). *Karl Popper's requirement for falsifiability is not applicable to statistical truths.*

Although the complexity of the situation (large containers with more apples than we can reasonably count) means that we are obliged to rely on probabilities rather than certainties, the situation in principle is still fundamentally deterministic. On this basis we are able to predict that the next bucket *is likely* to contain something in the region of 80 per cent green apples, and 20 per cent red.

In sum, positivist empirical science generates two kinds of knowledge – absolute and statistical. As we will come to see, corruptions occur when statistical truths are misrepresented as absolute ones.

Confidence levels and statistical significance

While hard facts are true 100 per cent of the time, the findings of modern science hardly ever reach this exalted state. Even when dealing with the inanimate universe (chemicals, the speed of light, the weight of object X, etc.), the confidence level of scientific claims is always less than 100 per cent.

This is even more the case when dealing with anything animate – in particular with human beings. Experiments conducted with, or on, human beings are never, ever, anywhere near certainty (apart from 'death and taxes' of course) because humans are not constants, they are continually changing beings. Invariably it is found that a hypothesis is true only some of the time and under certain conditions, and so is consistent with only some of the evidence. Statistical truths are always positioned on a scale somewhere between 100 per cent (always true) and 0 per cent (never true).

The status of hard truth claims are, in a manner of speaking, easy to sort out: they are either true or false. What about statistical truths?

Having conducted some statistical experiment (repeatedly filling a bucket with apples from a large container) and arrived at a result, how do I know that the findings are meaningful and not due to random chance? Statisticians perform a calculation which they call 'statistical significance'. If the chance of getting a particular set of results is less than 5 per cent, then the result is said to be 'statistically significant' (this is a technical statistical term). In other words, we can trust these results because the likelihood of them arising out of random events is less than 1 out of 20. This is written out as $p < .05$. (less than .05, which is the same as 5 per cent or 1 out of 20).

The thing to note is that although 5 per cent is a number, there is nothing *objective* about it. 5 per cent is simply the figure that has been *agreed to be reasonable* by statisticians. Because the figure that has been arrived at consensually, there is no reason in principle why the consensus should not shift to 4 per cent or 7 per cent. And indeed, in some situations, statisticians require the figure to be much more testing, say, 1 per cent. The point is that what counts as statistically significant is simply a figure that has been settled between persons in discussion, and so the conclusions are necessarily imbued with human subjectivity.

The commonplace unlikely

But even if the results are found to be statistically significant, this does not guarantee their truth value. The results could still be due to chance (an aspect of the problem of induction). When the numbers are big enough, the fluke and the impossible are everyday occurrences; the weekly winner of the lottery being a prime example. Over time, random activity is bound to generate something that looks like a meaningful pattern. For example: if I toss a coin a billion billion billion billion billion times, then it is likely that at some point it will come down heads a hundred times in a row. This would be a freak occurrence, *and it could occur at any point in this impossibly long experiment*. But say it occurred during my very first hundred throws. In which case I am likely to think that is a biased coin (hypothesis). To test this hypothesis, the experiment would need to be repeated several times. It is only when these reproduce the initial finding that we can say with some confidence that it is so.

We can see then the dangers of making a claim on the basis of a one-off trial. However convincing the results might look, they might be due to a chance occurrence – and particularly so if the number of participants is small.

It turns out that most of the published CBT research falls foul of both difficulties – they tend to be 'one-off' experiments with very small numbers of participants.

Statistical and clinical significance

Even if the findings of an empirical study are found to be statistically significant and this result is verified, the next and real question is whether the results are also *clinically significant*. In other words, will it make a difference in the world itself? One way to think about it is through an analogy with the lottery.

If I buy a lottery ticket, my chance of winning is about once chance in fourteen million. Throwing caution to the winds, I buy two tickets. In one move, I have doubled my chances of winning! To put it even more dramatically, my chance of winning has increased by 100 per cent!

'Doubled' and '100 per cent' makes it sound like the difference between one and two tickets is enormous. But as I well know through experience, this is of little practical (that is, clinical) significance. This is so even if I increase my chances tenfold to a dizzy 1000 per cent by rashly buying ten tickets. This distinction between the *absolute increase* (from one in fourteen million, to two in fourteen million) and the *relative increase* (doubled my chance, increased it by 100 per cent) is critical.

Whether I buy one ticket or a thousand tickets, it makes very little difference to the probability of a win. In actual fact, statistically speaking, there is hardly any difference to the probability of winning between one ticket and no ticket; but of course, practically speaking, there is a world of difference between one ticket and no ticket. If the recently discovered Beijing Man (who lived 40,000 years ago) bought a ticket every day of his life, and the practice was continued by his progeny and their progeny to this day, his family ought not to be surprised that they have not yet won the jackpot. But as we have already noted, when the numbers are big enough the unlikely is commonplace. Someone (neither Beijing Man, nor me, alas) does win the lottery most weeks.

Mostly, the results of psychological studies that are published are ones that show the relative benefit of a treatment rather than the absolute benefit – but they make no mention of this fact. In this way they come to look more convincing than they actually are. So, when researcher's claim that their study has halved or doubled the possibility of some outcome, we should always ask: half or double of what? And does it really matter?

I find that I have already embarked on the subject of the next chapter – the corruptions of science.

Chapter 12

The corruptions of science

Having established what some of the activities and processes of good science look like, I now turn to how CBT research science is actually conducted. There is bad science which is sloppy, careless science, and there is corrupt science in which intentional bad science is knowingly displayed as good science. But the boundaries differentiating the two are malleable. If on one side of the border is acceptable empirical science, then everything on the other side is unacceptable. However, the unacceptable can be made acceptable by the simple device of moving the border. This chapter then is in part about the movement of boundaries which has resulted in the once unacceptable now made to seem not only acceptable, but also normal.

Today, psychology departments (along with the rest of the university) are akin to factories, obliged to churn out prodigious amounts of research papers in order to put their departments and universities in good standing with the regulatory authorities and funders. Hyper-rationalist performance indicators become the measure of the standing of the university. Publications play a crucial role in this 'measuring' process. The greater the number of publications, the higher the university's score. It is this pressure to publish that has fostered the industrialization of psychological research, which in turn has become pedestrian, formulaic and ritualistic.

An analogy with religious faith is instructive. Some believers engage with their faith in a tokenistic and formulaic way—perhaps saying their prayers by rote whilst making a cup of tea. Their attitude to prayer might be an instrumental one, as a form of bargaining with the Deity. They might be motivated to investigate the efficacy of prayer in order to find ways of making it more effective: vocal vs. silent prayer, praying longer, more often, and so on. What it never occurs to them to do, is to question the fundamental basis of their belief, whether prayer works in this way and whether there is a Deity listening into them.

Something similar takes place within cognitivist psychological science. Contemporary mainstream psychology research takes the existence of mental disorders as given and the diagnostic categories for granted. They also take as given the belief that CBT treatments are 'The Way' of modifying these mental disorders. All this is never questioned. Instead, the research limits itself to the testing and tweaking the treatment (analogous to tweaking prayer). In this way the values of good science are diluted.

Harriet Hall has termed this kind of thing Tooth Fairy Science. If you accept the existence of the Tooth Fairy, you might design a study to check whether the Tooth Fairy leaves more money for molars or incisors. You might look to see what difference social class makes, and be excited to discover a very strong correlation between class and the amount of money the Tooth Fairy leaves. What you never question is the existence of the Tooth Fairy and the belief that the Fairy leaves money in exchange for teeth.

Westen et al. put this in succinct scientific language: CBT researchers utilize scientific methods for hypothesis testing, but not for hypothesis generation. In other words 'the assumptions underlying the methods used to test psychotherapies were themselves empirically untested' (2004, p. 632). And so unsurprisingly, like in the case of the Tooth Fairy, it very often leads to scientifically invalid conclusions.

The way that this kind of conveyor belt research proceeds is as follows. First, choose a category of mental illness from the DSM. Second, choose a specific CBT treatment package to test. Third, test it. Fourth, if the outcome is positive (statistically significant), then repeat the test. Fifth, if the second set of results is also positive, then apply to NICE for validation and recognition. Sixth, create a manual which consists of the steps followed in the research. Seventh, oblige practitioners use this manual to follow the same steps as during the research to reproduce its success rate. Eighth: choose another category from the DSM. Ninth: Repeat the whole process for the new category.

Now to the detail.

The first corruption: amplification

The evidence for evidence based treatments seems to be overwhelming. But when one looks a little more closely, it often turns out to be somewhat underwhelming. Here is an instance. Dialectical Behaviour Therapy (DBT) is a third wave CBT treatment that takes elements from a range of therapies, person centred, systemic, psychodynamic, gestalt, and mixes them with a version of Eastern psychology. In the decade or so following the introduction of the treatment into the literature in 1987, over 25 data driven scientific papers were published in support of the treatment. The evidence base was looking compelling. But then a researcher called Scheel noticed that each and every one of these publications drew on just 'one adequately controlled supportive outcome study to date, and that of limited size' (Scheel, 2000, p. 68). Scheel is being kind. The sample size in the study were not 'limited', they were miniscule—20 in the DBT group and 22 in the TAU group. This is an incredibly small number of persons on which to make predictions and generalizations about humanity at large.

The situation gets worse. Almost all the 25 publications were written by the members of the original treatment team. To underline the point, there were

25 publications, but just one study; and the authors of the 25 publications were the same ones that did the original one-off study. So if one only took account of the number of papers published, then the 'science' behind the treatment looks much more convincing than it actually is.

The content of the 25 publications mainly consisted of reanalysing data from the original study chopped up for different subgroups of the original research. For example the subgroup of consisting of members of the TAU group who had elected to receive some form of psychotherapy over the duration of the study. This being a subset of the original data, the numbers in in the sample size are even smaller—in the region of six or so people in each group. This makes the 'findings' even more shaky, inconsistent and unreliable. For example it was found that six months into the follow up year, DBT subjects were doing better than TAU subjects in regards to parasuicidal episodes (suicide attempts with no real intention of killing oneself). But by twelve months there was little meaningful difference between the groups. But when 'number of days in hospital as inpatient' was used as a measure, then the results were reversed: at six months there was no difference between the groups, but at twelve months the DBT group were doing better. There is no way of knowing whether these ups and downs are meaningful or whether they are due to random chance, particularly because the number of 'episodes' that we are talking about are also very very small—they averaged *just one or none over the period of a year*. Scheel concluded

> All positive published outcome findings are from a single study . . . [and] rest on no more than 24 DBT subjects . . . all remaining positive findings are based on 13 or fewer DBT subjects, and all process and most follow-up conclusions are based on seven or fewer DBT subjects.
>
> (Scheel, 2000, p. 80)

This sort of amplification is not specific to, nor limited to, DBT. Suffice it to say, that whichever way the data cookie crumbles, the researchers being invested in the treatment packages they are testing, find ways to read the crumble in ways that are favourable to that treatment.

The second corruption: overgeneralising

The second corruption is the means by which a statistical truth (likely to be true some of the time) comes to be camouflaged and misrepresented as a hard truth (true all the time).

Whether you want to test the efficacy of the fictitious drug called Zon for disease X, or test the efficacy of the equally fictitious Arbitrary Cognition Therapy (ArCoT), the research protocol is broadly the same—although it ought not to be the same for reasons that will become evident in the sixth corruption. I begin with Zon.

You start by finding (for the sake of argument) a hundred people suffering from X. However, out of the hundred, you discover that many of them are also suffering from Y or/and Z. Further, many of the hundred are over seventy years old, and you don't want to include them in your study, because they are prone to developing all sorts of health issues over the time period of the 'experiment', and so they will introduce more complications, variables and unknowns. By the time you have removed all the people you don't want to put through the test for various reasons, you are left with say, 20. The 20 are now randomly allocated to one of two groups of 10 (RCT: Randomized Control Trial).

Members of one group are given a placebo, and the other the drug Zon. However, both experimenter and subject are made deliberately 'blind' in that neither knows who is being given which treatment (double-blind protocols). Six years later, you look at the progress of the disease in each individual. You discover that seven out of the ten who were on Zon are in remission from disease X (70 per cent); whilst in the control group, only three are still well (30 per cent). A result! The experiment is repeated, and let us say that the results are similarly good. So the claim is made: The drug Zon is now scientifically proven to cure X!

But this is a vast overstatement. All they should actually claim is that the drug Zon has helped an additional 40 per cent (= 70 per cent–30 per cent) of those suffering from X. What this means is that 60 per cent are likely not to be helped by Zon. Add to this another conveniently 'forgotten' fact, which is that Zon has been tested on a particularly narrow and skewed population, on just 20 per cent of all those known to be suffering from X. When you put all this together, what this means is that Zon has been of benefit to 40 per cent of a particularly narrow 'ideal' population. But the language used on billboards and in the abstracts of research papers is often without caveats: as though it has been proved that Zon is the treatment of choice for *all those suffering from X—the entire hundred*. It is on this basis that anyone and everyone suffering from X is prescribed a course of Zon in the expectation that it *will be beneficial*.

Unreal research populations

The populations used for researching treatments of this kind are very skewed. One study found that just 6 per cent of representative asthma sufferers would have been eligible to participate in asthma treatment trials (Travers et al., 2007). In Finland researchers discovered that out of 7,411 patients suffering from a bone condition, 6,000 of them would not have been eligible to participate in the treatment trials (Jarvinen et. al., 2011). Another study discovered that only a third of those actually being treated for depression would have been able to participate in any of 39 trials of treatments for depression. And quite astonishingly, out of every eight people suffering from depression who had *volunteered* to take part in treatment trials, only one was deemed eligible to participate (Zimmerman et al., 2004).

The populations that treatments are tested on are so highly selected that they bear little resemblance to the real life general population. It is habitual to screen out those that have comorbidities, as it is called in the trade. Comorbidity means that the person has two or more conditions—say depression and obsessive compulsive behaviour. Even if one accepts that mental health 'conditions' exist in the first place, and that they can be separated out in the second place, the problem that it leaves is that most people looking for therapy do not fall into these neat categories. Comorbidities are the rule, not the exception. What this actually means is that the findings of these sorts of studies are not generalizable—a key requirement of positivist science.

Nevertheless, this is how the 'evidence-base' for CBT is generated and over-generalized: CBT is the treatment of choice for (fill in the blank) depression, anxiety, and so forth. It is presumed that the treatment works for all people all the time; in other words, the treatment is deemed to be 'perfect'.

So when real world populations are pushed through these treatments, many do not feel better, and many actually feel worse. Of course (it is said) this cannot have anything to do with the CBT treatment itself, which by definition, works (remember the table tennis balls). Therefore the reason for the failure must lie either with the patient—who is given a new label 'CBT-Resistant', or with the particularly pernicious form of the disease that they are thought to be suffering from—'treatment-resistant depression' (in the same sort of way that some bacteria are resistant to certain antibiotics). Accordingly, the treatment for these 'resistances' is more CBT, better CBT.

Recovery and Relapse

The literature repeatedly says two opposing things without noticing the irony, nor the contradiction. On the one hand it claims that people *recover* following CBT treatment. But in the very same breath they also say that people habitually tend to *relapse* after treatment. For example,

> Despite real progress over the past 50 years, many depressed patients still do not respond fully to treatment . . . Moreover, most patients will not stay well once they get better unless they receive ongoing treatment.
>
> (Hollon et al., 2002, p. 70)

This point to be underlined here is the way that success is defined in CBT treatments. As we have seen, if certain scores drop below a particular level, then this is counted as a success. But even with a so called successful treatment, the patient's symptoms are not eradicated, they are merely reduced. And further, the benefits as such are known to evaporate over time. This is what the research actually shows. For example, Westen et al (2004, p. 646) found that after 'successful' treatment for bulimia, the average bulimic patient continued to binge 1.7 times per week and purge 2.3 times per week. They also found that the 'average panic patient continued to panic about once every 10 days and had slightly over four out of the seven symptoms required for a DSM—IV panic disorder diagnosis, enough to qualify for limited-symptom attacks' (Westen et al., 2004, p. 645). These results for panic were the best of the bunch. After a review of the entire field, Westen et al concluded:

> With the exception of CBT for panic, the majority of patients receiving treatments for all the disorders we reviewed *did not recover*. They remained symptomatic even if they showed substantial reductions in their symptoms or fell below diagnostic thresholds for caseness; they sought further treatment; or they relapsed at some point within 1 to 2 years after receiving ESTs conducted by clinicians who were expert in delivery of the treatment, well supervised, and highly committed to the success of their treatment of choice.
>
> (Westen et al., 2004, p. 650)

Westen et al. concluded that 'the consistent finding in RCTs . . . [is] that the average patient remains symptomatic at the end of a trial of brief psychotherapy and seeks further treatment [after it]' (Westen et al., 2004, p. 647).

The attempt in the literature to paper over the tension between recovery and relapse generates baffling oxymorons such as 'recovered recurrently depressed patients' (Teasdale et al., 2000, p. 615). What is never up for question is the possibility that it is the CBT treatment itself that is ineffective. The situation is not unlike that of the old joke: operation successful, patient dead.

Here is a recent attempt to combat the afore mentioned 'treatment resistant depression'. A paper entitled 'Cognitive behavioural therapy as an adjunct to pharmacotherapy for primary care based patients with treatment resistant depression', was published in the prestigious scientific medical journal *The Lancet* (Wiles et al., 2013). The press release drawn from the abstract says:

> The CoBalT team, comprising researchers from the Universities of Bristol, Exeter and Glasgow, recruited 469 patients aged 18- to 75-years with treatment-resistant depression for the randomised controlled trial. Patients were split into two groups: 235 patients continued with their usual care from the GP, which included continuing on antidepressant medication, and 234 patients were treated with CBT in addition to usual care from their GP. Researchers followed-up 422 patients (90 per cent) at six months and 396 (84 per cent) at 12 months to compare their progress.
>
> At six months, 46 per cent of those who received CBT in addition to usual care [group A] had improved, reporting at least a 50 per cent reduction in symptoms of depression, compared to 22 per cent of those who continued with usual care alone [group B]. This beneficial effect was maintained over 12 months.
>
> The findings demonstrate that CBT provided in addition to usual care including antidepressant medication is an effective treatment that reduces depressive symptoms, and improves the quality of life in patients whose

depression has not responded to the most common first-line treatment for depression in primary care.

(Press Release, Bristol University, 2012)

Although this CBT treatment did not fare anywhere near as well as that of our mythical Zon, it is nevertheless being claimed that the research has scientifically demonstrated that it is an 'effective treatment'.

The first thing to note is the way that the figures are presented. Why are the outcomes not presented (as is the norm) as the difference between the treatment group and the control group? As you might suspect, it is because the actual figures are not all that impressive.

The fact that 46 per cent said that they felt better—means that more than half did not. But even if about a half of those who received the treatment did in fact benefit, then that is no bad thing. However, this figure does not take into account the 22 per cent in the control group who recovered 'spontaneously'.

We have to assume, as is usually the case, that 22 per cent of the treatment group would also have recovered without the benefit of the treatment. That, after all, is the point of having a control group. The benefit of the treatment is measured by the difference between the treatment group and the control group.

So when we take the control group into account as we are obliged to do as good scientists, then this leaves just 23 per cent (= 46per cent–22 per cent) per cent of the treatment group feeling better (perhaps) because of having received CBT. *In other words, the research showed that about two out of ten people came to feel better having received this CBT treatment.* When it is put like this, then it becomes blindingly obvious that by no means can this be called 'an effective treatment', or at least not without a gross distortion of the English language. What this also means is that this treatment is *not likely to help eight out of ten people.* And this is a scientific fact.

Even more, this 'improvement' has taken place in combination with the treatment as usual, presumably, drug therapy. And given the fact that relapse is common place as regularly mentioned in CBT research studies, we might guess that the benefits as such are not likely to prevail for very long.

In sum, at the conclusion of CBT treatments patients remain symptomatic, only less so. That is a worthy end, but CBT discourse does not present its achievements in this way, it inflates them to present itself as a cure, and a cure that endures.

The third corruption: the objectification of subjectivity

There is now yet another inflated claim smuggled into the reportage of the above study. Notice, that even the 'successful' 23 per cent were by no means cured of depression. What the subjects reported was that their symptoms of depression were *reduced by about 50 per cent.*

The use of the term 'measurement' suggests that that which is being measured is in some way measurable, and being measurable it must be objective, real, and therefore factual. The number of people at a bus stop is countable, and therefore is a fact. But what does it mean when subjects are reported as experiencing at least 'a 50 per cent reduction in symptoms of depression'? In what sense is this 'finding' a fact? 50 per cent certainly sounds a like a fact. How is it arrived at?

The so called measurements are the scores generated by the questionnaires we met earlier. One such questionnaire that is in regular use is the Clinical Outcomes in Routine Evaluation (CORE) form. The first of 34 statements is: 'I have felt terribly alone and isolated'.

The client ticks one of five boxes: 'not at all', 'only occasionally', 'sometimes', 'often', 'most or all of the time'. Each answer is allocated a numerical value from 0 to 4.

Numbers allocated to the answers of numerous questions are added up to arrive at some overall score. And this being a number, immediately gives the impression that something objective and concrete has been 'measured'.

It would seem then that the answer 'I'm very, very depressed' is subjective and not scientific; but if the same subjective experience is reported as the number '4', then it is suddenly deemed to be objective. This is what got Layard so excited. When these sorts of pseudo numbers are put through calculations to produce entities such as cumulative distribution functions and scalar random variables, all of which are written out in mysterious algebraic notations, the result is entirely incomprehensible to the lay person. It is through this sort of hyper-rationalist means that the researchers make the pseudo-mathematical claim that the participants are 50 per cent less depressed than before. The presence of decimal points increases the impression of precision. But however objective these numbers seem, they remain subjective experiences which have been given the gloss of objectivity.

So the 'results' of the CoBalT study actually ought to be announced in this way:

> About two out of ten people came to feel somewhat better because of having received CBT; however, although better, they are still depressed, only less depressed. By the way, *eight out of ten people receiving this treatment will not be helped.* And that's a fact.

If the treatment had been able to do the reverse, actually help eight out of ten, then the use of the term 'effective' would make sense.

The culmination of this kind of research claims in prestigious scientific journals has meant that it is now become established scientific 'fact' that CBT is unquestionably an entirely effective therapy. For example the statement on the website of the prestigious (Scientific) Royal College of Psychiatrists, is entirely without caveats. It says:

> CBT has been shown to help with many different types of problems. These include: anxiety, depression, panic, phobias (including agoraphobia and social phobia), stress, bulimia, obsessive compulsive disorder, post-traumatic

stress disorder, bipolar disorder and psychosis. CBT may also help if you have difficulties with anger, a low opinion of yourself or physical health problems, like pain or fatigue.

(www.rcpsych.ac.uk/expertadvice/treatments/cbt.aspx)

The fourth corruption: spinning, lying and hacking

The above is an example of spin. Spin is a form of deliberate confusion making. Its intention is to fool the listener into believing a false reality to be true. Another term for spin is propaganda. Another is fake news. But the researchers themselves are not likely to think this; they are just using gamesmanship to present their results in a good a light as possible—using all possible means at the limit of what is considered to be legitimate. A colleague who happened to be a researcher in psychology was very anxious because his results after a lengthy empirical study did not look very impressive. When I met him again some weeks later, he was much relieved because a statistician at his (prestigious) British university reassured him saying that it is always possible to manipulate data to put it in a good light. This he did; and his paper was eventually published.

   As it happens, this anecdote is an illustration of the general trend that was discovered by Theodore Sterling over fifty years ago.

> [In 1959] a psychologist called Theodore Sterling . . . went through every paper published in the four big psychology journals of the time, and found that 286 out of 294 reported a statistically significant result. This, he explained, was plainly fishy: it couldn't possibly be a fair representation of every study that had been conducted, because if we believed that, we'd have to believe that almost every theory ever tested by a psychologist in an experiment had turned out to be correct . . . In 1995, at the end of his career, the same researcher came back to the same question . . . and found that almost nothing had changed [Sterling, 1959, Sterling et al., 1995]
>
> (Goldacre, 2012, pp. 21–2)

How is this possible? Recall the discussion on statistical significance in the previous chapter. Sterling's findings suggest that researchers are regularly using statistical scams that make it appear that their findings are statistically significant ($p < 0.5$). This activity has gained the name p-hacking, and many are beginning to think that p-hacking is rife. It must be so because almost every published study magically ends up just under this threshold. p-hacking is made relatively easy because it is an institutionalized convention that researchers do not share their raw data, nor do they declare the way that they calculate p; all they do is to state its value embedded in a mix of dense hieroglyphics that immediately saps the uninitiated of the will to live, and can look like this:

$$\chi^2(1, N = 99) = 8.49, p < 0.005$$

The fifth corruption: desire driven results

When research results are talked up, the consequences that follow out of it are often calamitous. Today, it is the case that the regulators have agreed that all it need take is for two clinical trials to show benefits for a treatment to be allowed to apply for a licence. However, '*there is no limit to the number of trials that can be conducted in search of these two significant trials*' (Kirsch, 2011, p. 195).

It is common practice in the mental health research industry to conduct numbers of studies until they find two that produce favourable outcomes. There is no obligation on the researchers to publish the results of trials that do not produce significant results, and so they do not. There are moves to oblige all researchers to log their research before embarking on the research, but they will be under no obligation to publish their results. Why is this a problem?

Let us return to the large container of apples from the previous chapter and take it to be the case that customers prefer red apples over green apples. In this situation a shop keeper will want to buy containers from the farmer that contain more red apples. The scientist-farmer says, sure no problem. I will do the bucket experiment, and let you have the results; you can judge for yourself. S/he then proceeds with the experiment as before—filling eight buckets with apples at random, and then counting the colours in each of them.

But then, and this is crucial, s/he only shows the shop keeper the two buckets that contained mostly red apples; *and s/he hides* the six other buckets in which the green apples outnumbered the red.

Outrageous? Yes, certainly. But this is exactly the sort of deceitful practice that is the norm today in much of what passes for psychological scientific research. This was dramatically brought to light by a group of researchers, Turner et al. (2008) who tracked all registered clinical trials for all the anti-depressants that were launched between 1987 and 2004 (Turner et al., 2008). 38 of the trials concluded that the treatment being tested worked, and 36 found that the treatment did not. 37 of the 38 trials with positive results were published, whilst only 3 out of the 36 negative trials were. Of the remaining 33 trials with negative outcomes, 22 never saw light of day again, and quite astonishingly, the remaining 11 were written up as if the drug were a success. Consequently, when doctors looked to the published 'research' to help make an informed decision, they found 48 trials apparently demonstrating the efficacy of anti-depressants, set against 3 that did not. The published evidence made it appear that the efficacy of anti-depressants was uncontroversial.

Disturbing as this is, the situation is even more troubling and even harder to believe. It turns out that even when the regulatory agencies have knowledge of the existence of large numbers of negative trials as in the case above,

> [The] regulatory agencies [nevertheless] *discard the negative trials*. And they do this no matter how many there are. All they require are two positive

trials to give the green light for public use. The FDA in the US has publicly defended what may seem to you or me a dubious approval process.

(Davies, 2014, p. 71)

The situation is made worse by virtue of the fact that the bar is set at levels that are dismally low for a trial to be thought positive. For a research finding to be positive, all it need demonstrate is the difference between the treatment and placebo is statistically significant, not clinically significant. If you recall the analogy with the lottery from the last chapter, you will also recall that the difference between the two is indeed significant. And when you add to this the fact that *p*-hacking is rife, then we can make sense of the belief that 'you can prove anything with science'.

Here is another account illustrating the terrible consequences that follow out of this kind of malpractice. In his role as medical practitioner, Ben Goldacre prescribed the anti-depressant reboxetine (marketed as Edronax by Pfizer) to patients because *to his knowledge* the published findings on the drug were overwhelmingly positive. But then in 2010 a group of researchers discovered that there had actually been seven clinical trials comparing reboxetine against placebo, but only one of them had been published—the trial which showed a positive result for reboxetine. The six other trials that were buried showed that patients taking this drug did not feel any better when compared to placebo (sugar pills), and in many cases actually felt worse.

You would have thought that when the authorities were made aware of the six hidden negative studies, they would have immediately revoked the licence for reboxetine. But you would be mistaken: 'reboxetine is still on the market, and the system that allowed all this to happen is still in play, for all drugs, in all countries in the world' (Goldacre, 2012, p. 7).

What this means is that the scientist-farmer need not even go to the trouble of hiding the buckets that contain more green than red apples, as long s/he can show at least two buckets in which the majority of apples are red. That is all that seems to matter to the regulatory authorities. If the shop keeper complained about the deception, the regulatory authorities would back the farmer-scientist.

CBT researchers are using this same broken and corrupt system to test and validate their treatment as efficacious. Researchers being invested in the treatment modalities they are allegedly testing, repeatedly find ways of writing up findings that confirm their beliefs, even when they clearly do not. One such belief is that it is possible to sort out deep psychological problems in twelve to twenty hours. Believing this to be true, Hollon et al. (2002) looked into short-term Interpersonal Therapy (IPT) and CBT treatments for depression and found that initial outcomes were positive for the first 16 weeks of data. But three years later it was found that for 'patients who receive these 16-session psychotherapies relapse at unacceptably high rates relative to patients in medication conditions' (Westen et al., 2004, p. 640). What the researchers did next was to use these same short term treatments *repeatedly* over a three year period; after which they found that patients receiving IPT did considerably better. On this basis they claimed that the IPT story was a success story.

But what the research has actually shown is that these short-term therapies for depression had failed as evidenced by alarming rates of relapse following treatment. However, Hollon et al found a way of spinning the findings to validate short-term IPT as a success story

> On the basis of data showing that extending short-term interventions by several months substantially improves outcome, they [the researchers] concluded that *only long-term versions of these short-term treatments are empirically supportable* (Hollon et al., 2002). This conclusion makes sense of the available data, but the available data were predicated on a set of methodological assumptions that presume the disconfirmed hypothesis, that depression is malleable in the face of brief interventions.
>
> (Westen et al., 2004, p. 641)

Put more succinctly: short term treatments work when used long term. Therefore short term treatments work. QED.

These sorts of problems have been known about for over half a century, yet they are still not being addressed. The reason has to do in part, with the relationship between the regulators and the regulated which is a very cosy one, with poachers and game-keepers exchanging places freely and readily. And so it has come to pass that the standards set by the regulators for treatments to be granted official approval have been set at dismally low levels. Levels that are a long way away from that required by good scientific practice. This in turn allows all sorts of mischief and mistruth to pass itself off as empirical evidence-based scientific knowledge.

The sixth corruption: TAU

CBT researchers claim to produce high quality empirical research in accordance with the so called 'gold standard', the Randomised Control Trial (RCT). The gold standard requires the research procedure to test the treatment against a placebo, and for the study to be conducted in accordance with 'double blind' protocols. This is to ensure that neither researcher nor patient influence the results. The way this operates when testing medication is as follows: A researcher Jane puts pills randomly into numbered envelopes—half of the pills being the real drug, and the other half a placebo that looks exactly like the drug. Jane hands these over to researcher John who has no idea which envelopes contain the drug and which the placebo. He then distributes the envelopes in a random manner to those participating in the study. This way neither the researchers nor the subjects know who is getting what. It is only after the results are in that this information is revealed to the researchers.

This works fine in regard to tangibles like pills, injections, and treatments like Zon. But when it comes to some form of psychological treatment like the CBT and ArCoT (Arbitrary Cognition Therapy), there is no possibility of providing a convincing placebo, nor is it possible for those providing the treatment to be blind about what they are doing, nor is it possible for those receiving the treatment to be blind as to whether or not they are receiving a treatment. For these reasons CBT research methodology is not, and can never be that of randomized control trials, even though CBT researchers claim to be following 'gold standard' RCT methods.

Because there is no possibility of testing against a convincing placebo, CBT research is mostly tested against doing nothing—Treatment As Usual (TAU).

This is a problem because we know that people come to feel better by virtue of the simple fact of being attended to. The experience of feeling much better having simply visited the GP with some ailment is a familiar one. In my psychotherapy practice, new clients often say that they were astonished at how much better they felt after just one meeting. Over time, I have come to realize that this is not because I have delivered a spectacularly successful psychotherapy in the first 50 minutes. Much of this initial good feeling is born of simple relief at simply having finally spoken of the difficulties to another. Most astonishingly, 'fifteen percent of patients improve significantly after making the initial call to a therapist's office, *before attending the first session* (Kopta et al., 1994).

Add into this the fact that when researchers have an allegiance to the treatment package they are 'testing', the outcome will always be biased in favour of that treatment; so much so that 'Luborsky et al. (1999) found that . . . 92.5% of the time, they could predict which treatment will be most successful based on investigator allegiance alone' (Westen et al., 2004, p. 640).

All this is made even more apparent in a study conducted by Kirsch and Sapirstein (1998). They compared what happened to depressed patients after having received one of four procedures: anti-depressants, placebo medication, psychotherapy, and the fourth group were given no treatment at all. It turned out that the improvement for those who received the placebo was not very different from those who received anti-depressants or psychotherapy. The biggest difference was between those who received some treatment and those who received nothing, and *knew they were receiving nothing*. In other words *all those who thought they were receiving some treatment—any treatment*, came to feel better in comparison to those who *knew that they were not getting any treatment*. There are many studies that reinforce this sort of finding: the simple fact of receiving something that someone thinks might be helpful (whether or not it is actually helpful), has a positive effect on how people come to feel. It is quite likely that this would also be the case for angel therapy and other treatments of that ilk.

What this means is that studies in which the treatment group get something, and the control group gets nothing, are intrinsically biased and therefore flawed. Those in the treatment group are bound to show more benefit, simply because of having 'received' some treatment regardless of what the treatment is, and regardless of whether it actually helps or not. This fact necessarily biases the results in favour of 'treatment' *per se*. This constitutes a methodological crisis which cannot be overcome, even in principle.

CBT research is not scientific research of the kind that exists in the natural sciences. It tries to emulate it, but it cannot. It can only ape it.

It turns out that there is additional evidence to support the view that beginnings are often experienced as brighter than they actually are. Two Norwegian researchers conducted a meta-analysis examining the outcome of CBT research/treatments spread over about 15 years from 1997 to 2014. Their study concluded that the effectiveness of CBT treatments had steadily declined over this period. They speculate that this has occurred because of a version of the placebo effect.

> The placebo effect is typically stronger for newer treatments, however, as time passes and experience with therapy is gained, the strong initial expectations wane. One may question whether this is the case with CBT. In the initial phase of the cognitive era, CBT was frequently portrayed as the gold standard for the treatment of many disorders. In recent times, however, an increasing number of studies . . . have not found this method to be superior to other techniques. Coupled with the increasing availability of such information to the public, including the Internet, it is not inconceivable that patients' hope and faith in the efficacy of CBT has decreased somewhat, in recent decades.
>
> (Johnsen and Friborg, 2015, p. 768)

When translated into plain English, what these researchers are saying is that the initial positive outcomes were due to the effects of the propaganda that surrounds CBT, and as this propaganda is slowly starting to be exposed for what it is, propaganda, the magical effects of CBT have started to wane.

Interlude: a passing prediction

With all this in mind, here is a prediction. I know from experience that on the occasions that I am able to take a new perspective on some predicament that is causing me tension, then more often than not, it throws new light on the predicament, and eases my tension to some degree. The new perspective might be from the viewpoint of a person I am having conflict with, or from a more detached objective viewpoint 'above' the predicament, and so on.

I will now turn this 'insight' into a form of cognitive therapy, which I will call *New Viewpoints and Perspectives Cognitive Therapy* (NVPCT). NVPCT treatment will be aimed at helping those who get into arguments all the time because they suffer from RCD, Repeated Conflict Disorder (a disorder that the authors of the DSM are as yet unaware of). The treatment itself will consist of eight sessions. After scene setting in the first session, the next six will consist of examining the conflict from a different perspective each time: from the viewpoint of the client's mother, father, sibling, boss, friend and spouse. The sixth session from the viewpoint of person(s) the conflict is with. The final session is a wrap-up session, which will measure the shift in comparison to the first session. I will be the researcher/therapist in this endeavour and will test the treatment against TAU. I have of course to choose the population for study very carefully in order to ensure that the kinds of conflict being experienced will be amenable to being examined in this way.

My prediction is this: NVPCT will be found to be statistically significant. I think that this will be so for two reasons. First, investigator allegiance (me) will bias the findings in favour of the treatment; and second, many within the treatment group will declare themselves feeling better simply because of having received some form of treatment. If only on this basis, I am pretty confident that at the end of eight sessions more of those who received this treatment *will be* feeling better about things when compared to those who received nothing, Treatment As Usual.

Impressed? I imagine, not very. But this is exactly how CBT treatments are invented and then researched.

The seventh corruption: restricting research

NICE research protocols are deliberately framed in ways that not only favour CBT research protocols, they actually go out of their way to exclude other kinds of legitimate research protocols which fall well within the norms of good scientific practice. It is this exclusion that puts CBT research outside the bounds of good scientific practice to make it scientific malpractice. The way it works is this.

It makes both common and scientific sense that research ought to compare the efficacy of different kinds of treatments. But NICE does not entertain this sort of research. It declares that the only kinds of research that it is willing to countenance are those that test the outcome of *one* specific treatment tested on *one* specific mental disorder. It takes no notice of any research that *compares* the efficacy of other psychotherapeutic modality with CBT.

If I were genuinely trying to find a remedy for some ailment like cancer, then I would be testing out a range of different *kinds* of potential treatments. Say, diet versus radio therapy, versus surgery, versus acupuncture versus chemotherapy, versus angel therapy and so on. It would be rather stupid to limit the research *exclusively* to radio therapy. It is of course quite reasonable to study the consequences of varying the intensity and duration of radio therapy treatment; but what is not reasonable is to then *not compare* the results of this treatment with another, say surgery. So if I declared that I was only going to research the effects of radio therapy and none of the other possible potential interventions, you might well think it preposterous. Of course I would not actually put it this way. All I would have to do is to put in a number of scientific sounding constraints and protocols, the effect of which make it impossible to research the other treatment modalities. You might then discover that I had had shares in the company producing radio therapy instrumentation. But that would not matter if I convinced the funding bodies to decree that they would only fund research proposals that test variations in radio therapy; the circle is closed and everything else falls by the wayside.

NICE's claim that it is interested to discover and promulgate 'best practice' is rendered meaningless when it only takes account of one particular kind of practice. When the different kinds of practice are compared, as we saw earlier with Shedler and Kirsch and Sapirstein, then CBT is revealed as having no particular benefit over any other treatment.

The eighth corruption: packages and magical rituals

There is a lacuna residing at the heart of CBT research, a lacuna that has to do with the content and structure of the treatment. The way that CBT research habitually proceeds is by testing an already fully formed manualized CBT treatment *package* on a specific population. What is entirely left out is the question of how did this package come into existence in the first place? What was the rationale for the design of the treatment being tested?

The question never arises, because in the language of Norbert Elias, CBT research culture has effectively inserted an 'absolute beginning' in such a way that the question never surfaces. The treatment is 'a given' in the research process and so the *content and structure of the treatment* itself is never up for question or investigation. The beliefs that CBT treatments are based on are never put to the test, they are treated as incontrovertible axiomatic truths. We are back with Westen et al.'s critical insight that although scientific methods are being used to test hypotheses, the hypotheses themselves are not subject to scientific scrutiny.

You might think that perhaps that does not matter as long as CBT treatments produce good results. But it does matter, because if it did not, then we would no longer be in the region of science, but magic. Let me explain what I mean.

On Tuesday I decided to wear my three-piece grey suit and forgot to put on a tie. I left the house without my phone and had to go back for it. Because I was now late, I took a short cut along a muddy lane that I do not usually take. I ran for the bus and to the right of the lamp post in order to avoid a puddle. When I eventually got to work, my day was extraordinarily successful.

Being somewhat superstitious, I think that there was something about the sequence of events that took place that morning that made my day so wonderful. However, I don't know which of the elements are crucial and which are irrelevant. So in order to try to reproduce the spectacular day, I do *exactly* what I did previously. Grey suit, no tie, leave without phone, go back for it. Run along the muddy lane, go to the right of the lamppost.

I have created a magic spell: a sequence of ritualized gestures that should magically generate a particular reality. Magically, because I don't know how it works or why it works. To be safe, it is best to do everything I did before, because I don't know whether it is the uttered 'Abracadabra' or the hand gestures or something else entirely that is crucial to the efficacy of the spell.

This is exactly the situation with CBT treatment. CBT is unclear which of the elements of the sequence, A followed by B followed by C followed by D followed by E, helps in the recovery and which of the elements actually detract from recovery.

> most of the treatment effects demonstrated in studies of cognitive therapy for depression occur by the fifth session . . . studies using CBT to treat bulimia nervosa similarly have found that patients who do not reduce purging by 70% by the sixth session (prior to most of the interventions aimed at cognitive restructuring) are unlikely to respond to treatment (Agras et al., 2000; see also Wilson, 1999)
>
> (Westen et al., 2004, p. 639)

Perhaps recovery, such as it is, is being generated by something else entirely. For example Kroll (1993) found that both Dialectic Behaviour Therapy and psychodynamic treatment produced positive results with borderline personality disorder conditions. What was common to them (in contrast to other treatment modalities) was that both DBT and psychodynamic researcher/therapists were in close supervision. On this basis Kroll argued that supervision—*something that takes place outside the consulting room*—was one of the key ingredients to working successfully with this patient group. If Kroll is right, then in this instance the beneficial ingredient was something outside the treatment itself rather than the content of the treatment.

The point is important. What is being tested is an entire treatment *package*. The reasons why certain ingredients were selected for the package, and the way that they are arranged are not visible, because they reside behind their absolute beginning.

> researchers generally solidify treatment packages (manuals) so early and on the basis of so little hard data on alternative strategies, even within the same general approach, that clinicians have to accept *on faith* that the treatment as packaged is superior to the myriad variants one could devise or improvise with a given patient.
>
> (Westen et al., 2004, p. 640)

To underline the point once more: CBT research calls on scientific method for hypothesis testing, but generates the hypotheses themselves out of thin air. The hypotheses themselves are simply assertions of cognitivist ideology.

Quite simply, we don't know what works or why it works. Many studies suggest that it is simply the demeanour of the therapist that is crucial to patients feeling better. Maybe it is the repetitive form-filling each and every session that is beneficial in some mysterious way. Who knows? CBT researchers don't, and nor are they that interested in finding out. They bring the same injunction to bear on themselves as they do on the treatment itself: reasons are not relevant. All that matters is the mechanism. All that matters is the spell. As long as it works.

If only it did.

The ninth corruption: researchers versus clinicians

With this corruption we return to Kant' distinctions between cause and reason; between determinism and free will (more accurately, constrained autonomy); between predictability and emergent novelty; and finally, between mechanism and human.

CBT treatments are research driven and research derived. Clinicians are supposed to follow closely in the footsteps previously taken by the researchers; footsteps which are set out in the manuals. Within this hierarchical arrangement the needs of the researcher continually trump those of the clinician to such a degree that there is a real question as to whether CBT practitioners should even be called clinicians; Westen thinks that their role has been reduced to that of research assistants.

The intention of CBT research is to discover certain kinds of *predictable cause/ effect* relationships. This treatment (cause) *will* reduce symptoms to that degree and in that way (effect). For this reason the design of treatments ought to be such that they should enable researchers to draw clear causal conclusions. Because of this, treatments tend to be designed to meet the needs of the researcher and research methods, rather than of the treatment itself. Westen et al. say: 'treatments are required to fit the requisites of [research] methods rather than vice versa . . . [and so] the methodological tail [has come] to wag the clinical dog' (2004, p. 641–2).

Next, having discovered this 'predictable' cause/effect relationship (the treatment), the researcher now also requires the practitioner to be 'predictable'—to be trusted to exactly follow the footsteps of the original research. If they deviate from the steps for whatever reason, then they will have introduced 'noise' into the treatment. What this means is that there is a strong injunction arising out of the requirements of research, an injunction against practitioners using their clinical judgements as might arise within them from moment to moment. These sorts of novel thoughts will necessarily deviate from the manual and so constitute a contamination of the research protocol. In effect, the practitioner is not allowed the *autonomy* to make clinical decisions because their actions are already *determined* by the manual.

Any exercise of clinical judgment represents a threat to internal validity in controlled trials because it reduces standardization of the experimental manipulation and hence renders causal inferences ambiguous. A good clinician . . . is one who adheres closely to the manual, does not get sidetracked by material the patient introduces that diverges from the agenda set forth in the manual, and does not succumb to the seductive siren of clinical experience. The more researchers succeed in the scientifically essential task of reducing the clinician to a research assistant . . . the more they are likely to view psychotherapy as the job of paraprofessionals who cannot—and should not—exercise clinical judgment in selecting interventions or interpreting the data of clinical observation.

(Westen et al., 2004, p. 638–9)

Consequently both, suffering patient and cognitivist practitioner, are rendered by the researcher into predictable mechanisms—controllable by the principles of cause and effect. On the occasions when the practitioner gets out of control and succumbs to the seductive siren songs of reason and meaning, and is in danger of transmuting into a psychotherapist, then the managerialists within IAPT are called forth to coerce the practitioner back into line.

Manuals as Patents

'The Manual' is the source of tension between (real) clinicians and researchers. For the researchers the manual should be simply a descriptive record of the experiment—what they did, how they did it, what happened. But in actual fact the manual is written before the experiment is even begun—this is the afore mentioned treatment package. And so the researchers too are also following the steps written into a pre-determined manualized treatment—allegedly to see whether the package works. Mysteriously, it always seems to.

If the manual were in fact a record of the experiment, then it would primarily be of interest to other researchers, who would use it to try to replicate the findings by following the previously taken steps. But when it comes to practitioners, the manual is transformed into an instruction-manual, a set of directives that sharply constrain the actions of the practitioner. However, the manual also serves two other functions—as a colonizing process and also as a way of patenting treatments. As soon as a technique features in a treatment manual, it becomes the property of that treatment. It matters not who was using it previously; if they had not tested and recorded the fact in approved ways then it belonged to no one, and all reports are simply anecdotal (recall the Neem tree story once more).

Some odd things follow out of this kind of patenting process. The story that follows (Westen et al., 2004, p. 642–3) could sit equally well within the eighth corruption—the use of untested hypotheses to design treatment packages.

The story starts with a group of researchers (Fairburn et al., 1986) testing a short term CBT treatment for bulimia against a control treatment which was supposedly nonspecific and nondirective—allegedly psychodynamic. The therapists in the control treatment were required to tease out the precipitating underlying difficulties in the early sessions and then to remain focussed exclusively on them for the rest of the treatment. They were required to do this because apparently this is what psychodynamic practitioners spend most of their time doing—looking for the match that caused the forest fire. In their next trial (Fairburn et al., 1991), they replaced the original control treatment with Interpersonal Therapy (IPT) because 'it was similar . . . [and] had the advantages of being better known and having a treatment manual available" (Fairburn, 1997, p. 280).

The new protocol required the IPT therapist to spend the first four sessions determining the interpersonal context surrounding the bulimia, after which the eating disorder as well as the emotional responses to it, were not to be spoken about at all. The reason for this strange prohibition was not driven by theoretical or clinical considerations, but rather in order to distinguish the control treatment from the steps being followed in the manualized (and therefore patented) CBT treatment. Because CBT 'owned' these strategies, IPT was not allowed to use them.

Initially those in the CBT group did well. But then in the months after the treatments had ended, the researchers were surprised to discover that those in the IPT group improved until they were on par with the CBT group. Astonishingly, what happened next was that the control treatment (IPT) was manualized and promoted as the new 'go to' treatment for bulimia. Even more astonishingly, the manual required that after delineating the interpersonal context the treatment, the patient and practitioner were prohibited from mentioning anything to do with the eating disorder itself. Why? Because this is what was done when it was a control treatment; but the reason that it was done there was in order to distinguish IPT from the CBT treatment. However, this strange injunction was now legitimated and rationalized by saying that the eating disorder itself was distraction from the difficulties existing in the interpersonal context.

To my mind the examination of the interpersonal context around the eating disorder makes therapeutic sense, but what does not make sense is a *prohibition* about speaking about the disorder itself. In terms of the existing research base, there was no prior reason to believe that talking directly about the eating disorder would be therapeutically counterproductive. In actual fact the CBT treatment thought the reverse to be the case: that it was therapeutic to attend closely to the eating disorder. In sum,

> The reason the IPT manual proscribes any focus on the symptoms is that doing so made for a clean experiment, in which the effects of the two experimental conditions could be readily distinguished. And when, by accident, IPT turned out to be helpful to many patients, suddenly an experimental

manipulation never intended as anything but a credible-enough control found its way into review articles as an EST for bulimia, despite the lack of any empirical evidence for one of its key components (or noncomponents), the counterintuitive injunction against discussing one of the main things the patient came in to talk about.

(Westen et al., 2004, p. 643)

Chapter 13

Statistical spin, linguistic obfuscation *or* how 14 per cent is turned into 50 per cent

The website dedicated to Mindfulness Based Cognitive Therapy (MBCT) declares:

> The UK *National Institute for Clinical Excellence* (NICE) has recently endorsed MBCT as an effective treatment for prevention of relapse. Research has shown that people who have been clinically depressed 3 or more times (sometimes for twenty years or more) find that taking the program and learning these skills helps to reduce considerably their chances that depression will return. The evidence from two randomized clinical trials of MBCT indicates that it reduces rates of relapse by 50% among patients who suffer from recurrent depression.
>
> (MBCT website).

It all sounds legitimate and the claims seem pretty convincing. NICE has endorsed this treatment on the basis of two studies that tested out the efficacy of 'Mindfulness Based Cognitive Therapy' (MBCT). The first: 'Prevention of relapse/recurrence in major depression by mindfulness–based cognitive therapy' (Teasdale et al., 2000), and the second: 'Mindfulness-based cognitive therapy for depression: replication and exploration of differential relapse prevention effects' (Ma and Teasdale, 2004).

NICE endorsed the treatment because the second study reproduced the findings of the first study. This was taken to mean that this piece of research had arrived at the Holy Grail of Empirical Science; this being that they have demonstrated their findings to be *verifiable, repeatable* and therefore, *predictable*. The treatment has been scientifically proven to work. Having fulfilled the condition of two positive results, NICE has validated the use of the treatment. In what follows I will take issue with CBT research on its own rationalist, positivist terms, to show that if it is an empirically-based science, then it is a pretty shabby one.

These two published trials are considered to be exemplars of what good empirical research in psychology should look like and what the standards they should aspire to achieve. It is also the case that the lead researcher, John Teasdale, is a long standing and highly respected senior researcher in the field. All this is to say that the object of the critique that follows is not of some marginal 'Aunt Sally' text that it is easy to take cheap shots at. Rather, this is a critique of the methods, claims and practices that reside near the apogee of psychological research and treatment. And because the research protocols followed in these two studies are standardized norms within CBT research and academic psychology, the critique also raises deeper and more serious questions about current research practices within cognitive psychology.

By the conclusion of this chapter it should be clear that CBT has failed to live up to the scientific mark that it claims to live up to. We will see that the success rates are actually meagre, but then we will also see how results are generally inflated to make them appear more convincing than they actually are.

The rationale for researching MBCT treatment is as follows: Some people experience repeated periods of depression throughout their lives. There already exists a range of CBT treatments which are delivered to people whilst they are actually in the grip of depression, in the acute phase. These are the second wave CBT treatments. But large numbers of those that recover from the depression through these kinds of CBT treatment, tend to relapse. This is the group that MBCT treatment will target. MBCT will be delivered to those *who are currently in remission having previously recovered from depression*. The hope is that having gone through a course of MBCT, they will be less likely to 'relapse' and have another attack of the mental illness depression. The research question then is, can MBCT training delivered in this way, help prevent further relapses?

MBCT is a part of the third wave and so it is much 'softer' than the second wave; its ethos is that of mindfulness and acceptance rather than that of control. The third wave teaches you to accept your suffering self. Don't fight your negative feelings, don't engage in a battle with them. Instead, detach yourself from them. Observe them. You are not the same as your feelings. And if you watch these feelings long enough, they will dissipate. If you do this, you will end up in a calmer, more peaceful state of mind.

Prevention and reduction

The very first word in the title of the first paper is compelling: '*Prevention* of Relapse/Recurrence in Major Depression by Mindfulness-Based Cognitive Therapy'. 'Prevention' suggests that the treatment will *halt* the recurrence of major depression. Which is exactly what the journal abstract proudly claims has been achieved: '[This research demonstrates that] MBCT offers a promising cost-efficient psychological approach to *preventing* relapse/recurrence in recovered recurrently depressed patients' (Teasdale et al., 2000: 615; italics added).

However, within the body of the paper their research question is much more modest in its aspirations, where it speaks of 'reduction' not 'prevention': 'Does this intervention, when offered in addition to TAU, *reduce* rates of relapse and recurrence compared to TAU alone? (Teasdale et al., 2000: 617; italics added). In the body of their paper they freely bounce from 'prevent' to 'reduce' and back again as it suits them: 'The finding that MBCT *prevented* relapse . . .' (p. 622); 'can significantly *reduce risk* of future relapse/recurrence' (p. 623); 'MBCT offers a promising cost-efficient psychological approach to *preventing* relapse/ recurrence . . .' (p. 615); '*reduce* future risk of relapse and recurrence of depression . . .' (p. 618) and so on (all italics mine).

Well, which is it and does it matter? Is the intention of the research to *prevent* (a very strong and compelling claim), or is it merely to *reduce* (worthy, but perhaps not so sexy). Anticipating the argument, it does matter; and it matters because as we will come to see, the treatment can only claim to *reduce* the frequency of relapse and not at all to *prevent* it. To claim prevention is, to put it most kindly, an exaggeration, and less kindly but more accurately, it is obfuscation. And more, even this lesser claim also turns out to be deeply problematic for a number of other reasons that we will come to. The elision of prevention and reduction, allow these researchers to have their cake and eat it too, as is illustrated in *the very first sentence* of this 'scientific' paper: 'Relapse and recurrence following successful treatment of major depressive disorder (MDD) *is common* and often carries massive social cost' (Teasdale et al., 2000: 615; italics added).

This is an instance of the point made in the second corruption in the previous chapter, and so it is worth pausing a moment longer to reflect on this statement. If relapse and recurrence are common, then surely the treatments are ineffective, otherwise the relapses would not be 'common'. This state of affairs – where relapse is common following treatment – would be completely unacceptable in other arenas of medicine. It seems to me that in revealing this reality in their very first sentence, the authors have blown CBT's cover its claim that the beneficial effects of CBT treatment are sustained over many years. The research literature is littered with this sort of statement, that 'relapse following recovery is common'. There is nothing wrong with the CBT treatment itself. It works fine. It is just unfortunate that so many people fall ill again after having been cured by the treatment. It is a case of operation successful; patient dead.

What is MBCT?

In their own words,

> MBCT is a manualized group skills-training program . . . It is designed to teach patients in remission from recurrent major depression to become more aware of, and to relate differently to, their thoughts, feelings, and bodily sensations . . . The program teaches skills that allow individuals to disengage from habitual . . . depression-related ruminative thought patterns, as a way to reduce future risk of relapse and recurrence of depression.
>
> After an initial individual orientation session, the MBCT program is delivered by an instructor in eight weekly 2-hr group training sessions involving up to 12 recovered recurrently depressed patients. During that period, the program includes daily homework exercises.
>
> (Teasdale et al., 2000: 618)

The research period lasted one year. During the first eight weeks participants were put through the MBCT programme, after which there was a 52-week follow up phase. The question that the researchers had to answer was: at the end of the 60-week period, were the people who received MBCT any better off than those that did not receive MBCT?

Speaking for the evidence

It is always the case that the 'evidence', the data, never speaks for itself; it always has to be spoken for. Numbers are cited, and then they are interpreted and commented upon. In effect, the researcher looks at a number and then decides whether the number is meaningful or not, what it means, and on what basis. As we go through the numbers, it is interesting to note which numbers they highlight and make meaningful, and which they obscure by making no mention of them.

The trial started out with sample of 145 persons. At the end of the 60 weeks they had complete data on 137. Of the people that dropped out they say: 'Of the 13 patients allocated to MBCT not included in the per protocol sample, 6 failed to attend any training sessions and 7 . . . dropped out after attending fewer than four sessions' (Teasdale et al., 2000, pp. 618–19).

As is the convention in this kind of research protocol, the 13 are not included in any of the calculations. Here too it is worth pausing to think about this manoeuvre. The typical rationale for not including the 13 in the analysis would be: because they did not take part in 'the treatment', there is no data on them.

But in any analysis that is anything more than a simplistic arithmetic one, we would have to inquire *why* these six *adults decided* not to continue having attended the 'orientation session'. Was it a meaningful rational choice based on the information they gleaned in the orientation session, or were they simply disorganized, unmotivated, and therefore 'CBT resistant'?

So rather than saying that 'six *failed* to attend any training sessions', one should more properly say that 'six *elected* not to go any further because they were not persuaded by the information they were given about the principles of the treatment in the orientation session'. One might also say the same of the seven who elected to leave the 'treatment' having experienced it. On this basis I think the 13 should be included among those for whom CBT will not work its magic. In which case the results will be even less promising.

Notice also the anomaly: patients who drop out in the clinical context after two sessions are counted as having completed treatment by IAPT (they are added to the data); whilst in the research context, those who drop out having attended at least three sessions are removed from the data. This strategy works in the direction of making CBT look much more successful than it actually is.

Halving, doubling and disappearing

The participants were divided into two groups. One group, 71 people, received MBCT as well as TAU, and the other group, 66 people, received only TAU (sixth corruption).

At the end of the 60 weeks they found that out of the 71 people in the MBCT group, 31 had relapsed (44 per cent); and out of 66 in the TAU group, 38 people relapsed (58 per cent). Those that received MBCT were better off for it; but how much better and was it worth the effort?

To make sense of these sorts of results, it is worth representing the findings in simple diagrams, as the conventional means of representing the information, consisting as it does of a dense mix of statistical notation and highly digested claims, obscures more than it reveals (see Figure 13.1).

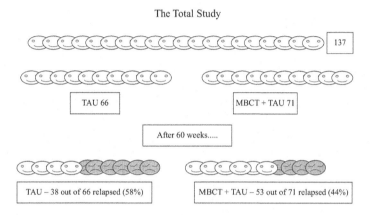

Figure 13.1

This leaves us with the result that just 14 per cent fewer people having relapsed in the treatment group at the end of one year.

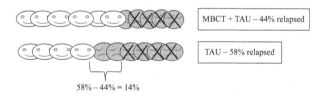

Figure 13.2

This is the total benefit: 14 per cent additional people did not relapse. In other words, the treatment was of benefit to about 1 or 2 out of 10 people. It is always instructive to state the reverse: 8 or 9 out of 10 people were not helped by the treatment.

Interestingly, these figures are *never stated* in this form in the paper. I had to search out numbers buried here and there in the paper and put them together to find this out. Why? Clearly, it is because these results show that *just one or two*

more people out of every ten people (14 per cent) in the MBCT group fared better. In other words, statistically speaking, *the treatment makes no difference*. And
if we add in the thirteen who elected not to continue with the treatment, then the
results would be even more invidious. Keep in mind also that this is not 14 per
cent of the general population, but a carefully selected ideal population that bears
little resemblance to the real general population (the second corruption).

Relatives and absolutes

However, things can be made to look more impressive by rearranging and regroup-
ing the data. It turned out that the figures for relapse are much better for a subset of
the total population. Following treatment, for some (unknown) reason, those who
had recovered from depression on three or more previous occasions, *relapsed less*
than those who had recovered from two or less previous episodes. It is this finding
that the paper highlights to such a degree that it obscures everything else, including
the fact that *in toto* the treatment does not do much at all (14 per cent).

They announce their finding about this specific subgroup, *those who suffered
and recovered from three or more previous episodes of depression* (105 out of the
137), in this way 'Over the total study period . . . 40% (22/55) of MBCT participants experienced relapse/recurrence compared with 66% (33/50) of TAU participants . . . *a 39% reduction in risk of relapse/recurrence in the MBCT condition*'
(Teasdale et al., 2000: 620; italics added).

They say that there is a '39% reduction in risk' following MBCT treatment.
39 per cent. This starts to look more promising. But wait. How did they get to 39 per
cent? Surely the difference is 26 per cent which we get by subtracting 40 per cent
from 66 per cent. Once again, let us resort to pictures

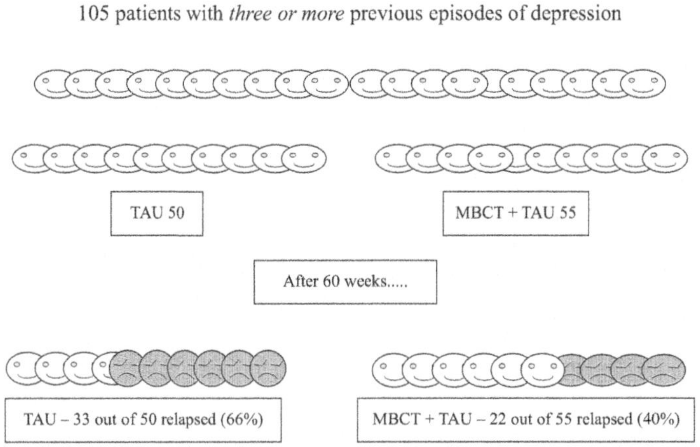

105 patients with *three or more* previous episodes of depression

TAU 50

MBCT + TAU 55

After 60 weeks.....

TAU – 33 out of 50 relapsed (66%)

MBCT + TAU – 22 out of 55 relapsed (40%)

Figure 13.3

Fewer of those who did receive the treatment are depressed. A result. The treatment has been helpful. But by how much? To find out we proceed as before: cancel out the equivalent number from each group, to leave 26 per cent.

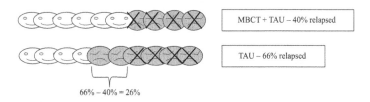

Figure 13.4

To my mind, this is the obvious way of reading the results. Which is say that 26 per cent (66 – 40 = 26) of those in the MBCT group were better off than those in the TAU group.

Curiously, the researchers make no mention of the 26 per cent and instead proffer the more impressive figure, 39 per cent and call it 'the reduction in risk'. What is going on? Let us go back to basics to think about this situation in regard to the three-or-more situation. The study shows us that if we did nothing different (TAU), then about 66 per cent of this group are likely to relapse over the year.

This is our base line; call this number X. The number of people relapsing in the treatment group *after* treatment (Y) becomes the measure of the success or not of the treatment.

> If the same numbers relapse in both groups, then the treatment makes no difference and is *useless* (Y = X).
> If fewer people relapsed in the treatment group compared to the control group, then the treatment is *beneficial* (Y < X).
> If more people relapse in the treatment group compared to the control group, then the treatment is *harmful* (Y > X).

Now, there are two ways of reading the relationship between Y and X. To my mind the obvious way of reading these figures is to say:

> The number of people who relapsed with no treatment (X) is 66 per cent.
> The number of people who relapsed after treatment (Y) is 40 per cent.
> Therefore, the people in the treatment group were better off by (X–Y) = 66% – 40% = 26%.

I have *subtracted* one figure from the other.

Teasdale meanwhile elects to *divide* one figure into the other to arrive at 39% in the following way:

$$\frac{Y}{X} = \frac{40}{66} = 0.61 = 61\%$$

$$100\% - 61\% = 39\%$$

To be sure they have performed some calculation, but what is it actually describing? What does it mean? They have elected *to name the result* a 'reduction in risk'. But is this what this calculation really means? Does this figure *really* describe a 'reduction in risk'?

This is where we need to recall the lottery ticket scenario that we touched on previously. My chance of winning with one lottery ticket is about one in fourteen million. And my chance of winning with four lottery tickets is about four in fourteen million. I could say that four tickets have increased my chances by 400 per cent, or I could say that my chances have increased from one out of fourteen million to four out of fourteen million. The first more impressive figure of 400 per cent is the *relative increase* in chance, relative to the initial chance. The second less impressive figure 4/14,000,000 is the *absolute increase*.

This is exactly the difference between the 26 per cent and the 39 per cent. The 26 per cent reduction is the absolute reduction in risk, and the 39 per cent is the relative reduction in risk, *relative to the 66 per cent*!

To my mind, as a sufferer of depression, what I would want to know is this: what difference will joining the MBCT group make to *my well-being*. Answer: if I join the MBCT group, I will *reduce my chances of relapse* by 26 per cent (but only if I have relapsed and recovered on *at least* three previous occasions). That is it. That is the big finding. Statistically speaking, even if I belong to this elite subset, I am much more likely not to feel any benefit from going through MBCT training – the likelihood of *not benefiting* being around 75 per cent. Nevertheless, the 26 per cent speaks directly and concretely to my experience and so I am able to put its meaning to me into words. The 39 per cent meanwhile, is an arithmetic mystification, by which I mean that I find it impossible to put into words what this means to *my experience* in any meaningful way. But of course, 26 per cent is not an impressive a number as 39 per cent.

It is part of the art of obfuscation not to trouble the reader by informing them that 'the reduction in risk' they are citing is *relative* rather than *absolute*, nor to trouble then with information about what the absolute reduction actually is, nor to reveal the actual calculations used to derive the figures in the first place. These practices are normative conventions within this research field. It begins to seem that we are in the territory of numerology masquerading as statistical science.

The art of amplification

Even so, let us allow them their 39 per cent, and look at what they do with it. They say, 'in participants with three or more previous episodes of depression . . . an "adequate dose" of MBCT *almost halved* relapse/recurrence rates over the follow-up period compared to TAU' (Teasdale et al., 2000, p. 621, my italics).

In this sentence, the 39 per cent (less than four out of ten) has been morphed into 'almost half'. To call it 'almost a half' is to increase 39 per cent by 11 per cent; and this 11 per cent is more than 25 per cent of the original figure of 39 per cent. That is a very, very big 'almost' – 25 per cent bigger. That would be like me saying to you: you owe me £75, so why don't you give me a £100 because a 100 is almost the same as 75.

The stealthy amplification continues a couple of paragraphs later, where we find that the caveat 'almost' is no longer deemed necessary, '*the halving of relapse* . . . rates in a group of high risk . . . would appear to be a clinically useful outcome' (Teasdale et al., 2000, p. 621, my italics).

In a few paragraphs we have jumped over 26 per cent (which does not even get a mention) to 39 per cent, to almost a half, to a half. Which is how we get to the 50 per cent we find on the MBCT website. Notice the transmutation process:

We start with *a number* 39 per cent. We then change the form of representation from number to language. This allows 39 per cent, which is just under 0.4 to be portrayed as 'almost half'. Next, because 'almost half' is so close to 'half, we may as well call it 'half'. Having got to 'half' the discourse reverts from the domain of language back to numbers. It is in this way, from numbers via language back to numbers, that 39 per cent has become 50 per cent.

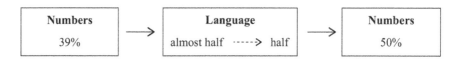

Figure 13.5

This then, is the message that is broadcast to all and sundry: that MBCT *halves* the relapse rates of all those prone to depression. And sure enough, this is exactly what we find on the official MBCT website, 'The evidence from two randomized clinical trials of MBCT indicates that it reduces rates of relapse by 50% among patients who suffer from recurrent depression' (MBCT).

The economic argument

The economic rationale for this treatment also falsely emphasizes 'prevention' in lieu of 'likelihood of reduction'. They say that the, '*Preventative* effect of MBCT was achieved for an average investment of less than 5 hours of instructor time per patient, suggesting [this is] . . . a cost-efficient strategy for *prevention*' (Teasdale et al., 2000, p. 622, my italics).

Fund holders are bound to be excited at the prospect of *preventing* depression for hardly any cost at all – for five hours work per patient. They would be less excited if they were told that what was being achieved was not 'prevention', but simply a 26 per cent *reduction in the likelihood of relapse*, and this too for a very narrow population. Fund holders are even less likely to be impressed if their attention is drawn to the fact that *the treatment will make no difference to 75 per cent* of those who had suffered three or more previous episodes of depression; they will continue to relapse as before. And they are likely to be even less impressed if their attention was also drawn to the fact that the treatment won't make any difference to eight out of every ten people in the general population.

Also, it is not clear how they arrive at the figure of less than five hours. To calculate the amount of instructor time invested, one needs to add up the orientation sessions, one hour per patient (12 hours), the training itself (8 groups × 2 hours/group = 16 hours), and the four follow up sessions per patient (12 patients each seen for 4 hours = 48 hours). This amounts to a total of 76 hours of instructor time, which divided between 12 patients, results in 6.3 instructor hours per patient.

To be sure this is not the most important part of the critique. But because they do not tell us how they calculated this figure, it could constitute yet another inflation of the actual results of the study.

Therapy or training?

But there is another element of note in the statement above: *there is no therapist present*; instead we find an 'instructor'. This is not an oversight. Ma and Teasdale (2004) inform us that MBCT was previously referred to as 'attentional control training'. And 'training' requires instructors not therapists. It is for this reason that Ma and Teasdale continue to speak of instructors, and in doing this they reveal that MBCT is better called an educational programme or a 'training', but not therapy, and even less, psychotherapy. Nothing wrong with that; we should just call a spade a spade.

Two or less episodes of depression

But what of those who had two or less previous episodes of depression? It would seem that MBCT did not help them. The researchers say, 'MBCT appeared to have *no prophylactic effects* in those with only two previous episodes' and 'MBCT prevented relapse and recurrence in patients with a history of three or more episodes of depression, *but not in patients with only two previous episodes*' (Teasdale et al., 2000, p. 622, my italics).

The mild neutral tone is repeated in the follow up paper four years later, 'The earlier finding that a group of patients with two previous episodes of depression . . . showed *no evidence of benefit* from MBCT was also replicated . . . MBCT can be *relatively unhelpful* for a particular group of patients' (Ma and Teasdale, 2004, p. 38, my italics).

But what are the actual figures regarding relapse for the two-or-less group? They tell us that 'Over the total study period . . . 56% (9/16) of MBCT participants experienced relapse/recurrence compared with 31% (5/16) TAU participants' (Teasdale et al., 2000, pp. 620–21).

Do look at the numbers again. *More* of the people who received MBCT relapsed, compared to those who did not get the treatment. Twenty-five per cent more of them. Yet the researchers do not say that the treatment made them ill, all they say is that there is *no evidence of benefit* of MBCT to this group. Their get-out clause is to say that this result is not statistically significant. Therefore, they are not meaningful. They say this despite the fact that this grouping became more ill in the second study too. In other words, the findings were *replicated* and *verified*.

Surely on the same grounds that they claim that MBCT is efficacious for the three-or-more group, 26 per cent, they ought to say that MBCT is positively harmful to those who have suffered two-or-less, 25 per cent. If we put the figures for the two-or-less group through the same arithmetic procedure as they did to arrive at 39 per cent, then according to those calculations, the treatment will *increase the chances of relapse by 80 per cent* relative to the original chance.

It is clear that for the two-or-less group the MBCT treatment is iatrogenic – it is making these people *more ill*. This embarrassing fact is obscured and packaged in bland neutral statements of 'no benefit', and that they have determined that the *p* value shows no statistical significance, 'As in Teasdale et al.'s (2000) study, these patients [two-or-less] showed a nonsignificantly greater tendency to relapse following MBCT' (Ma and Teasdale, 2004, p. 38).

Let me make clear what is going on here. The second study replicated and therefore verified the results of the first study, this being that those who suffered two or less previous episodes of depression, were more prone to relapsing following the MBCT treatment. In normal circumstances this would be a cause for celebration and it declared to be a scientific fact, because two of the key conditions of empirical science have been fullfilled – replication and verification. However, the authors say that although it looks like a fact, on this occasion it is not infact a 'fact', because the fact is not statistically significant. The notion of statistical significance is being used to erase the reality of the fact that in both studies, more of those belonging to this group became depressed following treatment. Is this an instance of the fourth corruption – *p* hacking?

Further issues

There are a number of other elements in the paper that fall short of the self-aggrandising rhetoric endemic to CBT discourse, that it is scientifically *rigorous* and so forth. If the authors of this study were truly rigorous and scientific, then they would be obliged to curtail their claims even further on the grounds that more than three quarters of the participants were women and close to 100 per cent of them were white. So properly speaking, the findings as such should also be limited to the category 'white women'.

It is also the case, as the authors of both papers, tell us that 'MBCT was most effective in preventing relapses *not preceded by life events*' (Ma and Teasdale, 2004, p. 31, my italics), and more effective when the depression was driven by 'autonomous ruminative-thinking' (Ma and Teasdale, 2004, p. 32). This then constitutes another major constraint that further limits their claims on the efficacy of MBCT. The point bears underlining: if you are depressed because of a tragic life event, then this treatment will be of no help you.

And finally, there is no way of emphatically knowing how and why those in the MBCT group relapsed less than those in the TAU group. Because apart from anything else, over the 60-week study period, those in the MBCT group accessed other forms of help *more* than the TAU group. The MBCT group visited their GP for a depression related issue 6 per cent more than the TAU group (58 per cent MBCT versus 52 per cent TAU); the MBCT group reached out for counselling 15 per cent more than the TAU group (49 per cent MBCT *vs.* 34 per cent TAU); and the MBCT group used medication 5 per cent more than did the TAU group (45 per cent MBCT *vs.* 40 per cent TAU). In fact, the researchers admit as much when they say, 'the design of the present study does not allow us to attribute the benefits of MBCT to the specific skills taught by the program versus nonspecific factors, such as therapeutic attention and group participation' (Teasdale et al., 2000: 622).

If the researchers were being truly rigorous, then the study would be unable to unequivocally claim that the reduction in relapse rates in the MBCT group was due to MBCT rather than the other kinds of help they accessed over the 60-week period.

The researchers are using the same strategy employed in the Full Guidelines to make tokenistic gestures towards the limitations of their study. In this way they lend their position an air of scientific humility, saying things like, 'the sample sizes in the two groups mean that estimates of risk have appreciable margins of error' (Teasdale et al., 2000, p. 622). They even confess, 'The relapse/recurrence rate in patients . . . *was clearly substantially above* the expected annual incidence rate . . . it is clear that the intervention did *not reduce risks of major depression to the "normal" range*' (Teasdale et al., 2000, p. 621, my italics).

All this is forgotten in the triumphalism we find in the journal abstract (which is all a busy professional is likely to have the time to read): 'MBCT offers a promising cost-efficient psychological approach to *preventing* relapse/recurrence in recovered recurrently depressed patients'.

In conclusion

When all is said and done, then the findings of this research should in fact be announced in this way:

Over the period of a year, MBCT is likely to reduce the chances of relapse into depression for something between two to three out every ten people who belong to a very restricted group of patients – those who are not currently depressed, but who have suffered and recovered from at least three previous episodes of depression. Further, their depressions ought not to be caused by actual life events but fed by 'autonomous ruminative thinking'. Therefore, about seven out of ten people within this group (three or more) – 'almost three quarters' – will continue to relapse despite the treatment.

These exciting claims, it should be remembered are for the grouping that has responded best to the treatment. Ethically, the abstract should also highlight the fact that: Eighty per cent of those who have suffered and recovered from two or less previous episodes of depression, are *more likely to become ill because of the treatment.* However, they will be relieved to know that their suffering caused by MBCT although personally problematic, is statistically not significant. And if the entire population of those who had previously suffered depression (but were currently in remission) were put through this treatment, then *only about one or two people out of every ten are likely to reduce their chances of relapse,* which means that it will make no difference to eight out of ten people.

So despite the range of caveats supplied by the researchers themselves, despite the fact that over three quarters of those who the treatment is meant to help will not be helped, despite the fact that those with two-or-less episodes will actually be made to feel considerably worse, despite the fact that this treatment is deemed inappropriate for anyone who is depressed because of a life event (most of human kind surely), the researchers feel able to end their abstract with the rousing statement, entirely devoid of caveats or qualifications, 'MBCT offers a promising cost-efficient psychological approach to *preventing* relapse/recurrence in recovered recurrently depressed patients'.

Chapter 14

The cognitive delusion

The cognitivist delusion is exactly that: the delusion that modern humans are primarily cognitive, rational-decision-making beings. The delusion continues: thoughts precede emotions and are separable from them. Emotions arise when they are triggered by thoughts (cognitions). Thoughts/cognitions themselves consist of the perception of the situation one finds oneself in, and the emotions are the response to that perception. In effect, mental life is said to be able to control emotional life. Irrational thoughts and perceptions produce problematic emotional states. Each kind of irrational perception constitutes a specific mental disorder and is listed in the DSM. Each of the irrational perceptions/cognitions can be corrected by a specific CBT treatment. Once corrected, once cognition matches reality, then the emotional life falls into line and the person is in recovery. This is readily achievable in anything between six and twenty sessions. Here endeth the delusion.

But that is not the end of the story, nor is it its beginning. I have been arguing that the reason that the delusion is able to flourish within psychology, is because it is shared by the managerialist beliefs, systems and structures that surround and sustain it: from its philosophy to its psychology; from the premises that the research is based on, to the way that the research is conducted and analysed; from the way that NICE is organized and the way that it operates. The final delusions are supplied by IAPT—who distort the way that CBT is delivered in order that reality is made to look like it matches the delusion.

Endemic to the whole enterprise has been the notion of control, a notion that manifests itself in different ways at every which level. Coercion and control are integral to the ethos and content of rule based CBT 'treatment' itself; it features in the research protocols which are carefully regulated to produce results that are statistically significant, and to ensure the exclusion of modalities that might question the basis of CBT's dominance and thereby threaten it; NICE meanwhile controls the membership of the GDGs to ensure that the majority are clinical psychologists of the positivist persuasion, and they in turn spin the data in ways that reinforce and validate their positivist paradigms; and finally managerialist protocols within IAPT are particularly pernicious in the ways that they control the way that the treatment is delivered and its requirements of the practitioners delivering the treatments. In effect, CBT treatments have been designed to fit with the requirements of research rather than of therapy, and the ways that the treatments have been delivered have been driven by political agendas and fiscal machinations rather than concern for the suffering individual. A tightly managed narrative is produced that binds together the whole endeavour, a narrative which papers over the cracks and fissures, so that we end up bewildered and believing their glossy tale of salvation.

It seems to matter little that CBT beliefs fly in the face of the findings of contemporary neuroscience. Nor does it seem to matter that CBT takes no notice of the cautions delivered by Kant many centuries ago—that humans are not mechanisms explainable by mechanistic causes, and therefore are not able to be reliably manipulated into positive states of mind by the application of rule based protocols. Rather human thoughts, feelings and actions are to be understood through reasons. In other words CBT has failed to notice that human suffering is meaningful and not mindlessly and mechanistically *caused* by mental disorders.

CBT has become so besotted by the symptom itself that it does not consider the possibility that the symptom might be meaningful, and even more, that it might in fact be a communication. As Foulkes and Anthony (1957, p. 260) say 'The language of the symptom, although already a form of communication, is autistic. It mumbles to itself secretly, hoping to be overheard'. But the CBT therapist is not listening; and so remains unaware that there is something there, still 'hoping to be overheard'. To put it differently, CBT has become so fixated on the pointing finger that it does not notice that the finger is in fact pointing, and so they do not trouble themselves to look for what the finger may be pointing to.

It is critical that we remember the caution sounded by the moral philosopher Raimond Gaita who said 'If our understanding of our inner life and its actuality are interdependent, if the concepts with which we identify and explore our inner life partly determine the character of that inner life, then a scientistic distortion of those concepts will not only distort our understanding, *it will distort the inner life itself.* (Gaita, 2008, p. 247; italics added). Worryingly, this in fact is what is occurring. CBT encourages, and often enough insists, that individuals distort their experience of their inner lives in order to try to fit into the cognitivist template.

All this is has been aided and abetted by the peculiar hyper-rationalist conventions that have come to reside within psychological research culture. For example, that all it need take is for just two studies with positive outcomes for a treatment to be licensed; this is so even when there are many more studies that show the lack of efficacy or even positive harm. Then there is the issue of p-hacking which seems to be endemic in psychological research; add to this the fact that all a person need do is attend two sessions for it to be counted as a completed treatment; add to that the gamesmanship endemic in NICE and IAPT. Add to that the fact that although CBT claims of benefit are of the statistical kind that speaks to likelihoods, it is sold as though it were generating certainties no different to the more objective disciplines of mathematics or physics; add to that the benefits such as they are, are cited in their relative form rather than absolute, making them look much more impressive than they actually are (recall the lottery).

The point that follows from this is particularly important. Both the supporters and detractors of CBT seem to be in agreement that in round figures, CBT is of benefit to about 50 per cent of the population. It is on this sort of figure that the Exchequer has been persuaded to part with eye-watering amounts of money. But this 50 per cent (already exaggerated) is the relative benefit. The actual (absolute) benefit tends to be around 25 per cent, and that too is for a peculiar and particular population that bears little resemblance to the general population. What CBT research itself shows, is that CBT will not be of benefit to at least 80 per cent of the population.

If it is the case that these sorts of figures which we came across in the MBCT study, are representative of the CBT research base in general (that the efficacy is not 50 per cent but 25 per cent), then something much more worrying is going on. Then we would have to ask: is the whole CBT research base infected and corrupted by these kinds of statistical malpractices? The answer appears to be an unequivocal yes.

I doubt that the Exchequer would be all that keen to empty the public purse on the more realistic but much more meagre promises of *reduction in likelihood of occurrence* rather than *prevention*, and a 25 per cent likelihood of reduction rather than 50 per cent prevention. And further, that the treatment will not deliver a cure, but only a 50 per cent *reduction in intensity of symptomatology*. Is the Exchequer aware that the treatments will not benefit about 8 out of the 10 people specially chosen for these studies? And is it aware that when it comes to members of the general population the results will be even more dismal? Is it aware that this is what the data actually shows when stripped of all obfuscation?

So it is quite extraordinary that so many of the great and the good—governments and policy makers—have been gullible enough to swallow the CBT fabulation in its entirety; and then, intoxicated by its heady hyper-rationalist promises, they have fostered the cognitivist delusion and in doing so nurtured the corruptions of science.

References

Alesina, A. and Ardagna, S. (2009). 'Large Changes in Fiscal Policy: Taxes vs. Spending', in J.R. Brown (ed.), *Tax Policy and the Economy*, vol. 24, pp. 35–68. Also published in NBER Working Paper No. 15639. Issued January 2010.

Artemis Trust (2011). In S. Callan and B. Fry (eds), *Completing the Revolution: Commissioning Effective Talking Therapies*. London: Centre for Social Justice.

Atkinson, P. (2014). 'Lies, Dammed Lies, and IAPT Statistics', *Self & Society*, 42(1–2): 18–19.

Bank of England (2014). 'Money Creation in the Modern Economy', available at www. bankofengland.co.uk/-/media/boe/files/quarterly-bulletin/2014/money-creation-in-the-modern-economy.pdf?la=en&hash=9A8788FD44A62D8BB927123544205CE4 76E01654.

Barbui, C., Furukawa, T.A. and Cipriani, A. (2008). 'Effectiveness of Paroxetine in the Treatment of Acute Major Depression in Adults: A Systematic Re-examination of Published and Unpublished Data from Randomized Control Trials', *Canadian Medical Association Journal*, 178(3): 296–305.

Barrett, W. (1990). *Irrational Man: Studies in Existential Philosophy*. New York: Anchor Books.

Barthes, R. (1984). *Mythologies*. London: Paladin.

Bell, S., Knapp, M., Layard, P., Meacher, M., Priebe, S., Thornicroft, G., Turnberg, L. and Wright, B. (2006). *The Depression Report: A New Deal for Anxiety and Depression Disorders*. London: Mental Health Policy Group, Centre for Economic Performance, London School of Economics.

bluegoat (2015). 'surviving targets', *ClinPsy*, available at www.clinpsy.org.uk/forum/ viewtopic.php?f=27&t=18474.

Boffey, D. (2013). 'MP's 11% pay rise set to embarrass party leaders', *The Guardian*, 8 December, available at www.theguardian.com/politics/2013/dec/08/mps-pay-rise-embarrass-party-leaders.

Booth, R. (2016). '"I didn't matter": The long wait for mental health treatment', *The Guardian*, 25 January, available at www.theguardian.com/society/2016/jan/25/nhs-mental-health-crisis-long-wait-for-treatment.

Bristol University (2012). *Press Release*, available at www.bristol.ac.uk/news/2012/ 8986.html.

Butler, S. (2017). 'Former Tesco executives pressured others to falsify figures, court told', *The Guardian*, 29 September, available at www.theguardian.com/business/2017/sep/29/ tesco-executives-court-christopher-bush-carl-rogberg.

Campbell, D. (2014). 'NHS chiefs' pay rises condemned as "double-standards" by nurses', *The Guardian*, 15 June, www.theguardian.com/society/2014/jun/15/nhs-chiefs-pay-rise-condemned-nurses.

Campbell, D. (2017). 'Private sector dominates NHS contract awards', *The Guardian*, 30 December, available at www.theguardian.com/society/2017/dec/29/richard-branson-virgin-scoops-1bn-pounds-of-nhs-contracts.

Carnap, R. (2012 [1934]). *The Unity of Science*, trans. M. Black. London: Routledge.

CiC (2013). 'Happiness at Work', *CiC-EAP*, available at www.cic-eap.co.uk.

Davies, J. (2014). *Cracked: Why Psychiatry is Doing More Harm Than Good*. London: Icon Books.

Davis C. and Abraham J. (2011). 'Desperately seeking cancer drugs: explaining the emergence and outcomes of accelerated pharmaceutical regulation', *Sociology of Health & Illness*, 1 July, 33(5): 731–47.

Deniker, P. and Lemperiere, T. (1964). 'Drug Treatment of Depression', in E.B. Davies (ed.), *Depression: Proceedings of the Symposium Held at Cambridge*. Cambridge: Cambridge University Press.

Department for Work and Pensions (2014). *Invitation to Tender; Entrenched Worklessness Provision; Cumbria and Lancashire Jobcentre Plus District*. Contract Reference: UI_DWP_101412, available at https://data.gov.uk/data/contracts-finder.../1b3e4225-a9dc-441b-a64a-6eb7d1fb2b1d.

Department of Health (2011). 'Talking Therapies: A Four-Year Plan of Action: A Supporting Document to 'No Health without Mental Health', available at www.gov.uk/government/publications/talking-therapies-a-4-year-plan-of-action.

Diagnostic and Statistical Manual of Mental Disorders – DSM (1980). Third Edition. Washington: American Psychiatric Association.

Dillow, C. (2007). *The End of Politics: New Labour and the Folly of Managerialism*. London: Harriman House.

Edgeworth, F. (1881). *Mathematical Psychics: An Essay on the Application of Mathematics to the Moral Sciences*. London: C.K. Paul & Co.

Ehrenreich, B. (2009). *Smile or Die: How Positive Thinking Fooled America and the World*. London: Granta.

Elias, N. (1994). *The Civilizing Process*, Oxford: Blackwell.

Fairburn, C.G. (1997). 'The management of bulimia nervosa and other binge eating problems', *Advances in Psychiatric Treatment*, 3(1): 2–8.

Fairburn, C.G. and Garner, D.M. (1986). 'The diagnosis of bulimia nervosa', *International Journal of Eating Disorders*, 5(3): 403–19.

Ferraro, D. (2015). 'Torture, psychology and the neoliberal state', *Overland*, available at https://overland.org.au/2015/01/torture-psychology-and-the-neoliberal-state/.

Foulkes, S.H. and Anthony, E.J. (1957). *Group Psychotherapy – The Psychoanalytic Approach*. London: Karnac Books.

Friedman, M. (1953). 'The Methodology of Positive Economics', in M. Friedman, *Essays in Positive Economics*. Chicago: Chicago University Press, pp. 3–34.

Friedman, M. (1962). *Capitalism and Freedom*. Chicago: Chicago University Press.

Friedman, M. (1970). 'The Social Responsibility of Business is to Increase its Profits', *The New York Times*, 13 September 1970.

Friedman, M. (1979). 'What is Greed?', *The Phil Donahue Show*, available at www.youtube.com/watch?v=StutmELY6po.

Gaita, R. (2008). *A Common Humanity: Thinking about Love, Truth and Justice*. Oxon and New York: Routledge.

Goldacre, B. (2012). *Bad Pharma: How medicine is broken and how we can fix it*. London: Fourth Estate.

Goodley, S. (2017). 'The chicken run: blood, sweat and deceit at a UK poultry plant', *The Guardian*, 28 September, available at www.theguardian.com/business/2017/sep/28/blood-sweat-deceit-west-midlands-poultry-plant.

Green, C. (2001). 'Operationalism Again: What Did Bridgman Say? What Did Bridgman Need?', *Theory and Psychology*, 11(1): 45–51.

Griffiths, S. and Steen, S. (2013). 'Improving Access to Psychological Therapies (IAPT) Programme: Scrutinising IAPT Cost Estimates to Support Effective Commissioning', *The Journal of Psychological Therapies in Primary Care*, Vol. 2: 142–56, November 2013.

Griffiths, S., Foster, J., Steen, S. and Pietroni, P. (2013). 'Mental Health's Market Experiment: Commissioning Psychological Therapies through any Qualified Provider', Centre for Psychological Therapies in Primary Care, Report 1.

Guy, A., Thomas, R., Stephenson, S. and Loewenthal, D. (2011). 'NICE under scrutiny: the impact of the National Institute for Health and Clinical Excellence guidelines on the provision of psychotherapy in the UK'. London: UK Council for Psychotherapy, available at www.easewellbeing.co.uk/downloads/nice%20report%20ukcp.pdf.

Hollon, S.D., Thase, M.E. and Markowitz, J.C. (2002). 'Treatment and Prevention of Depression', *Psychological Science in the Public Interest*, 3(2): 39–77.

Huxley, A. (1932). *Brave New World*. London: Chatto & Windus.

IAPT (2016). Improving Access to Psychological Therapies (IAPT) Executive Summary (May 2016). NHS Digital, available at https://digital.nhs.uk/media/29276/Improving.../IAPT-month-May-2016-exec-sum.

Jarvinen, T., Sievanen, H., Kannus, P., Jokihaara, J. and Kahn, K. (2011). 'The True Cost of Pharmacological Disease Prevention', *British Medical Journal*, 342: d2175.

Jennings, R. (1855). *The Natural Elements of Political Economy*. London: Longman, Brown, Green and Longmans.

Jevons, W.S. (1862). *General Mathematical Theory of Political Economy*. London: Macmillan.

Jevons, W.S. (1871). *The Theory of Political Economy*. London: Macmillan.

Johnsen, T.J. and Friborg. O. (2015). 'The Effects of Cognitive Behavioral Therapy as an Anti-Depressive Treatment is Falling: A Meta-Analysis', *Psychological Bulletin*, 141(4): 747–68. Advance online publication. http://dx.doi.org/10.1037/bul0000015.

Johnson, S. (2014). 'Why are NHS staff going on strike?', *The Guardian*, 8 October, available at www.theguardian.com/healthcare-network/2014/oct/08/everything-need-know-nhs-strike-pay.

Kant, I. (1784). 'Beantwortung der Frage: Was ist Aufklärung?', *Berlinische Monatsschrift*. English translation, 'What is Enlightenment?', available at www.columbia.edu/acis/ets/CCREAD/etscc/kant.html.

Kirk, S.A., Gomory, T. and Cohen, D. (2013). *Mad Science: Psychiatric Coercion, Diagnosis and Drugs*. Rutgers, NJ: Transaction Publishers.

Kirsch, I. (2011). 'Antidepressants and the Placebo Response', in M. Rapley, J. Moncrieff and J. Dillon (eds), *De-Medicalizing Misery: Psychiatry, Psychology and the Human Condition*. London: Palgrave, pp. 189–96.

Kirsch, I. and Sapirstein, G. (1998). 'Listening to Prozac but Hearing Placebo: A Meta-Analysis of Anti-Depressant Medication', *Prevention and Treatment*, (1): 2.

Kirsch, I., Deacon, B.J., Huedo-Medina, T.B., Scoboria, A., Moore, T.J. and Johnson, B.T. (2008). 'Initial Severity and Antidepressant Benefits: A Meta-analysis of Data Submitted to the Food and Drug Administration', *PLoS Medicine*, 5(2): e45.

Kirsch, I., Moore, T.J., Scoboria, A. and Nicholls, S.S. (2002). 'The Emperor's New Drugs: An Analysis of Antidepressant Medication Data Submitted to the US Food and Drug Administration', *Prevention and Treatment*, 5(23).

Krugman, P. (2015). 'The Austerity Delusion', *The Guardian*, 29 April, available at www.theguardian.com/business/ng-interactive/2015/apr/29/the-austerity-delusion.

Kutchins, H. and Kirk, S. (1997). *Making Us Crazy – DSM: The Psychiatric Bible and the Creation of Mental Disorders*. New York: Free Press.

Layard, R. (2005). *Happiness*. London: Penguin.

Layard, R. and Clark, D. (2014). *Thrive: The Power of Evidence-Based Psychological Therapies*. London: Allen Lane.

Le Guin, U.K. (2004). 'The Ones Who Walk Away from Omelas', in *The Wind's Twelve Quarters*. New York: Harper Perennial.

LIWY (2016). 'IAPT Waiting List Targets', available at www.clinpsy.org.uk/forum/view topic.php?p=180855.

Ma, S.H. and Teasdale, J.D. (2004). 'Mindfulness-Based Cognitive Therapy for Depression: Replication and Exploration of Differential Relapse Prevention Effects', *Journal of Consulting and Clinical Psychology*, 72(1): 31–40.

Marsh, S. (2017). 'Tens of thousands of NHS patients enduring long ambulance waits', *The Guardian*, 29 December, www.theguardian.com/society/2017/dec/29/111-nhs-hot line-calls-peaked-in-week-before-christmas.

Midlands Psychology Group (2010). 'Welcome to NICEWorld', available at www.midpsy. org/niceworld.doc.

MBCT (n.d). 'Mindfulness-based Cognitive Therapy: Does it work?', available at: http://mbct.com/about/does-mbct-work/.

Moncrieff, J. (2011). 'The Myth of Anti-Depressants: An Historical Analysis', in M. Rapley, J. Moncrieff and J. Dillon (eds), *De-Medicalizing Misery: Psychiatry, Psychology and the Human Condition*. London: Palgrave, pp. 174–88.

Moncrieff, J. and Timimi, S. (2013). 'The social and cultural construction of psychiatric knowledge: an analysis of NICE guidelines on depression and ADHD', *Anthropology and Medicine*, 20(1): 59–71.

NHS England (2016). *Joint Technical Definitions for Performance and Activity 2017/18, 2018/19*. Operational Information for Commissioning: Publication Gateway Reference: 05830; available at www.england.nhs.uk/wp-content/uploads/2015/12/joint-technical-definitions-performance-activity.pdf.

NICE (2004). 'Depression: Management of Depression in Primary and Secondary Care: Clinical Practice Guideline Number 23'. London: NICE.

NICE (2006). *Attention deficit hyperactivity disorder (ADHD): stakeholder consultation table*. London: NICE.

NICE (2009). 'Depression in Adults: Recognition and Management (updated 2016). Clinical Guideline Number 90', available at www.nice.org.uk/guidance/cg90. London: NICE.

NICE (2017a). 'Developing NICE guidelines: the manual', available at www.nice.org.uk/process/pmg20. London: NICE.

NICE (2017b). 'Depression in Adults: Treatment and Management. NICE guideline, short version – draft for consultation', available at www.nice.org.uk/guidance/gid-cgwave0725/documents/short-version-of-draft-guideline-2. London: NICE.

Norton-Taylor, R. (2009). 'Revealed: The £130bn cost of Trident Replacement', *The Guardian* 18 September, available at www.theguardian.com/politics/2009/sep/18/trident-replacement-hidden-cost-revealed.

Okun, A. (1973). *Equality and Efficiency: The Big Tradeoff.* Washington, DC: Brookings Institution Press.

Otto. M.W. and Wisniewski, S.R. (2012). 'CBT for treatment resistant depression'. *The Lancet*, 381: 352–3.

Pickett, K. and Wilkinson, R. (2010). *The Spirit Level: Why Equality is Better for Everyone.* London: Penguin Books.

Positive Money (2017). 'How Banks Create Money', available at http://positivemoney.org/how-money-works/how-banks-create-money/.

Radhakrishnan, M., Hammond, G., Jones, P.B., Watson, A., McMillan-Shields, F. and Lafortune, L. (2013). 'Cost of Improving Access to Psychological Therapies (IAPT) programme: An analysis of cost of session, treatment and recovery in selected Primary Care Trusts in the East of England region', *Behaviour Research and Therapy*, 51(1): 37–45.

Rapley, M., Moncrieff, J. and Dillon, J. (2011). *De-Medicalizing Misery: Psychiatry, Psychology and the Human Condition.* London: Palgrave.

redheadgingerbread (2015). 'surviving targets', *ClinPsy*, available at www.clinpsy.org.uk/forum/viewtopic.php?f=27&t=18474.

Reagan, R. (1980). *Address Accepting the Presidential Nomination at the Republican National Convention in Detroit*, available at www.presidency.ucsb.edu/ws/?pid=25970.

Reinhart, C.M. and Rogoff, K.S. (2010). 'Growth in the Time of Debt', *American Economic Review*, 100(2): 573–8.

Richards, D. and Whyte, M. (2011). Reach Out: National Programme Student Materials to Support the Delivery of Training for Psychological Wellbeing Practitioners Delivering Low Intensity Treatment. IAPT: Rethink Mental Illness, available at https://cedar.exeter.ac.uk/media/universityofexeter/schoolofpsychology/cedar/documents/Reach_Out_3rd_edition.pdf.

Rizq, R. (2011). 'IAPT, Anxiety and Envy: A Psychoanalytic View of NHS Primary Care Mental Health Services Today', *British Journal of Psychotherapy* 27(1): 37–55.

Ronson, J. (2011). *The Psychopath Test: A Journey Through the Madness Industry.* London: Picador.

Scheel, K.R. (2000). 'The Empirical Basis of Dialectical Behavior Therapy: Summary, Critique and Implications', *Clinical Psychology: Science and Practice*; 7(1): 68–86.

Seligman, M.E.P. (1972). 'Learned helplessness', *Annual Review of Medicine*, 23(1): 407–12.

Sen, A. (1977). 'Rational Fools: A Critique of the Behavioral Foundations of Economic Theory', *Philosophy and Public Affairs*, 6(4): 317–44, Summer.

Sen, A. (1987). *On Ethics and Economics.* Malden, MA: Blackwell.

Serioussham (2016). 'IAPT Waiting List Targets', available at www.clinpsy.org.uk/forum/viewtopic.php?p=180855.

Shedler, J. (2010). 'The Efficacy of Psychodynamic Psychotherapy', *American Psychologist*, 65(2): 98–109.

Smith, A. (1759). *The Theory of Moral Sentiments.* London: A. Kincaid and J. Bell.

Smith, A. (1776). *The Wealth of Nations*. London: W. Strahan and T. Cadell.

Sobel, D. (2011). *A More Perfect Heaven: How Copernicus Revolutionized the Cosmos*, New York: Walker & Company.

Spiegel, A. (2005). 'The Dictionary of Disorder: How one man revolutionized Psychiatry', *The New Yorker*, 3 January, available at www.newyorker.com/magazine/2005/01/03/the-dictionary-of-disorder.

Spitzer, R.L. (1980). 'Introduction', in *Diagnostic and Statistical Manual of Mental Disorders Third Edition*, Washington, DC: American Psychiatric Association.

Sterling, T. (1959). 'Publication decisions and their possible effects on inferences drawn from tests of significance – or vice versa', *American Statistical Association Journal*, 54(285): 30–34.

Sterling, T., Rosenbaum, L. and Weinkam, J. (1995). 'Publication decisions revisited – the effect of the outcome of statistical tests on the decision to publish and vice-versa', *American Statistical Association Journal*, 49(1): 108–12.

Syal, R. and Mason, R. (2014). 'MPs should get 10% pay rise, says regulator', *The Guardian*, 2 June, available at www.theguardian.com/politics/2015/jun/02/mp-pay-rise-go-ahead-cameron-public-sector-unions-opposition.

Taylor, K. (2017). 'Virgin Care just sued the NHS for a fortune – but the Tories and Lib Dems made it possible', *Left Foot Forward*, available at https://leftfootforward.org/2017/12/virgin-care-just-sued-the-nhs-for-a-fortune-but-the-tories-and-lib-dems-made-it-possible/.

Teasdale, J.D., Segal, Z.V., Williams, M.G., Ridgeway, V.A., Soulsby, J.M. and Lau, M.A. et al. (2000). 'Prevention of Relapse/Recurrence in Major Depression by Mindfulness-Based Cognitive Therapy', *Journal of Consulting and Clinical Psychology*, 68(4): 615–23.

Travers, J., Marsh, S., Williams, M., Weatherall, M., Caldwell, B., Shirtcliffe, P., Aldington, S., and Beasley, R. (2007). 'External validity of randomised controlled trials in asthma: to whom do the results of the trials apply?', *Thorax*, 62(3): 219–23.

Trevithick, P. (2011). 'Whose Knowledge Counts', *Inaugural Lecture*. Buckinghamshire New University, 25 October 2011, available at https://youtu.be/4k7BYqdESsM.

Turner, E., Matthews, A., Linardatos, E., Tell, R. and Rosenthal, R. (2008). 'Selective publication of antidepressant trials and its influence on apparent efficacy', *The New England Journal of Medicine*, 358: 252–60.

Vollrath, D. (2015). 'Mathiness versus science in growth economics', available at https://growthecon.com/blog/mathiness-versus-science-in-growth-economics (21 May).

von Tagle, J. (1995). 'The New DSM-IV: Is It Easier to Prove Damages?'. *California Trial Lawyers Association Forum*, 25(1): 13–19.

Watson, J.B. (1913). 'Psychology as the Behaviorist Views It', *Psychological Review*, 20: 158–77.

Watson, J.B. (1919). *Psychology from the Standpoint of a Behaviourist*. Philadelphia: Lippincott.

Watson, J.B. and McDougall, M. (1929). *The Battle of Behaviourism: An Exposition and an Exposure*. New York: Norton & Co.

Westbrook, D., Kennerley, H. and Kirk, J. (2008). *An Introduction to Cognitive Behavioural Therapy: Skills and Applications*. London: Sage.

Westen D., Novotny, C.M. and Thompson-Brenner, H. (2004). 'The empirical status of empirically supported psychotherapies: assumptions, findings, and reporting in controlled clinical trials', *Psychological Bulletin*, 130(4): 631–63.

Wiles, N., Thomas, L., Ridgway, L., Turner, N., Campbell, J., Garland, A., Hollinghurst, S., Jerrom, B., Kessler, D., Kuyken, W., Morrison, J., Turner, K., Williams, C., Peters, T. and Lewis, G. (2013). 'Cognitive behavioural therapy as an adjunct to pharmacotherapy for primary care-based patients with treatment resistant depression: results of the CoBalT randomised controlled trial', *The Lancet*, 381: 375–84.

Williams, J.B. et al. (1992). 'The Structured Clinical Interview for DSM-III-R', *Archives of General Psychiatry*, 49: 630–36.

Zimmerman, M., Chelminski, I. and Posternak, M.A. (2004). 'Exclusion criteria used in antidepressant efficacy trials: consistency across studies and representativeness of samples included', *The Journal of Nervous and Mental Disease*, 192(2): 87–94.

Index

hospitals: accident and emergency
    departments 91–2; Devon NHS mental
    health hospital 92–4
hugging 13–14
Hume, David 70, 71
hygiene 42
hyper-rationality 1–10, 19, 22, 23, 51, 69,
    83, 86, 89, 91, 112, 124, 141, 152, 180,
    181
hypotheses: making assumptions with 75,
    146; testing 74, 143, 146, 161

IAPT *see* Increasing Access to
    Psychological Therapies
identity formation 31–46
imipramine 58–9
Increasing Access to Psychological
    Therapies (IAPT) 7, 98, 109, 113–34;
    funding/financing 97, 98, 103, 118–19;
    targets IAPT 92, 121, 122, 124, 125,
    127, 133, 134
independence of NICE 99
individual, NICE guidelines and
    consequences for 103; *see also* other
    people
induction 139, 140, 141, 143
inequality 14, 25, 26
instructors (trained) 36; MBCT 168, 175
internal markets 90
International Monetary Fund (IMF) 83
interpersonal therapy (IPT) 110, 155–6;
    bulimia 164

jazz 42
Jennings, Richard 69
Jevons, W.S. 73
Jew in hiding from Nazis, Layard's moral
    dilemma for German citizen 21

Kant, Immanuel 2, 21, 69–71, 78, 140,
    162, 180
Keynes, John Maynard 73

Labour Party and Government 8, 14, 15,
    18, 79, 80, 82, 86, 87, 97
Layard, Richard 5, 6, 8–9, 14–15, 17,
    18–23, 25–6, 27, 28–9, 80, 94, 98, 111,
    118, 131, 152; Clark and 8, 15, 25, 27,
    33–4, 35, 38, 44, 45, 79–80, 80
learned helplessness 14, 36, 45, 105
Liberating the NHS: Greater choice and
    control 114–15

life events, adverse/tragic 1, 45; MBCT
    relapse prevention and 177, 178
life experiences (lived experiences): early
    (children and their family life) 27, 30,
    35, 48, 105; outcome measures and 129
linguistic obfuscation 166–78
LIWY (*ClinPsy* post by)
logical positivism 22, 140–1
low-intensity interventions 109, 119–20;
    workers in 132–3, 133, 134
lying 153

magical rituals 160–2
malpractices 124, 126, 155; data
    manipulation 124–6, 153
managerialism 5, 9, 10, 79, 86–94,
    113–34; IAPT and 98; privatization of
    mental health and 113–34
manuals as patents 153–4
marketing 92
marketization 90–1, 92
marketplace 88, 90, 114, 115, 116, 118
marriage 29
masochistic personality disorder 54–5
master-myths 33–46
measurement 88–9; fetishization of
    91–2; of happiness 22, 23–4, 72–3; of
    outcome of treatment 123–4, 128–31,
    152; of performance *see* performance;
    see also questionnaires
medical conditions, NICE examination of
    99
medical doctors (medics): psychiatrists vs
    (in US) 47, 52–63; psychologists vs
    (in UK) 63–5
medicalization of suffering and distress 6,
    7, 16, 59, 99
mental health 7, 15; NICE GDG,
    membership 99; privatization 78, 79,
    86–7, 113–34
mental illness (mental/psychiatric
    conditions/disorders) 5, 6, 6–7, 7,
    15, 15–16, 23, 53, 106, 132; children
    from single parent families and 29;
    depression classed as 57, 106; diagnosis
    see diagnosis; Diagnostic and Statistical
    Manual; drug-centred approach before
    1950s 58; genes and 27; harmful
    recovery 131–2; NICE and 99, 101,
    103; unemployment due to 84–5, 97,
    131–2; *see also specific disorders*
Mill, John Stuart 72

praising workers 93
predictions 139, 158–9; cause/effect relationship 162; in economic theory 75–6
premenstrual dysphoric disorder 54–5
prevention (of depression): of occurrence 181; of relapse 166–78
primary care 109; counselling 117
privatization (transfer to private sector) 78, 79, 86–7, 113–34
professionals and professional bodies/ organizations 39, 87, 88, 102
profit 77, 79, 87, 118
'psy' wars and 'psy' professions 9, 46, 47–65
psychiatric conditions *see* mental illness
psychiatrists vs medics (in US) 47, 52–63
psychoanalysis 44, 45–6, 47–9, 50, 51
Psychological Wellbeing Practitioners (low-intensity workers) 132–3, 133, 134
psychologists vs medical doctors in UK 63–5
psychology 23, 24, 34–6, 47, 50; clinical 47, 64–5, 99; cognitive *see* cognitivism; economic 71–9
psychotherapy (talking therapy) 9, 133; psychoanalytic 44, 45–6, 47–9, 50, 51; psychodynamic 100–1, 117; waiting lists 16; *see also* Increasing Access to Psychological Therapies
PTSD (post-traumatic stress disorder) 38, 56–7, 109
public services/utilities/industries: as businesses 79; cuts 97, 119–22, 123; efficiency/inefficiency 87, 90; selling of 79, 87, 116

questionnaires: diagnostic 76–7, 106–8; at end of every session 127
Quick Reference Guide (NICE) 102

randomised controlled trials 150, 156
rationality (and rational thought/thinking) 2, 39, 40, 71, 111–12; in choice-making 74, 83, 105, 169; Enlightenment 3, 73; power and 39; *see also* hyper-rationality
Reach Out 119
Reagan, Ronald 78, 79, 80
reality 4, 48; objective 4, 111; perceived 25
reason 44, 45, 73, 98, 138; rise of 69–71
reboxetine 155
recovery 125–6, 134, 139–50; harmful 131–2; onus on providers to

demonstrate 126; relapse after *see* relapse; targets 121
recurrence *see* relapse
redheadgingerbread (*ClinPsy* post by) 121–2
regulatory agencies and negative trials 154–5
relapse and recurrence in depression 149–51; MBCT trial in prevention of 166–78
relatives (relative risks/benefits) 181; MBCT trial on relapse prevention/ reduction 173, 176
religious faith 145
research 10, 135–81; NICE and 101, 146, 159–60; restricting 159–60; *see also* trials
results: desire-driven 154–6; payment by (PbR) 117–18, 128, 130, 131, 132
reverse engineering 13–14
rich and the poor 20, 25–6
Rizq, Rosemary, experiences of working in IAPT 132
role play 35
ruling elite *see* power

science 2, 137–65; bad/corrupt 10, 145–57; bureaucratization 97–103; economics as 73, 74, 76, 77; even harder 141–2; facts in (scientific facts) 14, 59, 99, 103, 127, 138, 139, 141, 151, 176; good 10, 137–44, 145, 151, 156, 159; of happiness 13, 14, 22–3, 93; hard 138–9; harder 140–1; politics 60; statistical 141–2
selective serotonin reuptake inhibitors (SSRIs) 57–8, 101
self (the) 38
Seligman, Martin 14, 36, 76–7, 105
Sen, Amartya 73–4
Serioussham (*ClinPsy* post by) 124, 126
serotonin: imbalance 57–8; selective serotonin reuptake inhibitors (SSRIs) 57–8, 101
services *see* public services
shame 42–3
Short Version (NICE) 102
significance: clinical 60, 101, 143–4; statistical 142–3, 153
single parent families, children 29–30
Skinner B.F. 49, 50
Smith, Adam 69, 71–2, 77, 79
social carnage 79–80
social phobia 109
social policy, cognitivist 28–30